Shades of
BLUE

VOLUME

1

JAMES S. HARRIS
RACHEL NACION
GREG GRUCEL
CAL SLAYTON

Shades of BLUE

Table of Contents

1. New Prologue - Page 5

2. Volume I, Issue 1 - Page 14

3. Volume I, Issue 2 - Page 33

4. Volume I, Issue 3 - Page 52

5. Volume I, Issue 4 - Page 76

6. Volume I, Issue 5 - Page 101

7. Epilogue - Page 125

8. Convention Special - Page 132

9. Artwork and Pin-Ups - Page 137

From the Author...

Thanks for picking up the book! If you're a returning reader, welcome back and we hope you enjoy the new eight page prologue which sheds a little light on the day Heidi got her powers. If you're a new reader, welcome, and we hope you'll enjoy our little story.

The reprinted issues contained here were self-published between July of 1999 and December of 2001 by me under the name "Amp Comics." In addition, we've added a brand new eight page prologue, as well as a four page mini-comic we made up for the 2001 convention season. AND we've included the six page Epilogue originally published in Digital Webbing Presents. We also have some great pinups and behind the scenes artwork from our own Cal Slayton. But more on all this later...

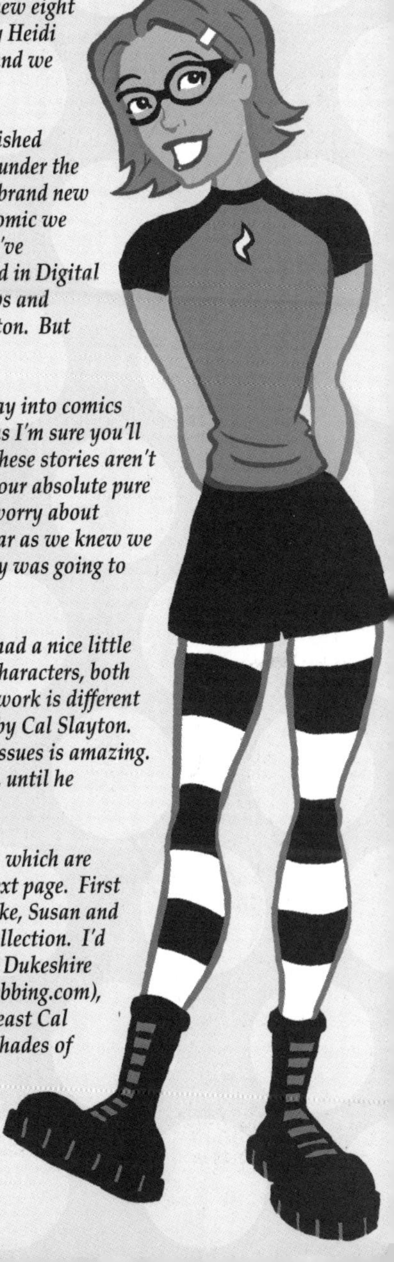

A little about us--Shades of Blue was the first foray into comics for all of us. There was a bit of a learning curve, as I'm sure you'll see over the course of this collection. Not to say these stories aren't as good as what came later; these stories contain our absolute pure love of comics. We didn't hold anything back or worry about keeping stories or jokes or whatever for later; as far as we knew we were living issue to issue and chances were nobody was going to read our stories anyway!

Well, as it turned out, people did read us, and we had a nice little run. It's kind of fun to see the progression of the characters, both in their looks and their words. Obviously the artwork is different from issues 1 and 2, by Greg Grucel, to 3, 4 and 5, by Cal Slayton. But just looking at Cal's progression in his three issues is amazing. The characters seemed to subtly morph each issue, until he perfected their looks in issue 5.

Anyway, enough blather and onto the thank yous, which are different from the dedications, which are on the next page. First and foremost, I'd like to thank Josh, Marshall, Mike, Susan and everyone else at Devil's Due for publishing this collection. I'd also like to thank Rachel Nacion, Greg Grucel, Ed Dukeshire and everyone at Digital Webbing (www.digitalwebbing.com), my mother, my father, and last but certainly not least Cal Slayton. Without Cal there would have been no Shades of Blue after issue 2 (well maybe there would have been but it probably would have blew).

Thanks to all listed and anyone I've forgotten.
Jim Harris

Published By

D³ DIGEST

Josh Blaylock:* *President

Mark Powers:* *Senior Editor

Mike Norton:* *Art Director

Chris Crank:* *Web Developer

Tim Seeley:* *Staff Illustrator

Sean Dove:* *Graphic Designer

Marshall Dillon:* *Project Manager

Susan Bishop:* *Office Manager

Sam Wells:* *Office Assistance

A division of
DEVIL'S DUE PUBLISHING, Inc.
4619 N. Ravenswood Ave. #204
Chicago, IL 60640

www.devilsdue.net

First Edition: MARCH 2005
ISBN 1-932796-26-6
PRINTED IN CANADA

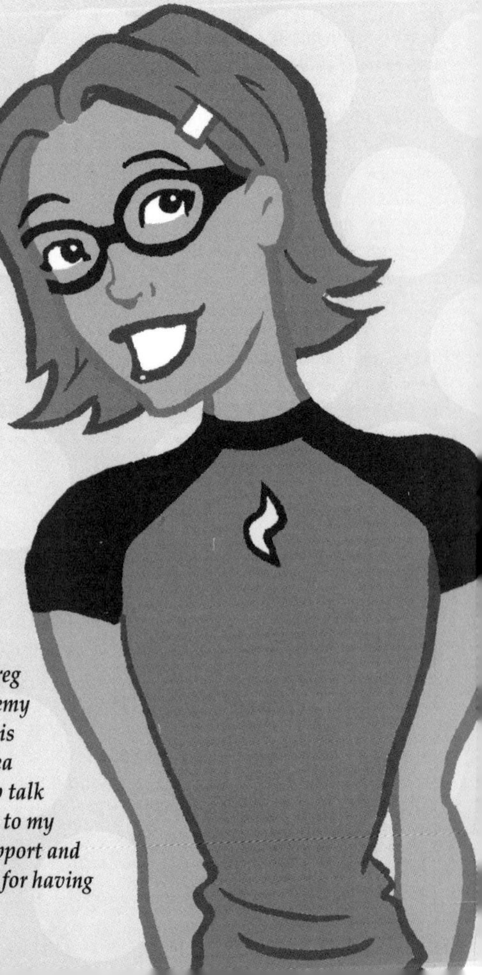

Dedications and Thanks:

Jim: For Michelle and Eliza, my best friends.

Cal: Thanks to my family and friends for their support. Thanks to Jim for being the first person to publish my work, I am forever grateful. Thanks to every artist that ever influenced me, they're too many to name. Thanks to Greg Thompson at Lone Star Comics and Jeremy Shorr at Titan Comics for supporting this book early on. Thanks to the Dallas Area Comic Creators Lunch Club for the shop talk and the inspiration. And special thanks to my lovely wife Heather for her constant support and encouragement, every day I give thanks for having you in my life.

PROLOGUE:
"Heidi's Origin,"
or
"How I Learned to Stop Being Unstylish and Love the Mall"

Writer:
James S. Harris

Art:
Cal Slayton

Lettering:
Ed Dukeshire

Editor:
Michelle Harris

Writer's Muse:
Miss Eliza Harris

An original story created for this collection and published here for the first time.

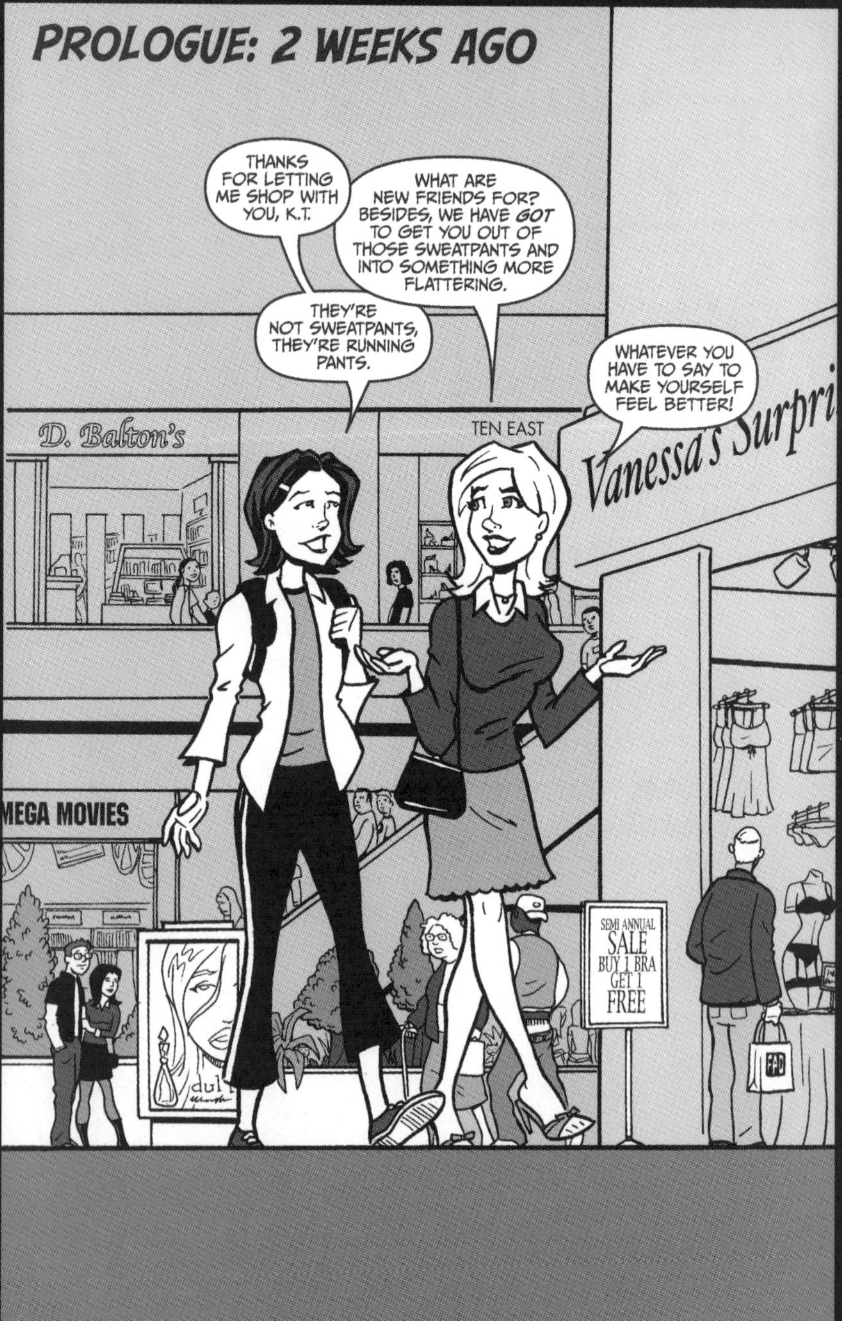
PROLOGUE: 2 WEEKS AGO
THANKS FOR LETTING ME SHOP WITH YOU, K.T.
WHAT ARE NEW FRIENDS FOR? BESIDES, WE HAVE *GOT* TO GET YOU OUT OF THOSE SWEATPANTS AND INTO SOMETHING MORE FLATTERING.
THEY'RE NOT SWEATPANTS, THEY'RE RUNNING PANTS.
WHATEVER YOU HAVE TO SAY TO MAKE YOURSELF FEEL BETTER!
D. Balton's
TEN EAST
Vanessa's Surpri
MEGA MOVIES
SEMI ANNUAL SALE BUY 1 BRA GET 1 FREE

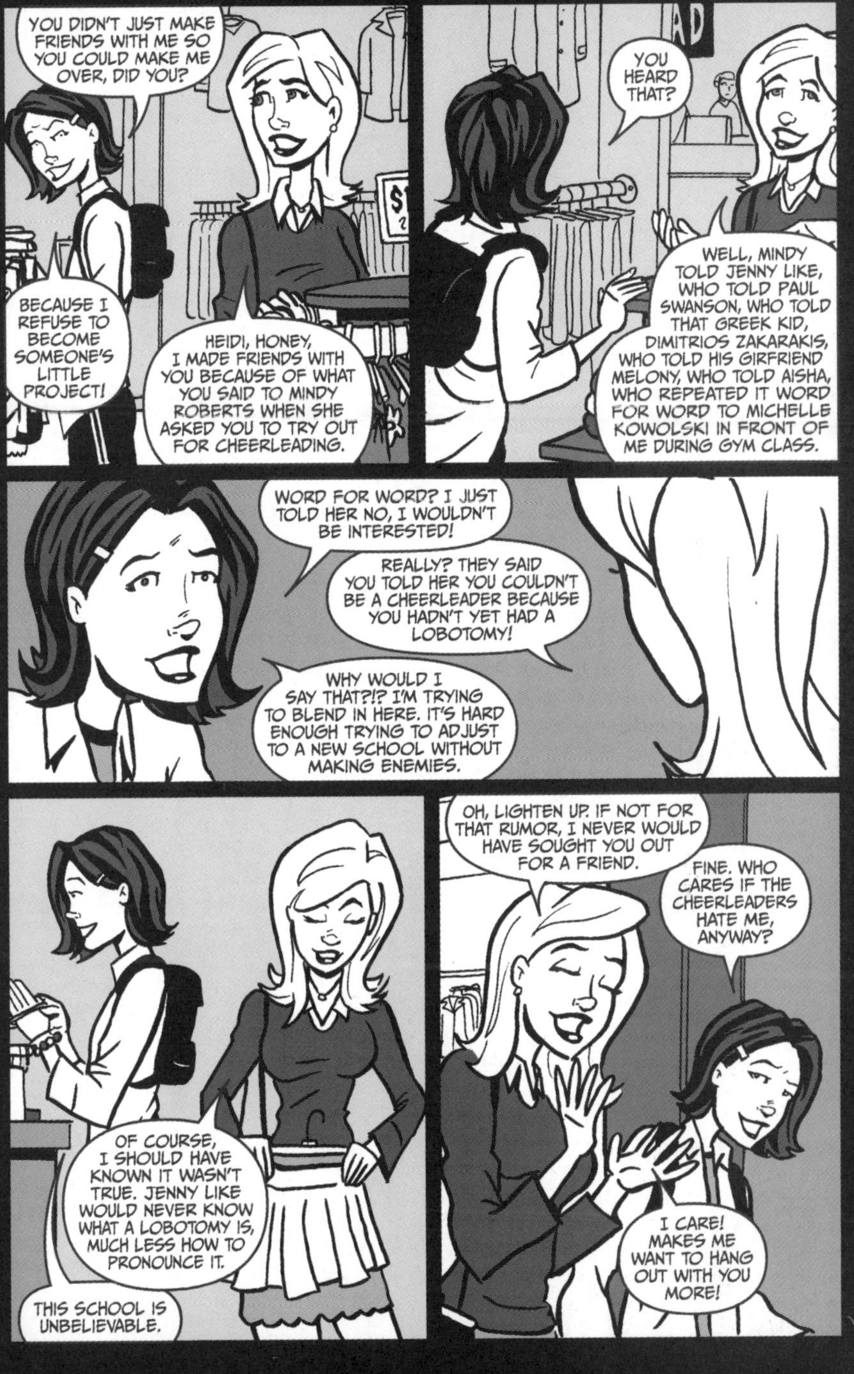
YOU DIDN'T JUST MAKE FRIENDS WITH ME SO YOU COULD MAKE ME OVER, DID YOU?
BECAUSE I REFUSE TO BECOME SOMEONE'S LITTLE PROJECT!
HEIDI, HONEY, I MADE FRIENDS WITH YOU BECAUSE OF WHAT YOU SAID TO MINDY ROBERTS WHEN SHE ASKED YOU TO TRY OUT FOR CHEERLEADING.
YOU HEARD THAT?
WELL, MINDY TOLD JENNY LIKE, WHO TOLD PAUL SWANSON, WHO TOLD THAT GREEK KID, DIMITRIOS ZAKARAKIS, WHO TOLD HIS GIRFRIEND MELONY, WHO TOLD AISHA, WHO REPEATED IT WORD FOR WORD TO MICHELLE KOWOLSKI IN FRONT OF ME DURING GYM CLASS.
WORD FOR WORD? I JUST TOLD HER NO, I WOULDN'T BE INTERESTED!
REALLY? THEY SAID YOU TOLD HER YOU COULDN'T BE A CHEERLEADER BECAUSE YOU HADN'T YET HAD A LOBOTOMY!
WHY WOULD I SAY THAT?!? I'M TRYING TO BLEND IN HERE. IT'S HARD ENOUGH TRYING TO ADJUST TO A NEW SCHOOL WITHOUT MAKING ENEMIES.
OF COURSE, I SHOULD HAVE KNOWN IT WASN'T TRUE. JENNY LIKE WOULD NEVER KNOW WHAT A LOBOTOMY IS, MUCH LESS HOW TO PRONOUNCE IT.
THIS SCHOOL IS UNBELIEVABLE.
OH, LIGHTEN UP. IF NOT FOR THAT RUMOR, I NEVER WOULD HAVE SOUGHT YOU OUT FOR A FRIEND.
FINE. WHO CARES IF THE CHEERLEADERS HATE ME, ANYWAY?
I CARE! MAKES ME WANT TO HANG OUT WITH YOU MORE!

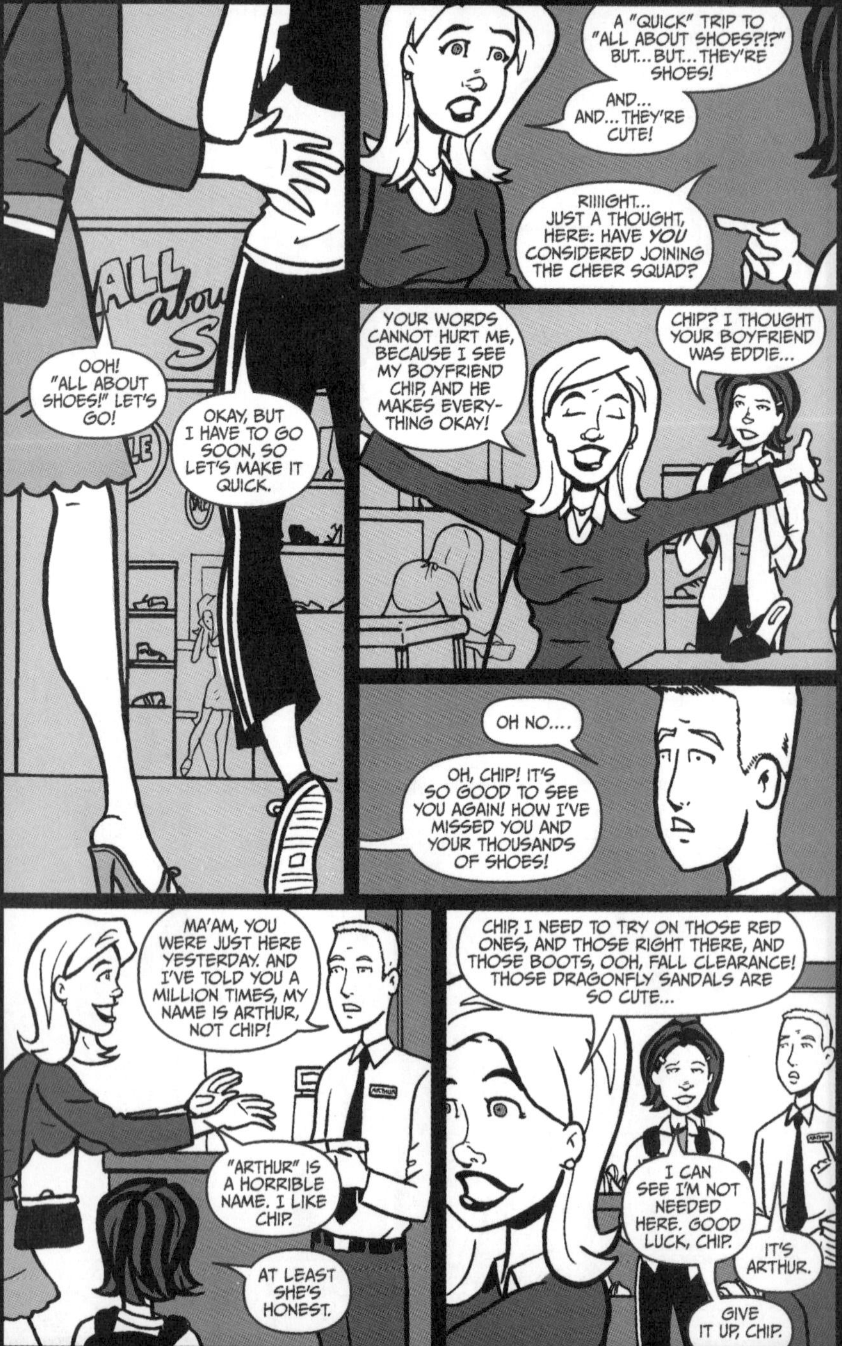
OOH! "ALL ABOUT SHOES!" LET'S GO!
OKAY, BUT I HAVE TO GO SOON, SO LET'S MAKE IT QUICK.
A "QUICK" TRIP TO "ALL ABOUT SHOES?!?" BUT... BUT... THEY'RE SHOES!
AND... AND... THEY'RE CUTE!
RIIIIGHT... JUST A THOUGHT, HERE: HAVE YOU CONSIDERED JOINING THE CHEER SQUAD?
YOUR WORDS CANNOT HURT ME, BECAUSE I SEE MY BOYFRIEND CHIP, AND HE MAKES EVERY-THING OKAY!
CHIP? I THOUGHT YOUR BOYFRIEND WAS EDDIE...
OH NO....
OH, CHIP! IT'S SO GOOD TO SEE YOU AGAIN! HOW I'VE MISSED YOU AND YOUR THOUSANDS OF SHOES!
MA'AM, YOU WERE JUST HERE YESTERDAY. AND I'VE TOLD YOU A MILLION TIMES, MY NAME IS ARTHUR, NOT CHIP!
"ARTHUR" IS A HORRIBLE NAME. I LIKE CHIP.
AT LEAST SHE'S HONEST.
CHIP, I NEED TO TRY ON THOSE RED ONES, AND THOSE RIGHT THERE, AND THOSE BOOTS, OOH, FALL CLEARANCE! THOSE DRAGONFLY SANDALS ARE SO CUTE...
I CAN SEE I'M NOT NEEDED HERE. GOOD LUCK, CHIP.
IT'S ARTHUR.
GIVE IT UP, CHIP.

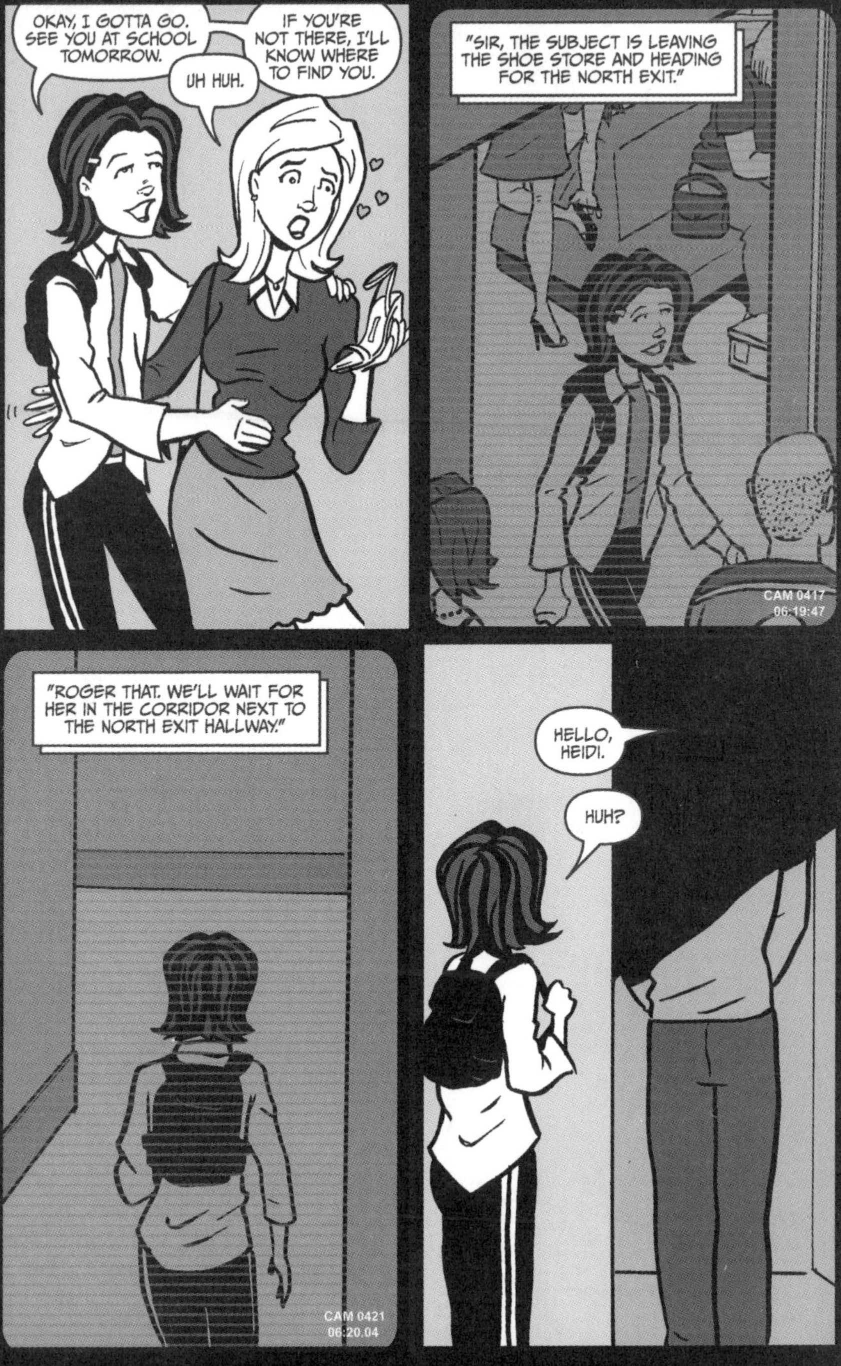
OKAY, I GOTTA GO. SEE YOU AT SCHOOL TOMORROW.
UH HUH.
IF YOU'RE NOT THERE, I'LL KNOW WHERE TO FIND YOU.
"SIR, THE SUBJECT IS LEAVING THE SHOE STORE AND HEADING FOR THE NORTH EXIT."
CAM 0417
06:19:47
"ROGER THAT. WE'LL WAIT FOR HER IN THE CORRIDOR NEXT TO THE NORTH EXIT HALLWAY."
CAM 0421
06:20.04
HELLO, HEIDI.
HUH?

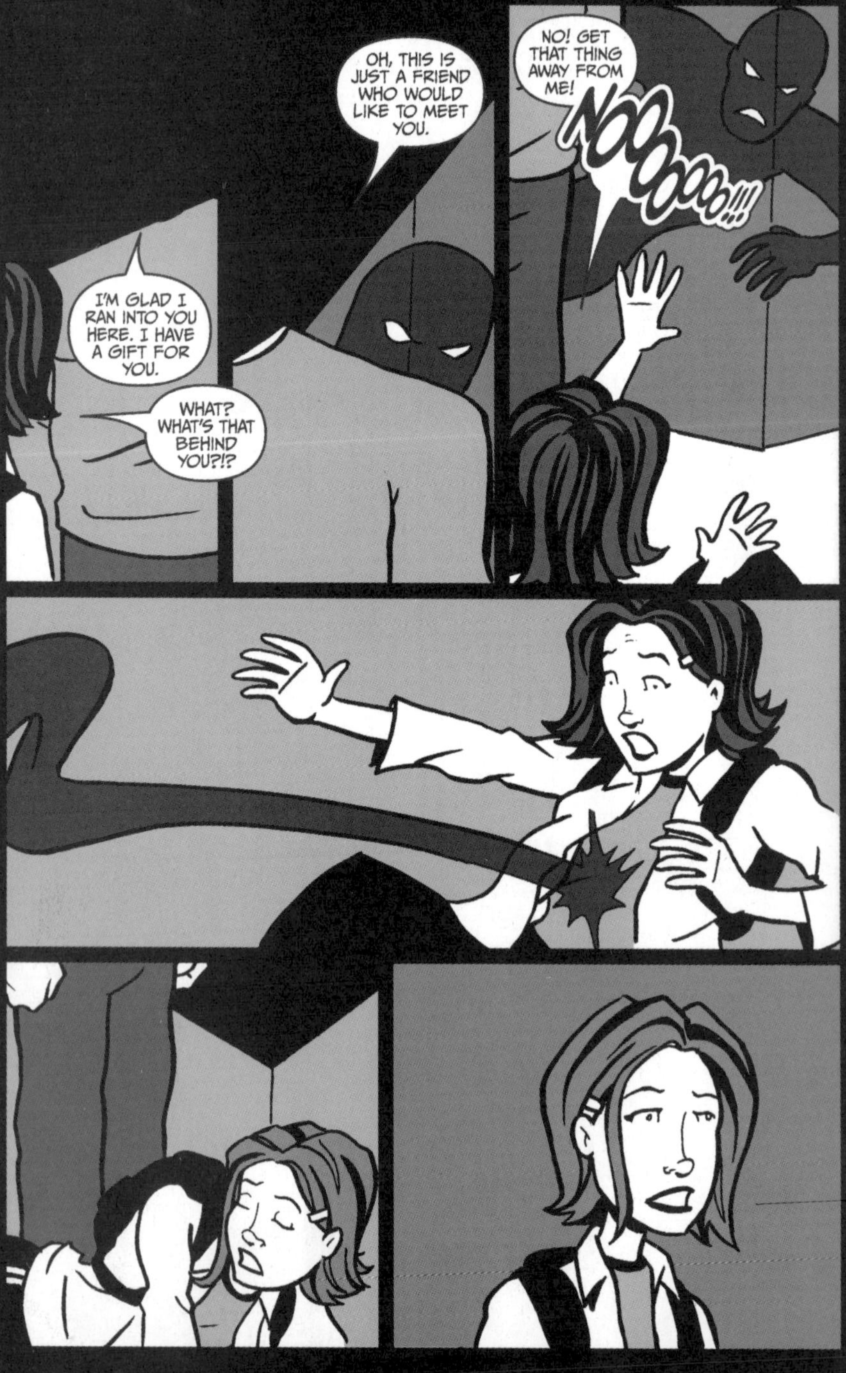
I'M GLAD I RAN INTO YOU HERE. I HAVE A GIFT FOR YOU.
WHAT? WHAT'S THAT BEHIND YOU?!?
OH, THIS IS JUST A FRIEND WHO WOULD LIKE TO MEET YOU.
NO! GET THAT THING AWAY FROM ME!
NOOOOOOO!!!

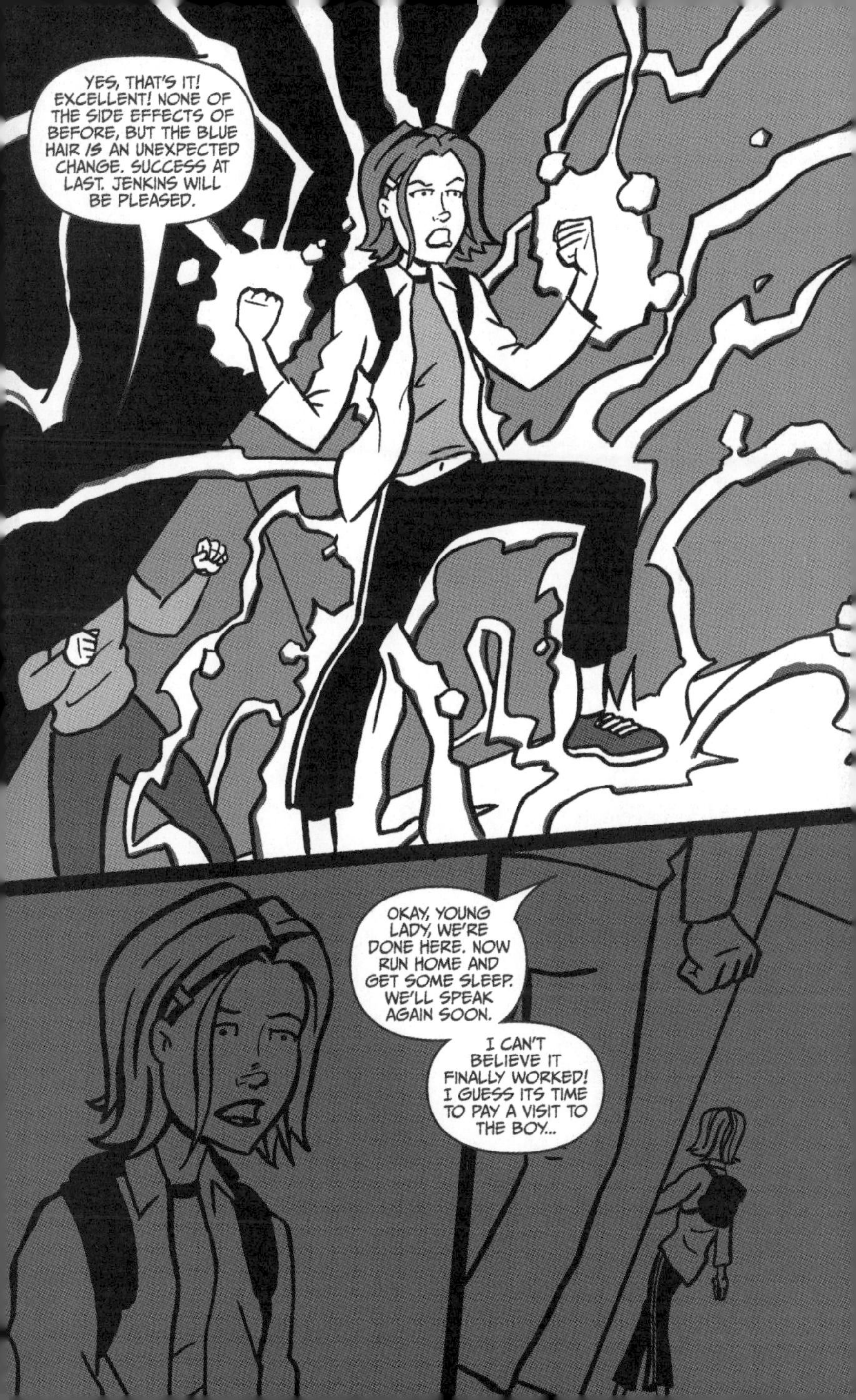
YES, THAT'S IT! EXCELLENT! NONE OF THE SIDE EFFECTS OF BEFORE, BUT THE BLUE HAIR *IS* AN UNEXPECTED CHANGE. SUCCESS AT LAST. JENKINS WILL BE PLEASED.
OKAY, YOUNG LADY, WE'RE DONE HERE. NOW RUN HOME AND GET SOME SLEEP. WE'LL SPEAK AGAIN SOON.
I CAN'T BELIEVE IT FINALLY WORKED! I GUESS ITS TIME TO PAY A VISIT TO THE BOY...

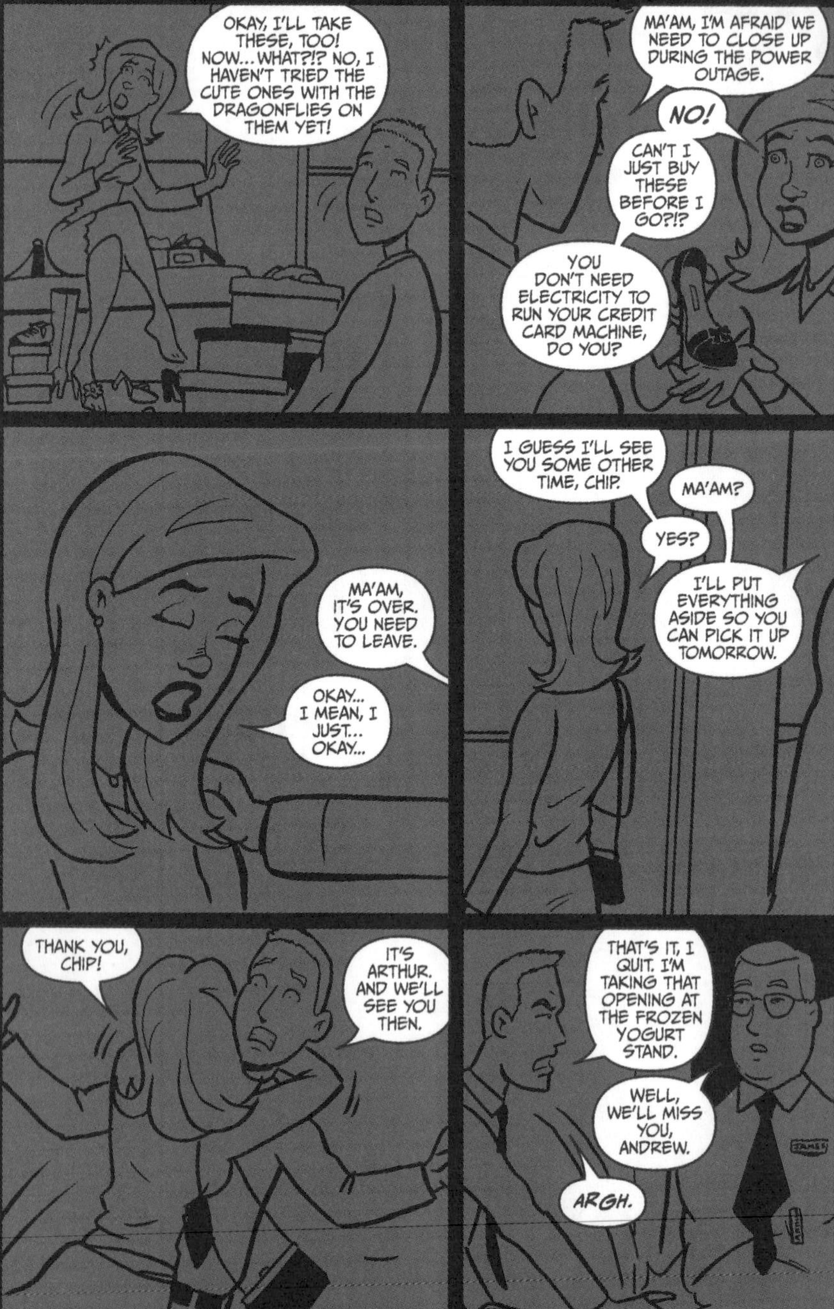

OKAY, I'LL TAKE THESE, TOO! NOW...WHAT?!? NO, I HAVEN'T TRIED THE CUTE ONES WITH THE DRAGONFLIES ON THEM YET!
MA'AM, I'M AFRAID WE NEED TO CLOSE UP DURING THE POWER OUTAGE.
NO!
CAN'T I JUST BUY THESE BEFORE I GO?!?
YOU DON'T NEED ELECTRICITY TO RUN YOUR CREDIT CARD MACHINE, DO YOU?
MA'AM, IT'S OVER. YOU NEED TO LEAVE.
OKAY... I MEAN, I JUST... OKAY...
I GUESS I'LL SEE YOU SOME OTHER TIME, CHIP.
MA'AM?
YES?
I'LL PUT EVERYTHING ASIDE SO YOU CAN PICK IT UP TOMORROW.
THANK YOU, CHIP!
IT'S ARTHUR. AND WE'LL SEE YOU THEN.
THAT'S IT, I QUIT. I'M TAKING THAT OPENING AT THE FROZEN YOGURT STAND.
WELL, WE'LL MISS YOU, ANDREW.
ARGH.

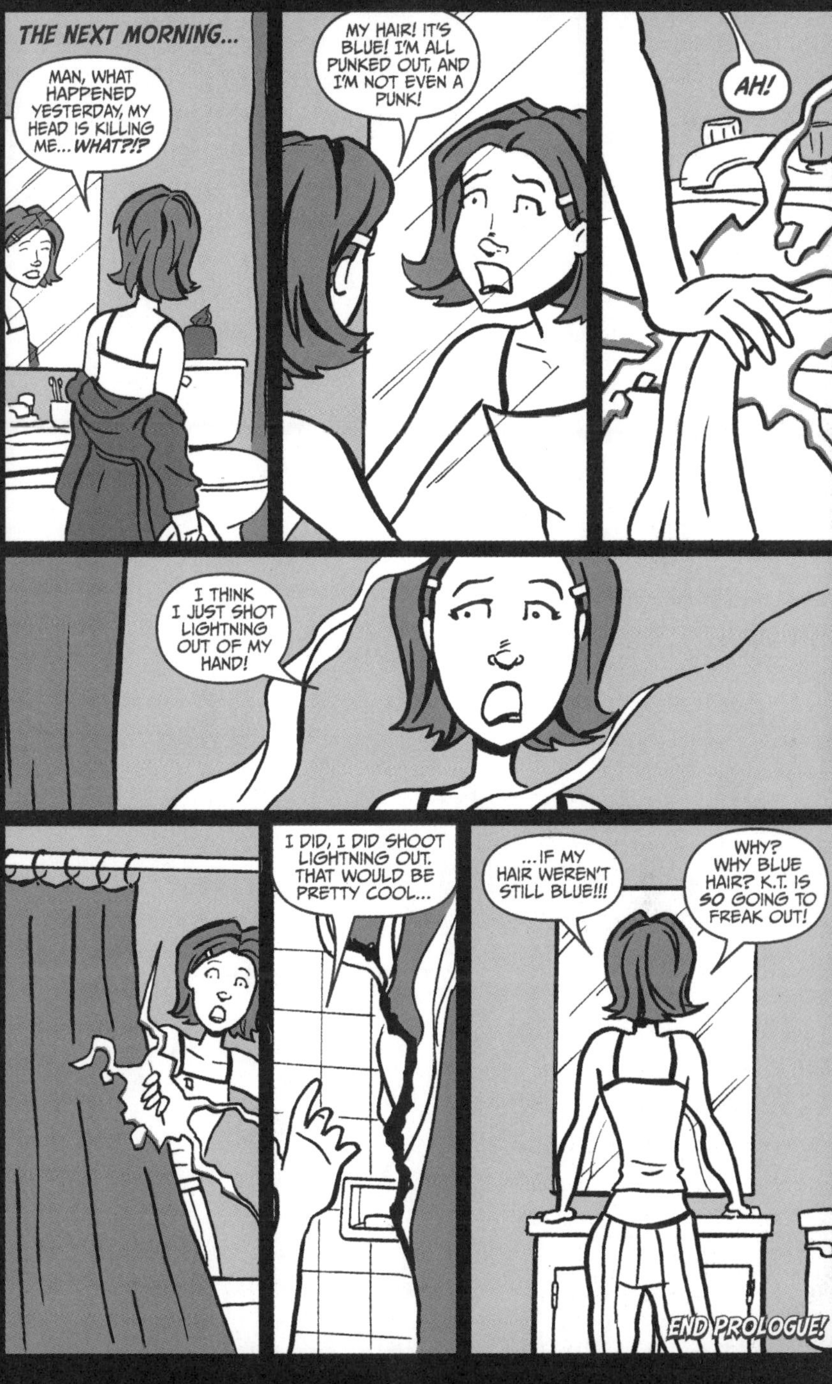
THE NEXT MORNING...
MAN, WHAT HAPPENED YESTERDAY, MY HEAD IS KILLING ME... WHAT?!?
MY HAIR! IT'S BLUE! I'M ALL PUNKED OUT, AND I'M NOT EVEN A PUNK!
AH!
I THINK I JUST SHOT LIGHTNING OUT OF MY HAND!
I DID, I DID SHOOT LIGHTNING OUT. THAT WOULD BE PRETTY COOL...
...IF MY HAIR WEREN'T STILL BLUE!!!
WHY? WHY BLUE HAIR? K.T. IS SO GOING TO FREAK OUT!
END PROLOGUE!

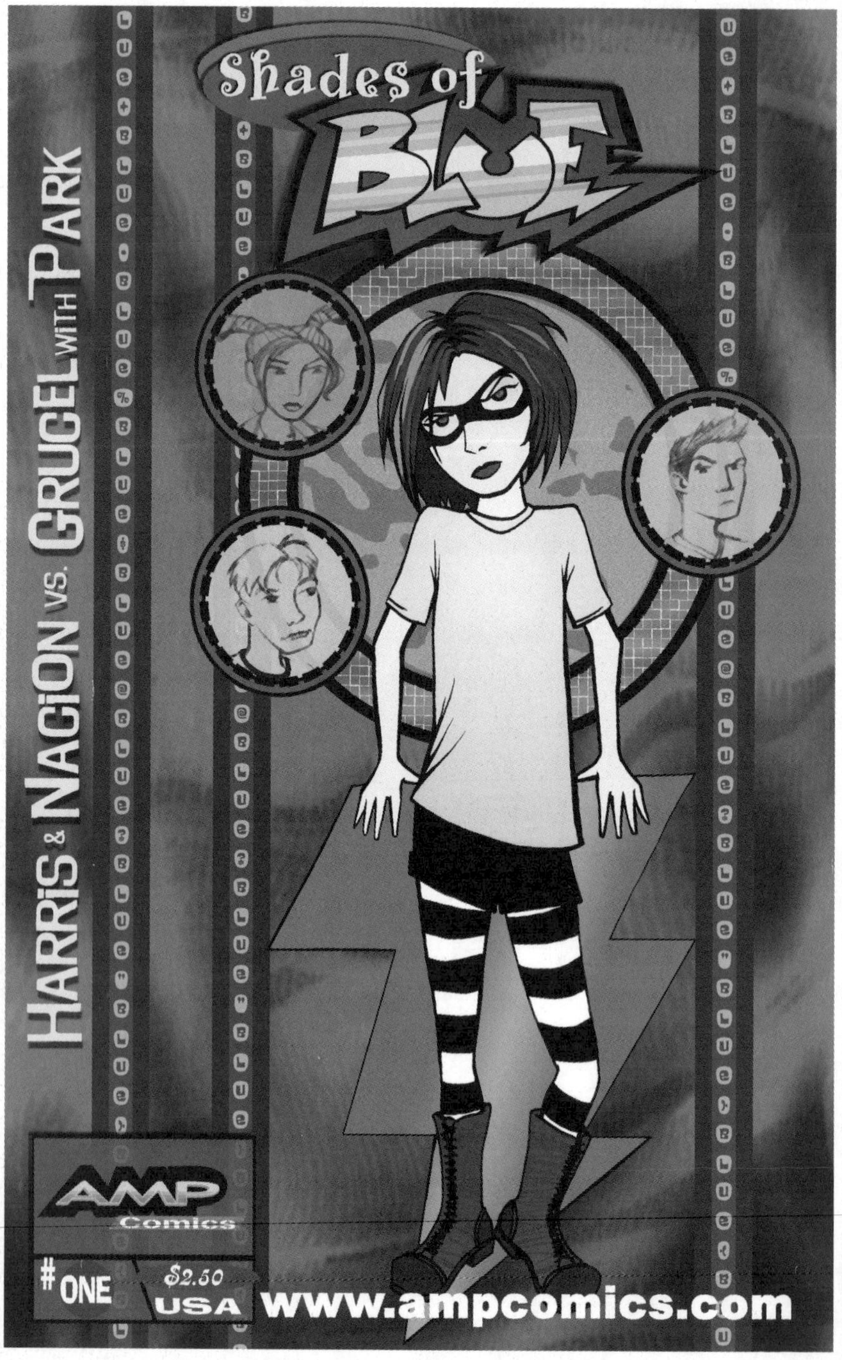

Shades of BLUE
HARRIS & NACIÓN VS. GRUCEL WITH PARK
AMP Comics
#ONE
$2.50 USA
www.ampcomics.com

"The Definition of Amok and Other Time-Killing Activities-- Part I"

Flowery Words:
James S. Harris & Rachel Nacion

Pretty Drawings, Striking Inks, Colors, Cover Design, and General Nice Guy:
Greg Grucel

Additional Artwork:
Roy Park

The Players:

Heidi Paige:
Reluctant Hero

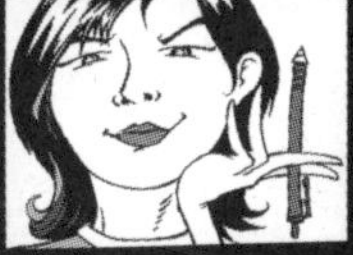

Jack:
Rebellious love interest

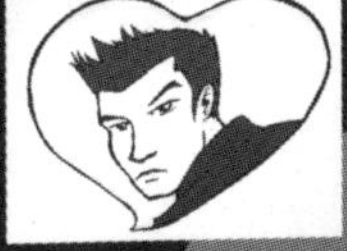

K.T. O'Hara:
Heidi's Best Friend

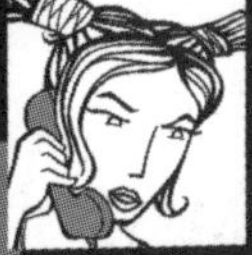

Marcus:
Geek with a car

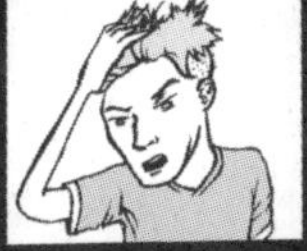

The story thus far: There hasn't been a story yet. Didn't you see the "First Issue" draped across the front cover? Sheesh! What, you thought maybe there was a special "Preview Edition," or some kind of 1/2 or zero issue? And that perhaps that particular comic came polybagged with some magazine that covers the comic industry? Yeah, right. Like that magazine covers indy books like ours. Get a clue. Oh yeah--and thanks for buying the book!

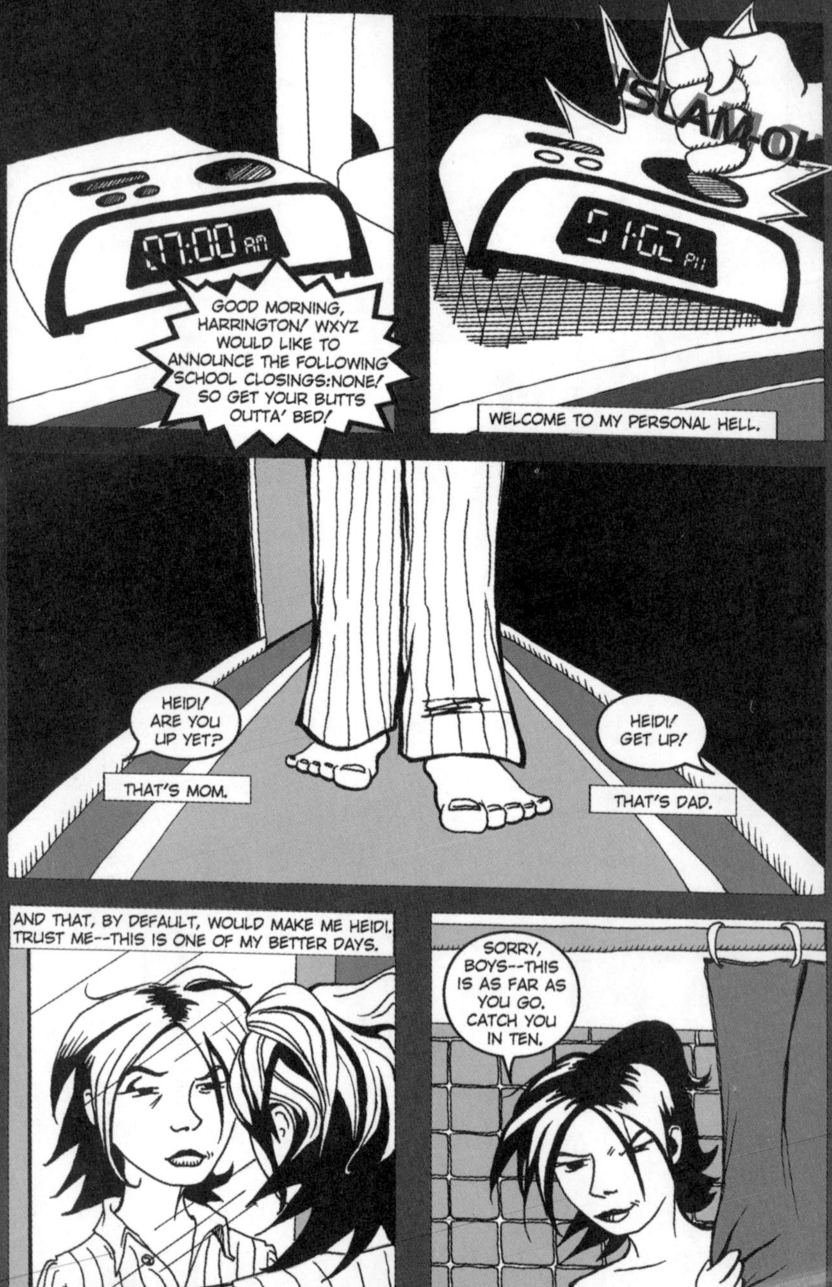
07:00 AM
GOOD MORNING, HARRINGTON! WXYZ WOULD LIKE TO ANNOUNCE THE FOLLOWING SCHOOL CLOSINGS: NONE! SO GET YOUR BUTTS OUTTA' BED!
SLAM-O!
WELCOME TO MY PERSONAL HELL.
HEIDI! ARE YOU UP YET?
THAT'S MOM.
HEIDI! GET UP!
THAT'S DAD.
AND THAT, BY DEFAULT, WOULD MAKE ME HEIDI. TRUST ME--THIS IS ONE OF MY BETTER DAYS.
SORRY, BOYS--THIS IS AS FAR AS YOU GO. CATCH YOU IN TEN.

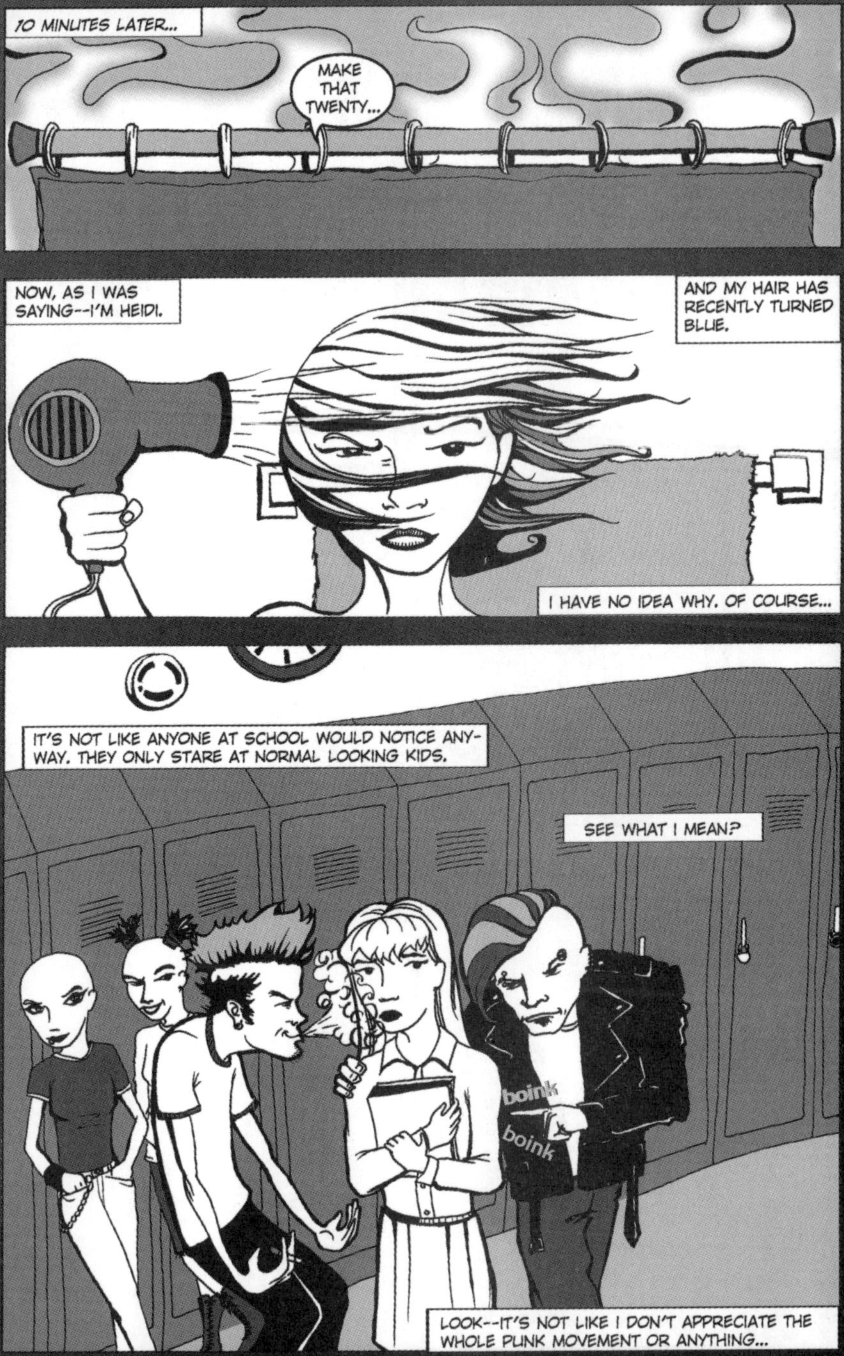
10 MINUTES LATER...
MAKE THAT TWENTY...
NOW, AS I WAS SAYING--I'M HEIDI.
AND MY HAIR HAS RECENTLY TURNED BLUE.
I HAVE NO IDEA WHY. OF COURSE...
IT'S NOT LIKE ANYONE AT SCHOOL WOULD NOTICE ANY-WAY. THEY ONLY STARE AT NORMAL LOOKING KIDS.
SEE WHAT I MEAN?
boink
boink
LOOK--IT'S NOT LIKE I DON'T APPRECIATE THE WHOLE PUNK MOVEMENT OR ANYTHING...

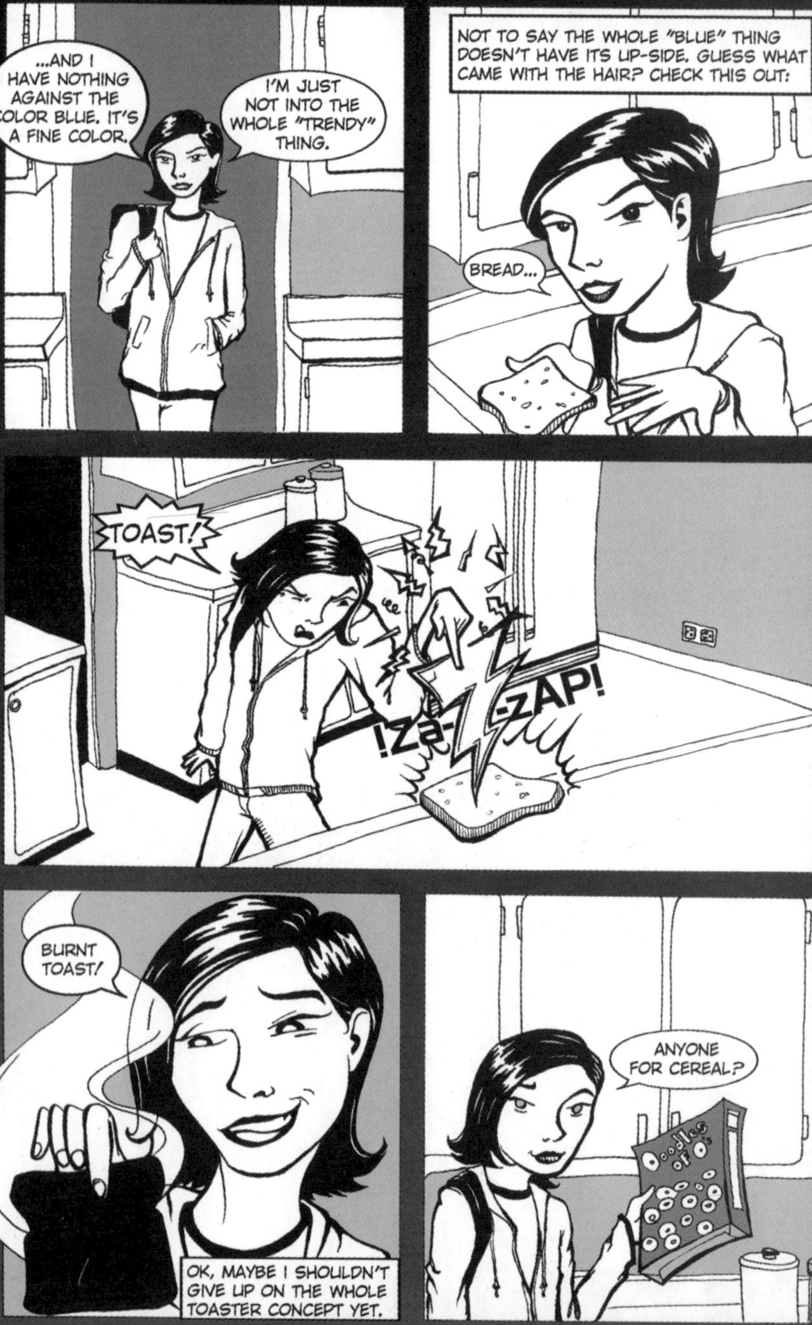
...AND I HAVE NOTHING AGAINST THE COLOR BLUE. IT'S A FINE COLOR.
I'M JUST NOT INTO THE WHOLE "TRENDY" THING.
NOT TO SAY THE WHOLE "BLUE" THING DOESN'T HAVE ITS UP-SIDE. GUESS WHAT CAME WITH THE HAIR? CHECK THIS OUT:
BREAD...
TOAST!
!ZA-
-ZAP!
BURNT TOAST!
OK, MAYBE I SHOULDN'T GIVE UP ON THE WHOLE TOASTER CONCEPT YET.
ANYONE FOR CEREAL?
Oodles OF O's

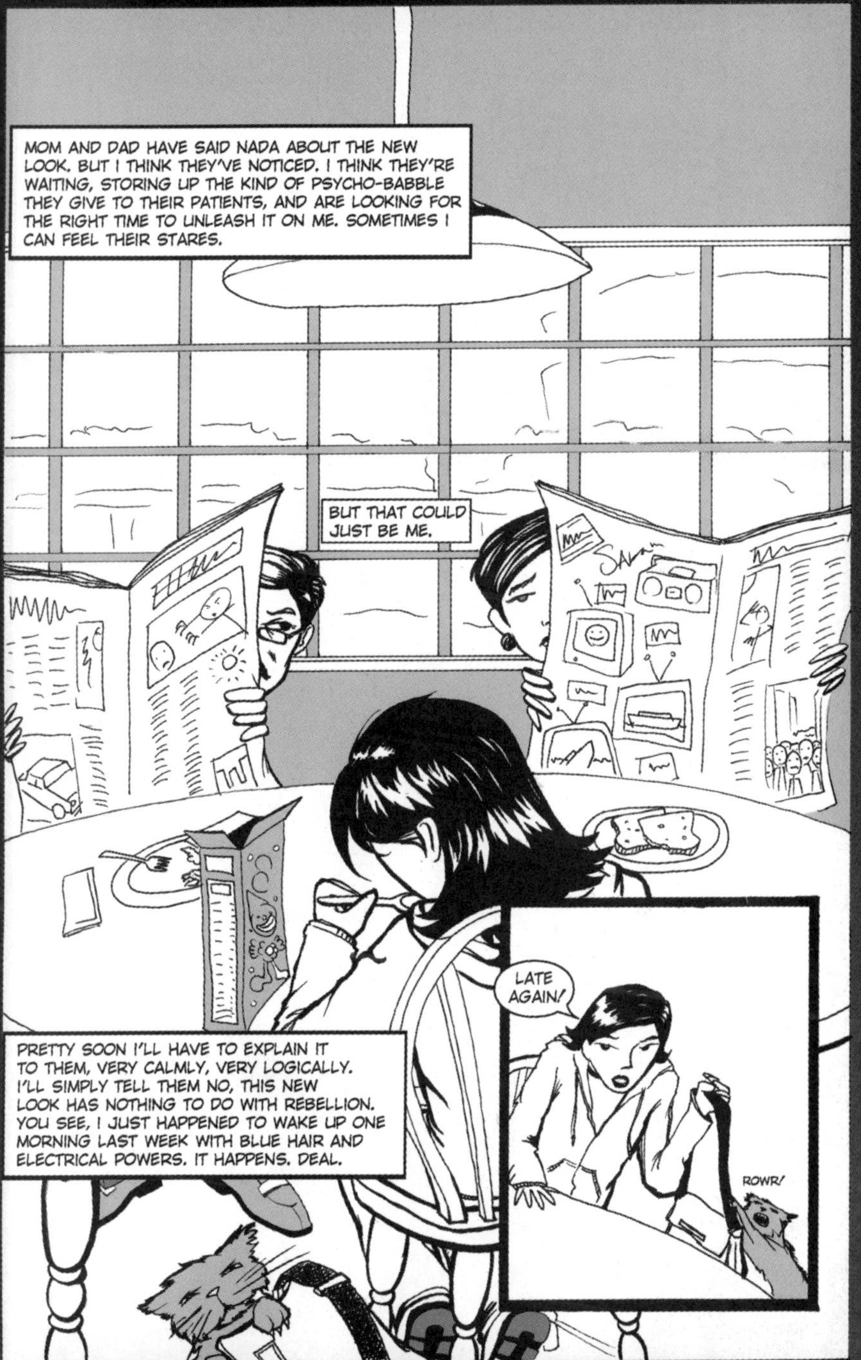
MOM AND DAD HAVE SAID NADA ABOUT THE NEW LOOK. BUT I THINK THEY'VE NOTICED. I THINK THEY'RE WAITING, STORING UP THE KIND OF PSYCHO-BABBLE THEY GIVE TO THEIR PATIENTS, AND ARE LOOKING FOR THE RIGHT TIME TO UNLEASH IT ON ME. SOMETIMES I CAN FEEL THEIR STARES.
BUT THAT COULD JUST BE ME.
PRETTY SOON I'LL HAVE TO EXPLAIN IT TO THEM, VERY CALMLY, VERY LOGICALLY. I'LL SIMPLY TELL THEM NO, THIS NEW LOOK HAS NOTHING TO DO WITH REBELLION. YOU SEE, I JUST HAPPENED TO WAKE UP ONE MORNING LAST WEEK WITH BLUE HAIR AND ELECTRICAL POWERS. IT HAPPENS. DEAL.
LATE AGAIN!
ROWR!

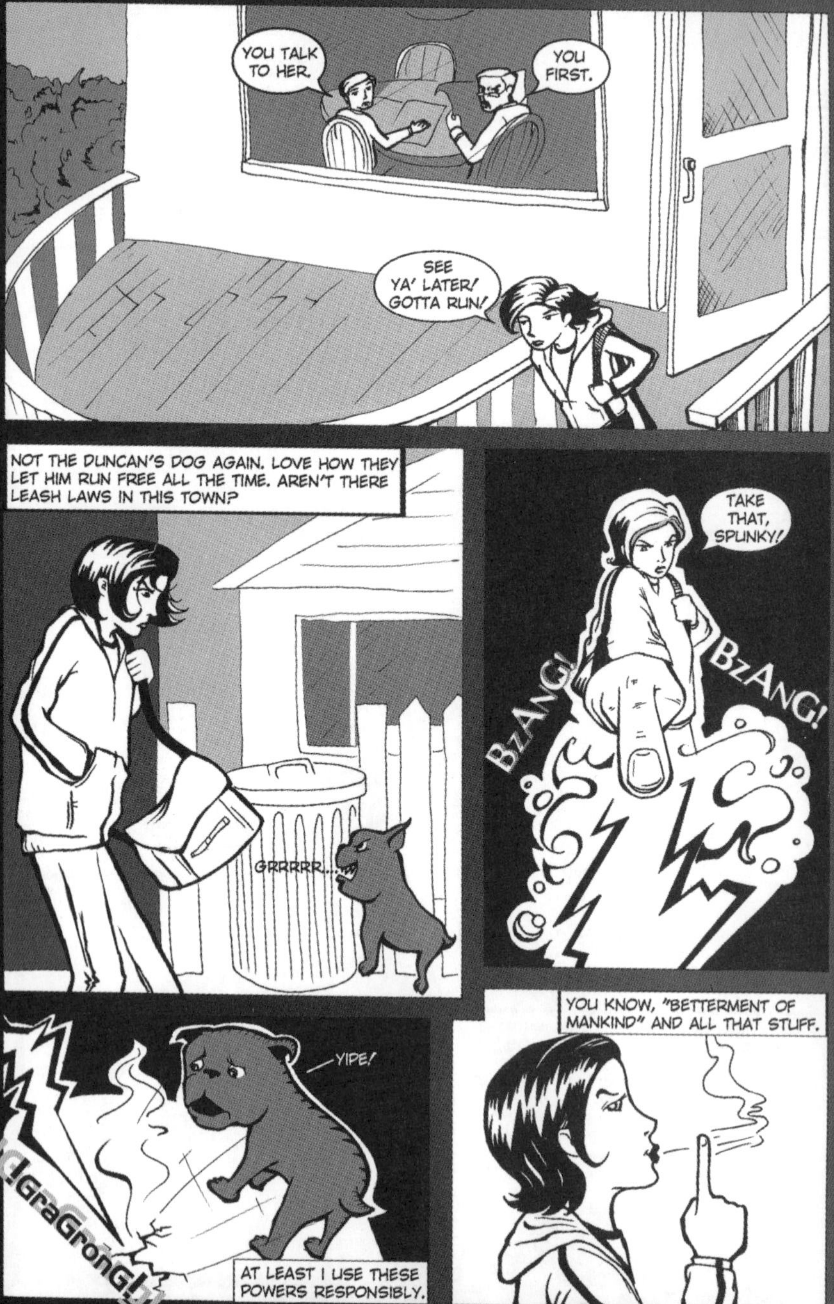
YOU TALK TO HER.
YOU FIRST.
SEE YA' LATER! GOTTA RUN!
NOT THE DUNCAN'S DOG AGAIN. LOVE HOW THEY LET HIM RUN FREE ALL THE TIME. AREN'T THERE LEASH LAWS IN THIS TOWN?
GRRRRRR...
TAKE THAT, SPUNKY!
BzANG!
BzANG!
GraGronG!
YIPE!
AT LEAST I USE THESE POWERS RESPONSIBLY.
YOU KNOW, "BETTERMENT OF MANKIND" AND ALL THAT STUFF.

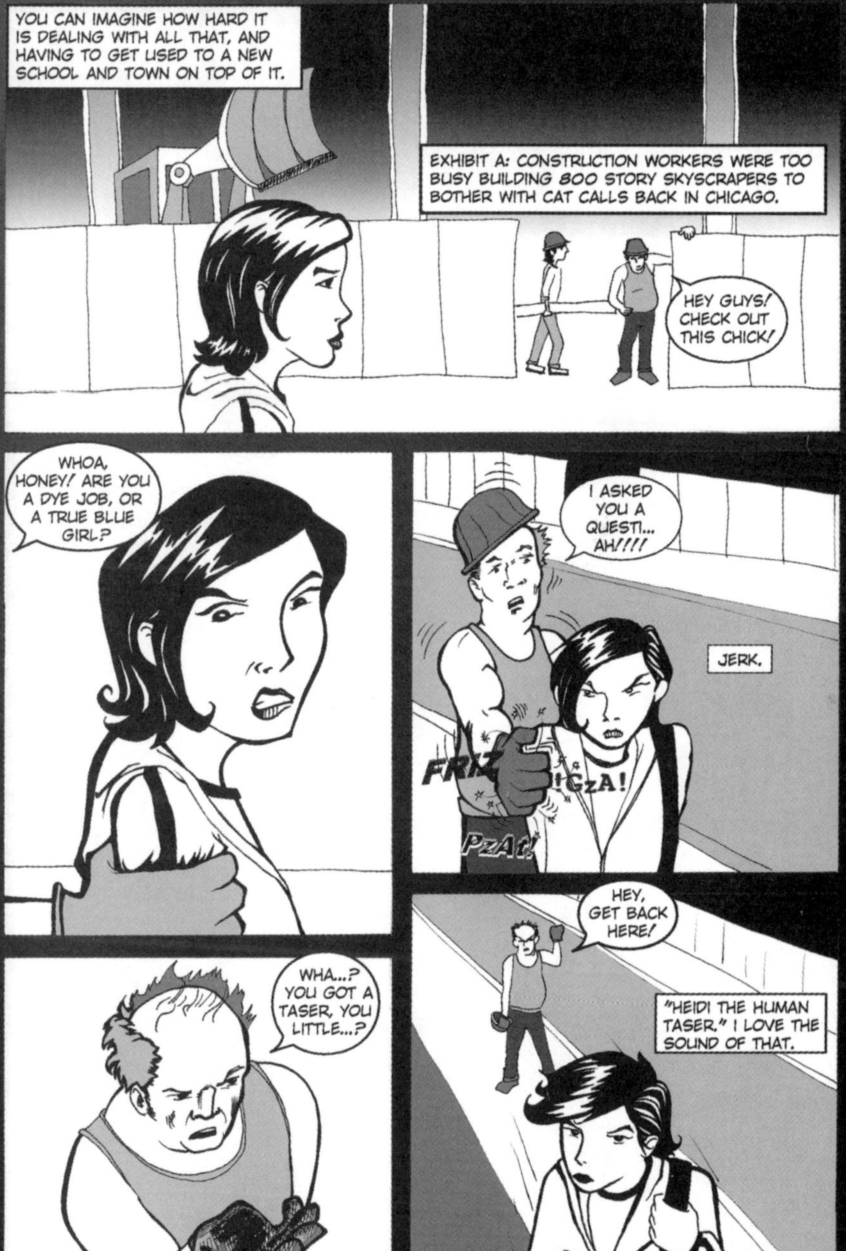
YOU CAN IMAGINE HOW HARD IT IS DEALING WITH ALL THAT, AND HAVING TO GET USED TO A NEW SCHOOL AND TOWN ON TOP OF IT.
EXHIBIT A: CONSTRUCTION WORKERS WERE TOO BUSY BUILDING 800 STORY SKYSCRAPERS TO BOTHER WITH CAT CALLS BACK IN CHICAGO.
HEY GUYS! CHECK OUT THIS CHICK!
WHOA, HONEY! ARE YOU A DYE JOB, OR A TRUE BLUE GIRL?
I ASKED YOU A QUESTI... AH!!!!
JERK.
FRIZ
IGzA!
PzAt!
WHA...? YOU GOT A TASER, YOU LITTLE...?
HEY, GET BACK HERE!
"HEIDI THE HUMAN TASER." I LOVE THE SOUND OF THAT.

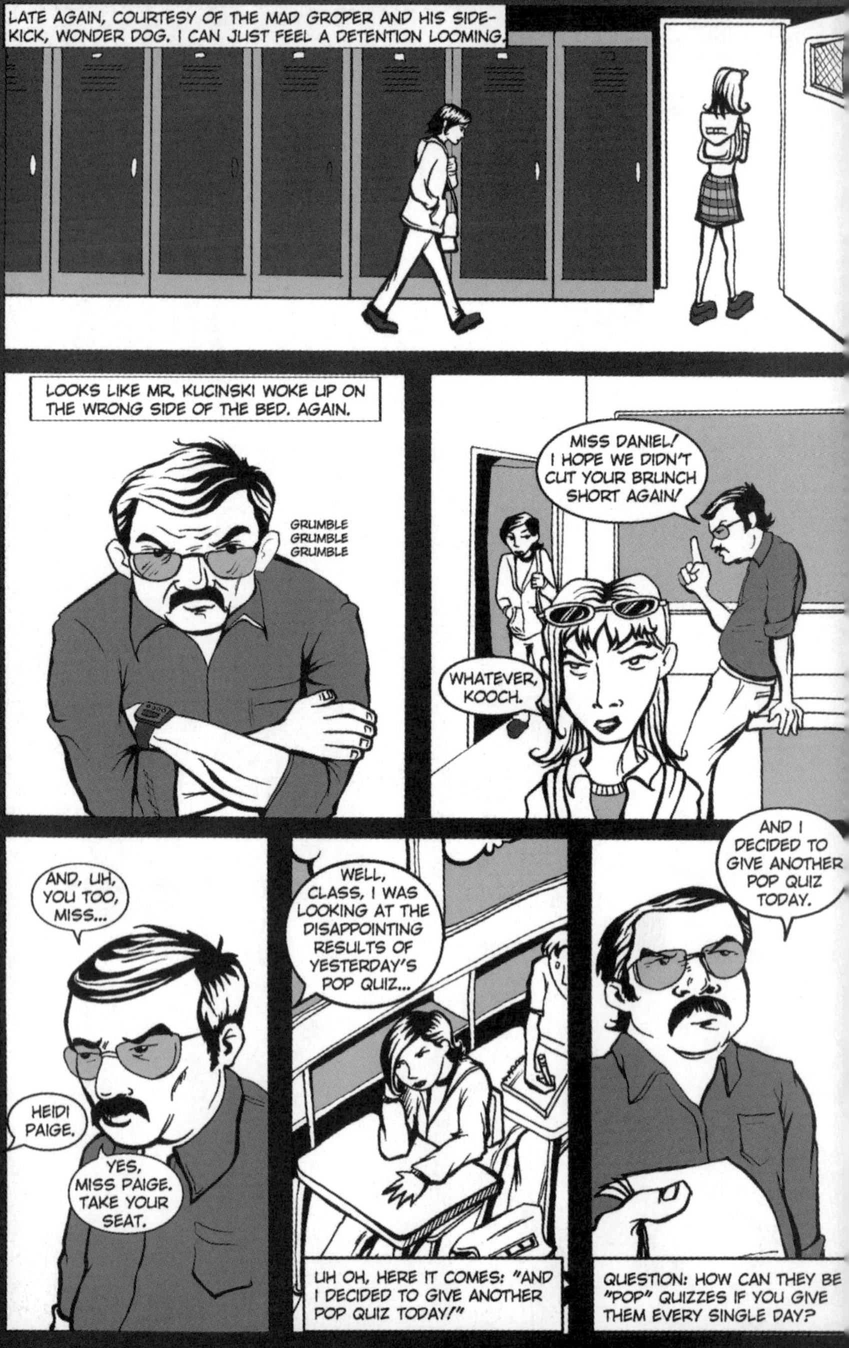
LATE AGAIN, COURTESY OF THE MAD GROPER AND HIS SIDE-KICK, WONDER DOG. I CAN JUST FEEL A DETENTION LOOMING.
LOOKS LIKE MR. KUCINSKI WOKE UP ON THE WRONG SIDE OF THE BED. AGAIN.
GRUMBLE GRUMBLE GRUMBLE
MISS DANIEL! I HOPE WE DIDN'T CUT YOUR BRUNCH SHORT AGAIN!
WHATEVER, KOOCH.
AND, UH, YOU TOO, MISS...
HEIDI PAIGE.
YES, MISS PAIGE. TAKE YOUR SEAT.
WELL, CLASS, I WAS LOOKING AT THE DISAPPOINTING RESULTS OF YESTERDAY'S POP QUIZ...
UH OH, HERE IT COMES: "AND I DECIDED TO GIVE ANOTHER POP QUIZ TODAY!"
AND I DECIDED TO GIVE ANOTHER POP QUIZ TODAY.
QUESTION: HOW CAN THEY BE "POP" QUIZZES IF YOU GIVE THEM EVERY SINGLE DAY?

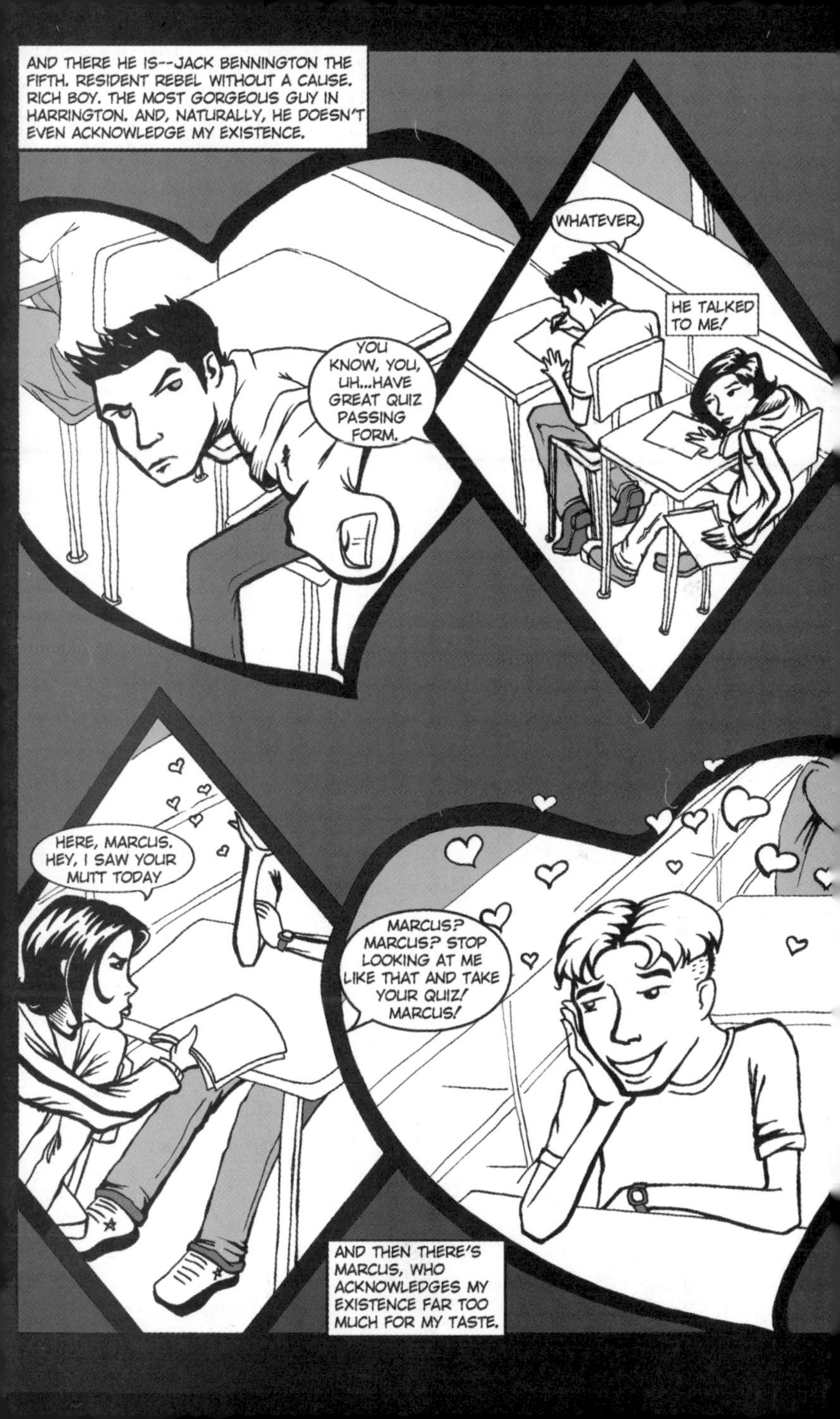
AND THERE HE IS--JACK BENNINGTON THE FIFTH. RESIDENT REBEL WITHOUT A CAUSE. RICH BOY. THE MOST GORGEOUS GUY IN HARRINGTON. AND, NATURALLY, HE DOESN'T EVEN ACKNOWLEDGE MY EXISTENCE.
YOU KNOW, YOU, UH...HAVE GREAT QUIZ PASSING FORM.
WHATEVER.
HE TALKED TO ME!
HERE, MARCUS. HEY, I SAW YOUR MUTT TODAY
MARCUS? MARCUS? STOP LOOKING AT ME LIKE THAT AND TAKE YOUR QUIZ! MARCUS!
AND THEN THERE'S MARCUS, WHO ACKNOWLEDGES MY EXISTENCE FAR TOO MUCH FOR MY TASTE.

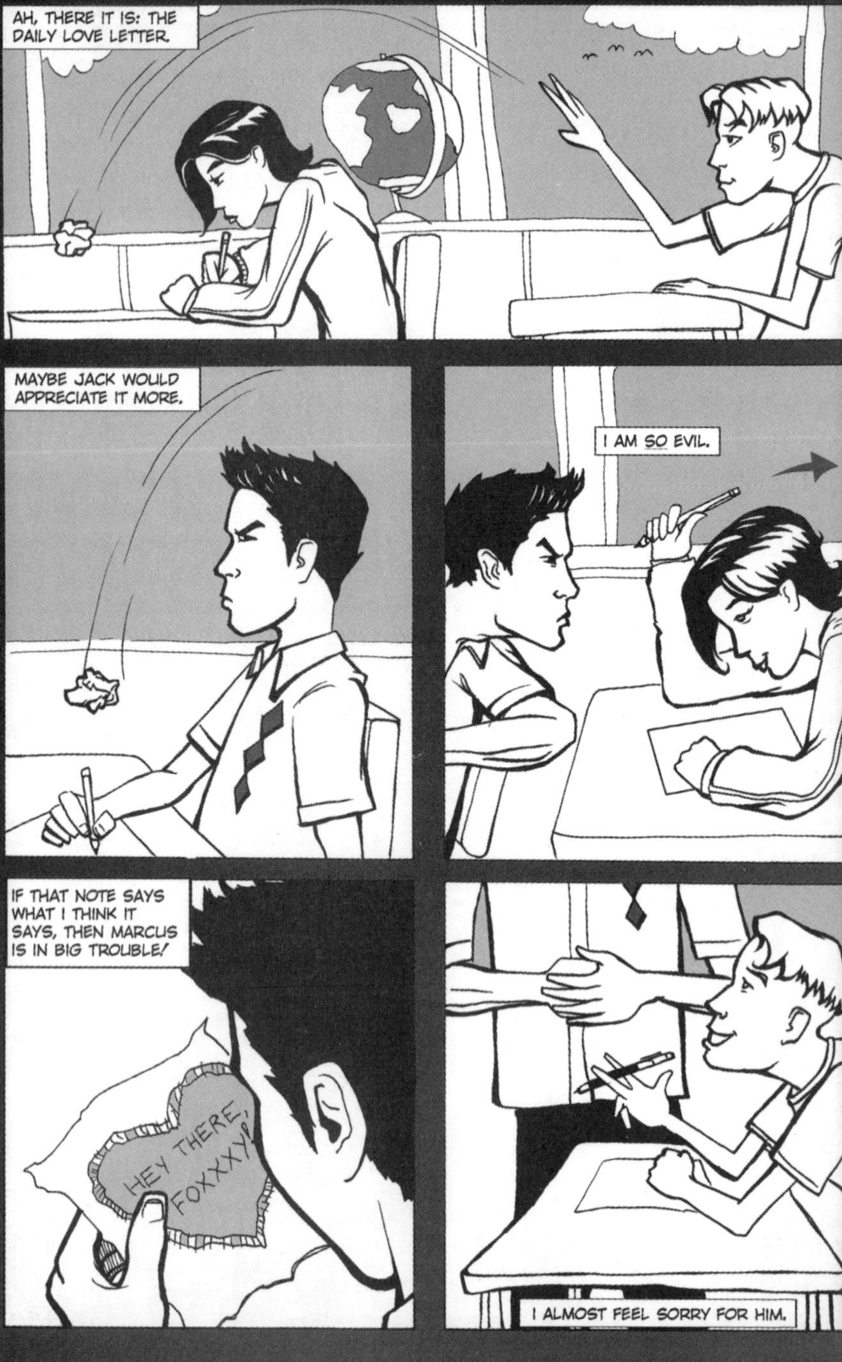
AH, THERE IT IS: THE DAILY LOVE LETTER.
MAYBE JACK WOULD APPRECIATE IT MORE.
I AM SO EVIL.
IF THAT NOTE SAYS WHAT I THINK IT SAYS, THEN MARCUS IS IN BIG TROUBLE!
HEY THERE, FOXXXY!
I ALMOST FEEL SORRY FOR HIM.

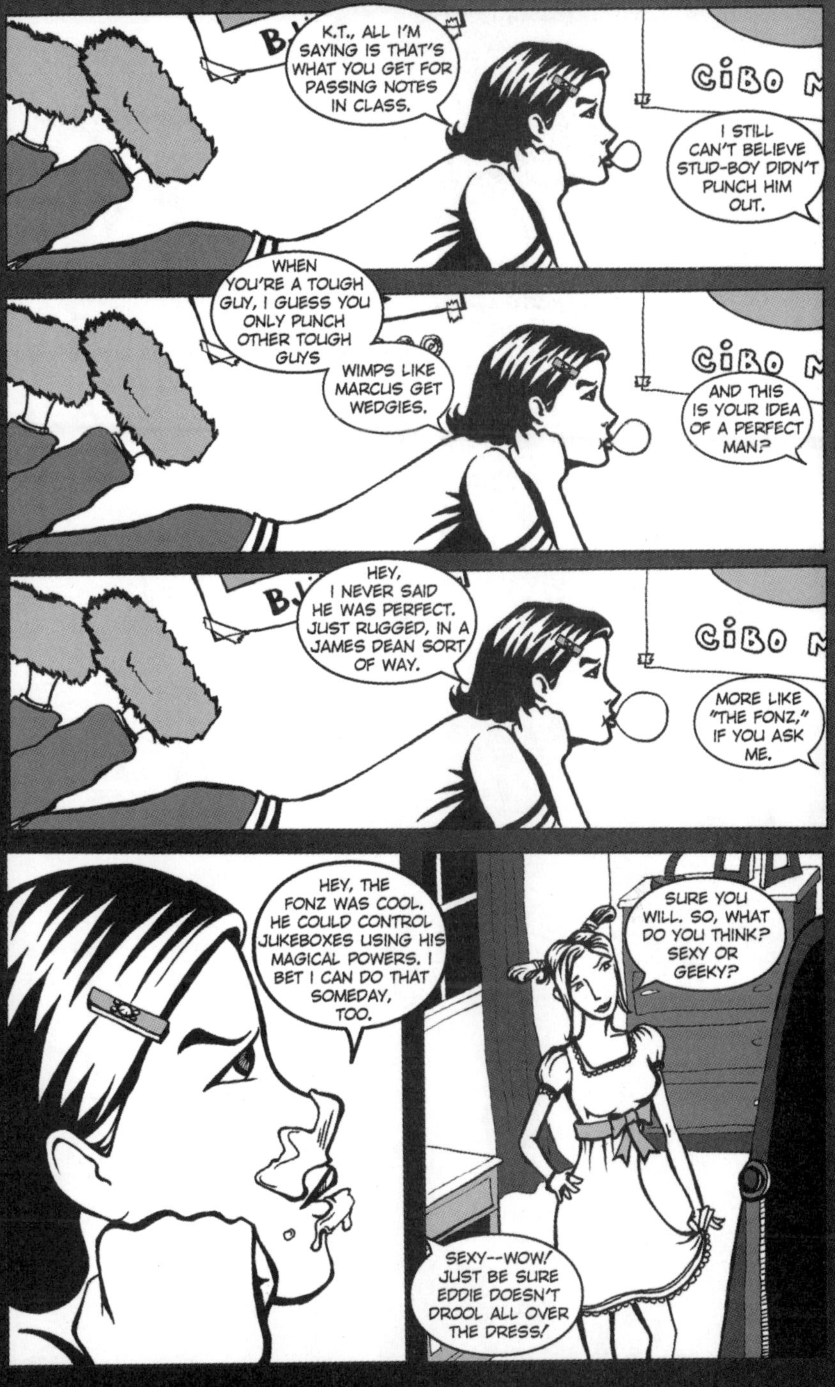

K.T., ALL I'M SAYING IS THAT'S WHAT YOU GET FOR PASSING NOTES IN CLASS.
I STILL CAN'T BELIEVE STUD-BOY DIDN'T PUNCH HIM OUT.
WHEN YOU'RE A TOUGH GUY, I GUESS YOU ONLY PUNCH OTHER TOUGH GUYS
WIMPS LIKE MARCUS GET WEDGIES.
AND THIS IS YOUR IDEA OF A PERFECT MAN?
HEY, I NEVER SAID HE WAS PERFECT. JUST RUGGED, IN A JAMES DEAN SORT OF WAY.
MORE LIKE "THE FONZ," IF YOU ASK ME.
HEY, THE FONZ WAS COOL. HE COULD CONTROL JUKEBOXES USING HIS MAGICAL POWERS. I BET I CAN DO THAT SOMEDAY, TOO.
SURE YOU WILL. SO, WHAT DO YOU THINK? SEXY OR GEEKY?
SEXY--WOW! JUST BE SURE EDDIE DOESN'T DROOL ALL OVER THE DRESS!

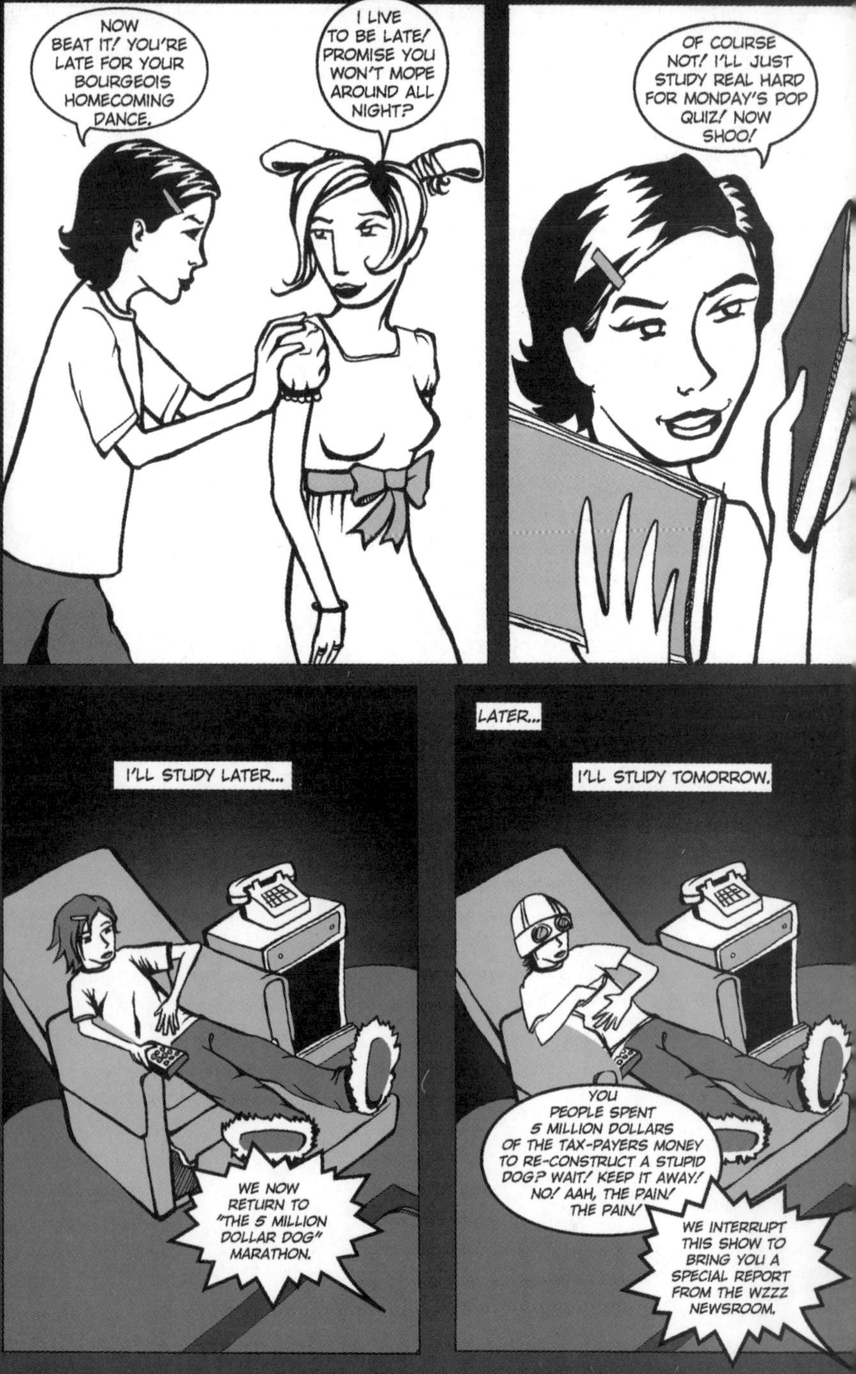
NOW BEAT IT! YOU'RE LATE FOR YOUR BOURGEOIS HOMECOMING DANCE.
I LIVE TO BE LATE! PROMISE YOU WON'T MOPE AROUND ALL NIGHT?
OF COURSE NOT! I'LL JUST STUDY REAL HARD FOR MONDAY'S POP QUIZ! NOW SHOO!
I'LL STUDY LATER...
WE NOW RETURN TO "THE 5 MILLION DOLLAR DOG" MARATHON.
LATER...
I'LL STUDY TOMORROW.
YOU PEOPLE SPENT 5 MILLION DOLLARS OF THE TAX-PAYERS MONEY TO RE-CONSTRUCT A STUPID DOG? WAIT! KEEP IT AWAY! NO! AAH, THE PAIN! THE PAIN!
WE INTERRUPT THIS SHOW TO BRING YOU A SPECIAL REPORT FROM THE WZZZ NEWSROOM.

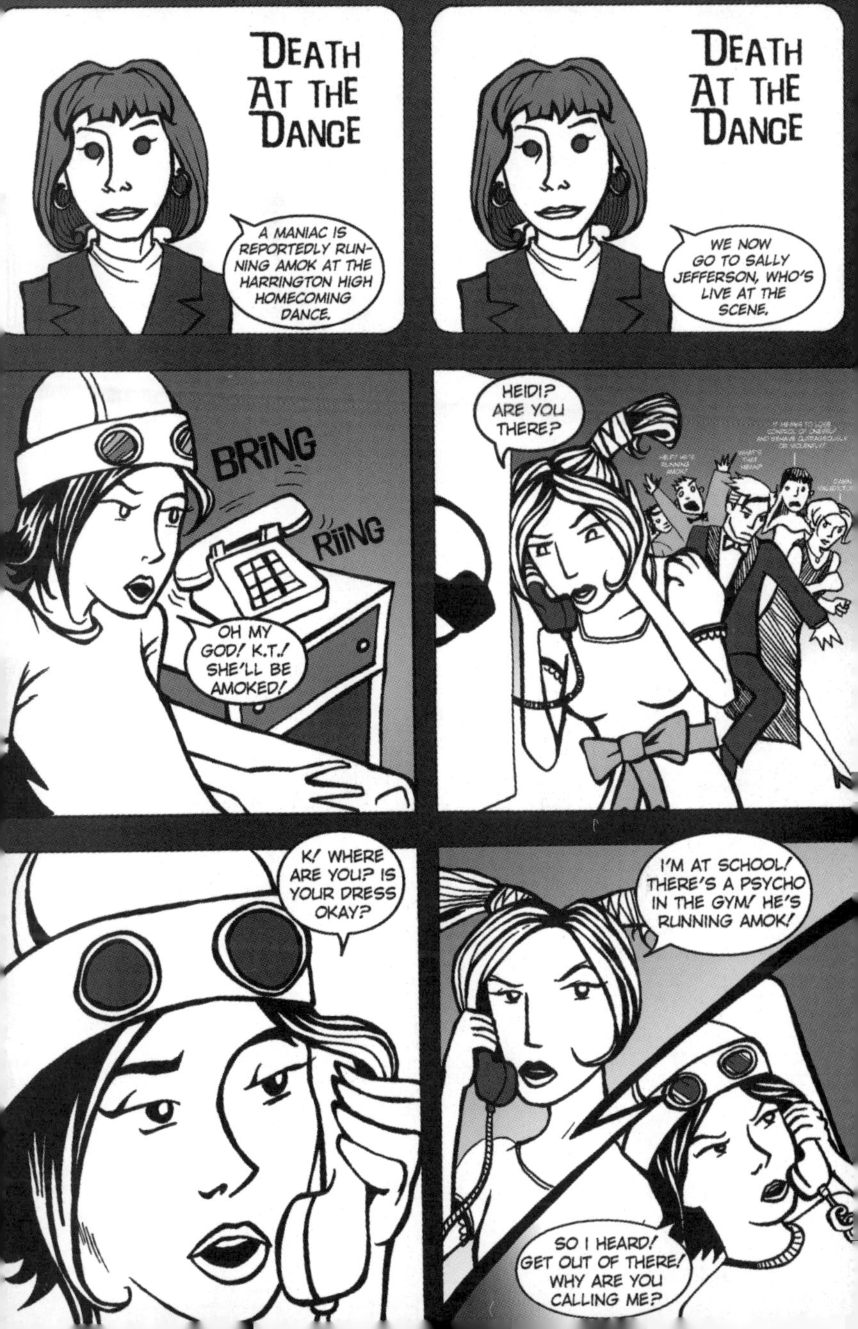
DEATH AT THE DANCE
A MANIAC IS REPORTEDLY RUN-NING AMOK AT THE HARRINGTON HIGH HOMECOMING DANCE.
DEATH AT THE DANCE
WE NOW GO TO SALLY JEFFERSON, WHO'S LIVE AT THE SCENE.
BRING
RIING
OH MY GOD! K.T.! SHE'LL BE AMOKED!
HEIDI? ARE YOU THERE?
K! WHERE ARE YOU? IS YOUR DRESS OKAY?
I'M AT SCHOOL! THERE'S A PSYCHO IN THE GYM! HE'S RUNNING AMOK!
SO I HEARD! GET OUT OF THERE! WHY ARE YOU CALLING ME?

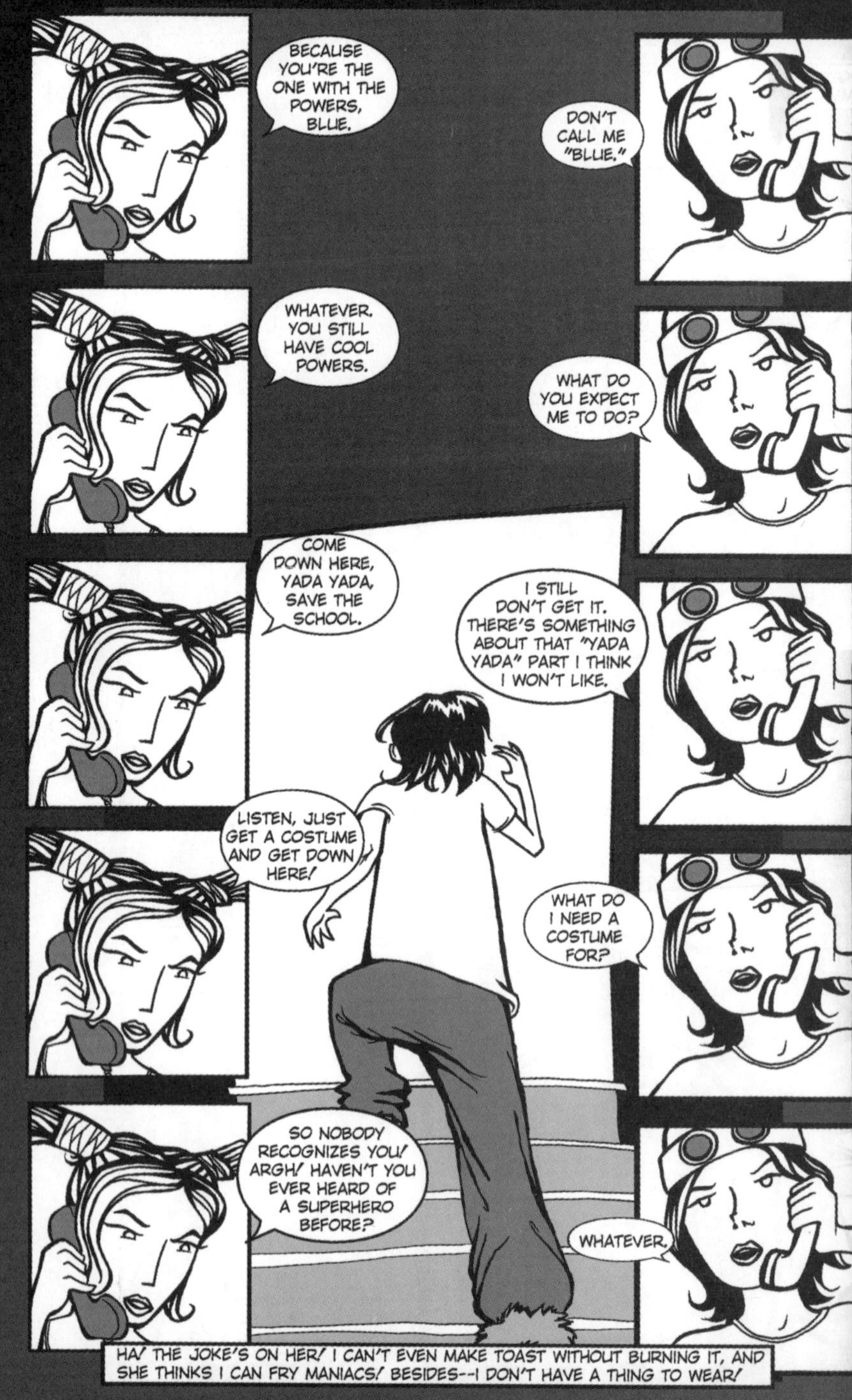
BECAUSE YOU'RE THE ONE WITH THE POWERS, BLUE.
DON'T CALL ME "BLUE."
WHATEVER. YOU STILL HAVE COOL POWERS.
WHAT DO YOU EXPECT ME TO DO?
COME DOWN HERE, YADA YADA, SAVE THE SCHOOL.
I STILL DON'T GET IT. THERE'S SOMETHING ABOUT THAT "YADA YADA" PART I THINK I WON'T LIKE.
LISTEN, JUST GET A COSTUME AND GET DOWN HERE!
WHAT DO I NEED A COSTUME FOR?
SO NOBODY RECOGNIZES YOU! ARGH! HAVEN'T YOU EVER HEARD OF A SUPERHERO BEFORE?
WHATEVER.
HA! THE JOKE'S ON HER! I CAN'T EVEN MAKE TOAST WITHOUT BURNING IT, AND SHE THINKS I CAN FRY MANIACS! BESIDES--I DON'T HAVE A THING TO WEAR!

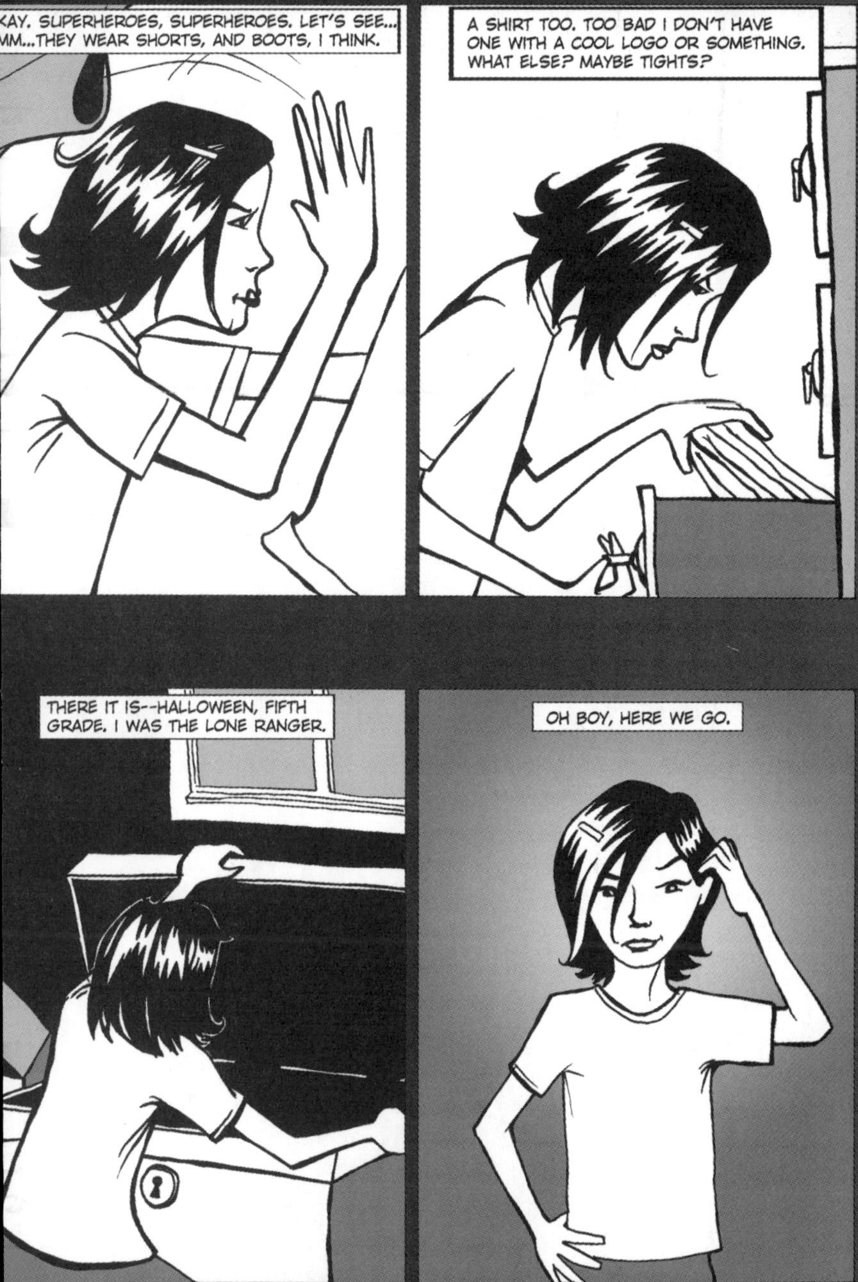
KAY. SUPERHEROES, SUPERHEROES. LET'S SEE...
MM...THEY WEAR SHORTS, AND BOOTS, I THINK.
A SHIRT TOO. TOO BAD I DON'T HAVE ONE WITH A COOL LOGO OR SOMETHING. WHAT ELSE? MAYBE TIGHTS?
THERE IT IS--HALLOWEEN, FIFTH GRADE. I WAS THE LONE RANGER.
OH BOY, HERE WE GO.

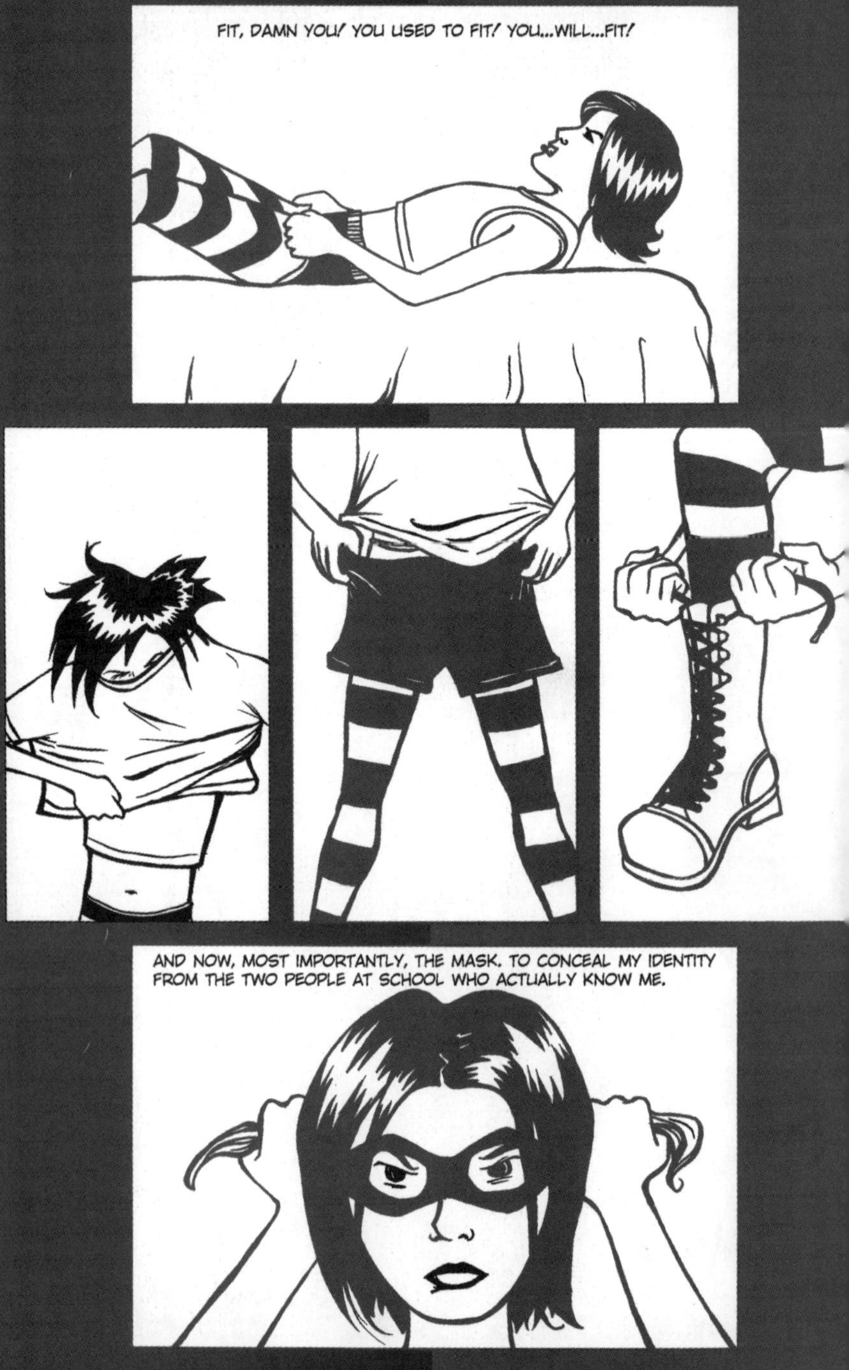
FIT, DAMN YOU! YOU USED TO FIT! YOU...WILL...FIT!
AND NOW, MOST IMPORTANTLY, THE MASK. TO CONCEAL MY IDENTITY FROM THE TWO PEOPLE AT SCHOOL WHO ACTUALLY KNOW ME.

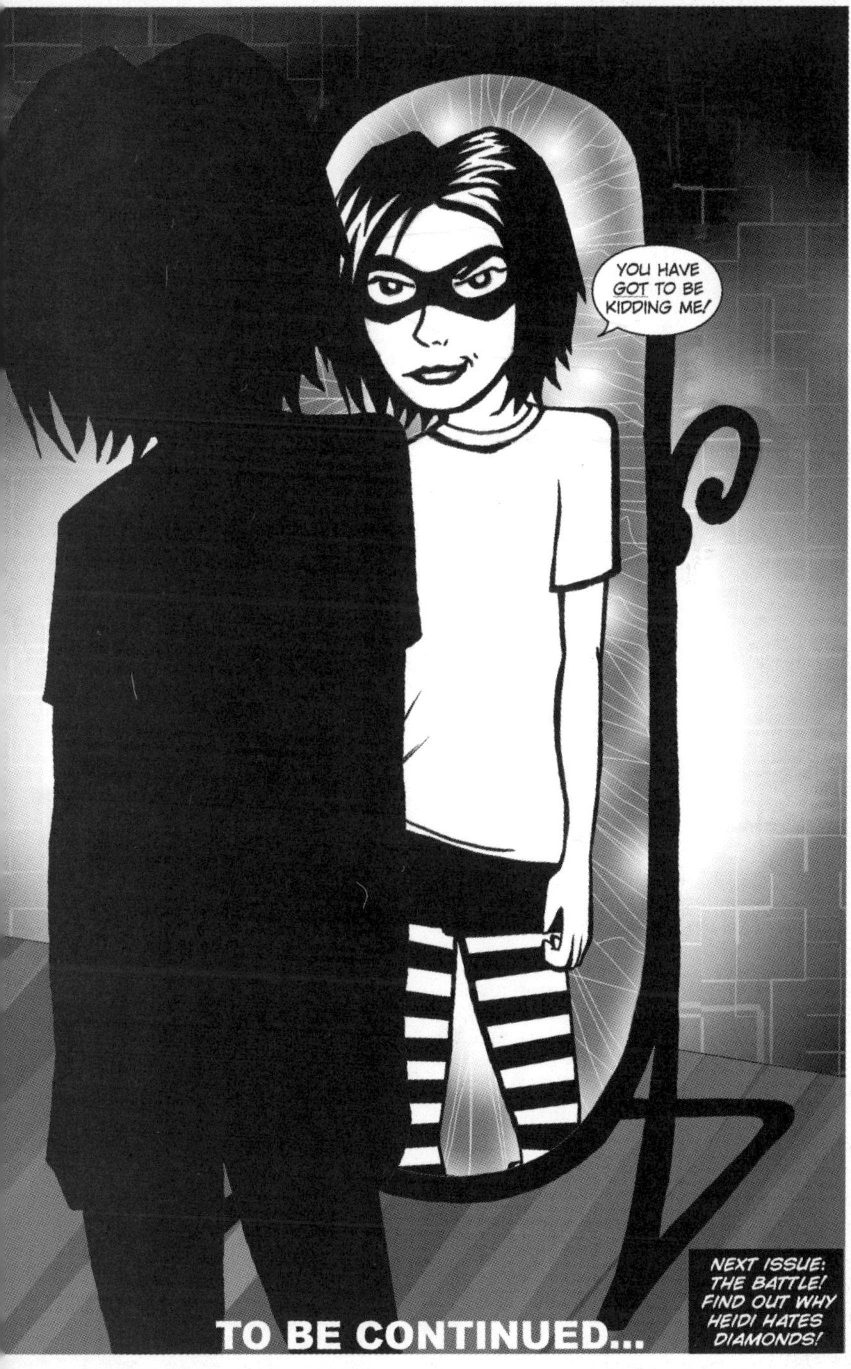
YOU HAVE GOT TO BE KIDDING ME!
TO BE CONTINUED...
NEXT ISSUE: THE BATTLE! FIND OUT WHY HEIDI HATES DIAMONDS!

Vol.53 No.27

Harrington Post-Gazette

www.ampcomics.com "Serving the Town of Harrington since 1946"

Cloudy, High 55 Details on Page 2   **Final Edition**

Census Says: Harrington Population Boom!

Mayor Schaul calls numbers "astounding"

The population in Harrington increased by nearly fifty percent over the last nine years, new census data has shown.

"The numbers are astounding," Mayor Melinda S. Schaul said during a press conference yesterday. "Clearly, this shows my plan to add an extra drinking fountain in Harrington Park has paid off!"

After the laughter in the room died down, Mayor Schaul said, "What? Why is everyone laughing? You think people moved here for some other reasons? It's a good fountain, people! Stop laughing!"

Schaul continued on in such a manner, pretending she was serious even though everyone knew she must be joking. At least, everyone hoped she was just joking.

Experts say the boom is clearly related to the growth of the Harrington Institute of Mental Health, and its accompanying University.

"Enrollment is up twenty-five percent at the University in the last five years," Institute President John Reeves, Jr., said, "and I can't tell you how thilling it is to see all my father's hard work come to fruition!" John Reeves, Sr. founded the town of Harrington in 1932.

Harrington Mall Re-Opens

Officials call power outage a mystery

Harrington Mall, closed since last Monday due to an electrical problem, will re-open this Friday, mall officials said.

"Harrington Power still hasn't discovered what caused the transformer to over-heat last week, considering there was no storm or increased power usage throughout the city on that day," Harrington Mall owner Phineas K. Whopmaster said.

"The 'why' is a mystery for another day," Harrington Power representative Roger Hourihane said. "For now, we're just happy to get the center open and in business again."

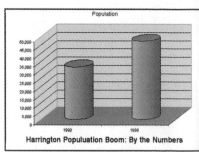

Harrington Populaution Boom: By the Numbers

Sunday's State Lottery Results:
7 9 13 23 33 91

In Today's Post-Gazette:

Meet Harrington's newest sports star. Follow Elsa Daniel as she gets ready for her first big challenge in her brand new town. Section C, Page 1

"Beloved" Teacher James "Kooch" Kucinski mysteriously disappears graciously retires. Find out why one of Harrington High's favorites is calling it a career. Section Z, Page 30

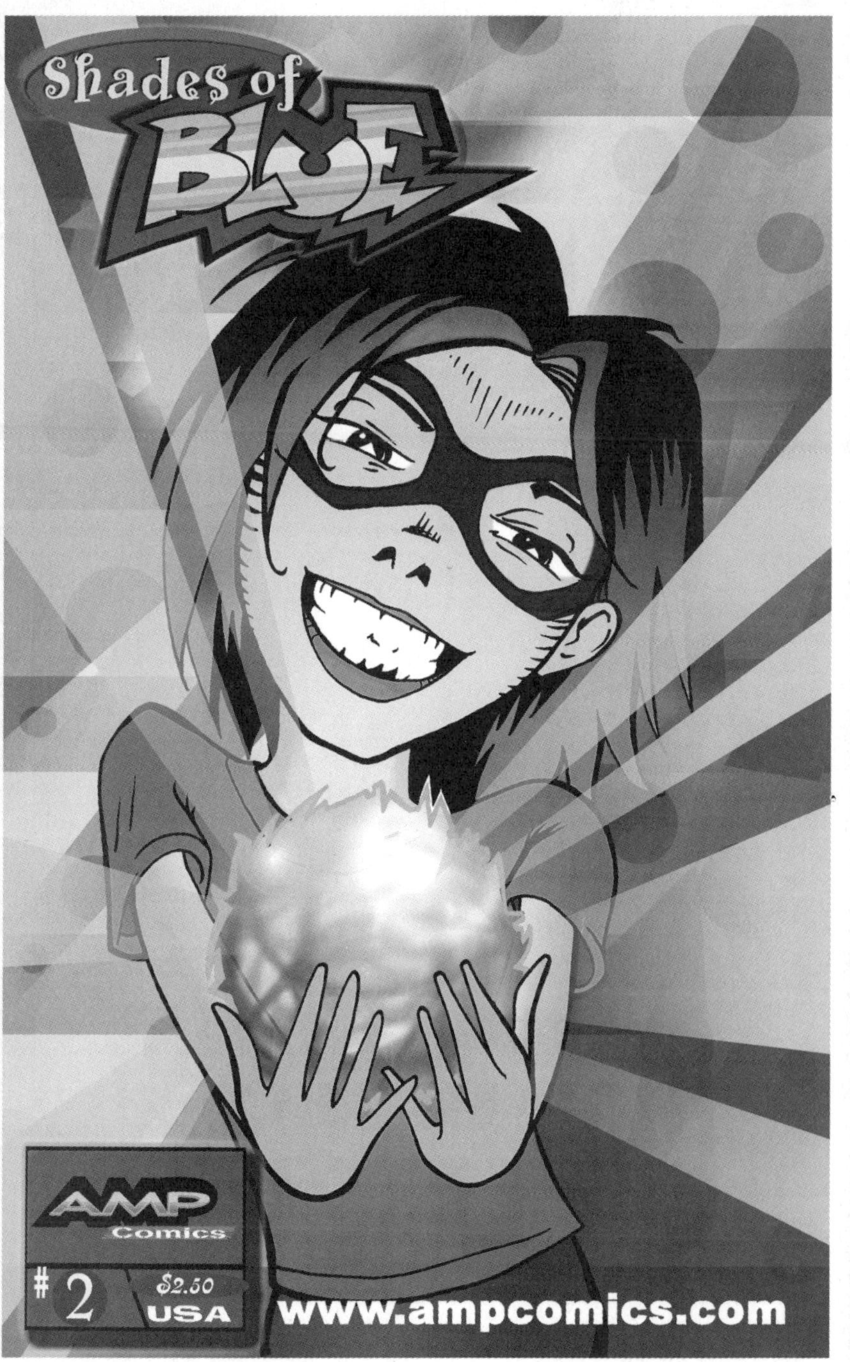
Shades of
BLUE
AMP
Comics
2
$2.50
USA
www.ampcomics.com

"The Definition of 'Amok' and Other Time-Killing Activities-- Part II"

Flowery Words:
Rachel Nacion & James S. Harris

Pretty Drawings, Striking Inks, Colors, Cover Design, and General Nice Guy:
Greg Grucel

The Players:

Heidi Paige:
Reluctant Hero

Jack:
Rebellious love
interest

K.T. O'Hara:
Heidi's
Best Friend

Marcus:
Geek with
a car

The story thus far: Heidi Paige was an average, jaded high school junior until a few weeks ago. One morning, Heidi woke up with blue hair and the power to control electricity. Well, control is a bit of an overstatement. Anyway, while spending a quiet Saturday evening watching the tube, Heidi gets a call from her best friend K.T. Seems some mysterious thug is running amok at the Homecoming Dance. K.T. is able to convince Heidi to put together a superhero costume, and use her newfound powers to save the Homecoming Dance (because really, is there anything more important than the Homecoming Dance? Well, maybe prom...)!

Shades of Blue, Vol. 1, Number 2, August, 2000. First Printing. Published by Amp Comics, 335 N. Seymour Ave., Mundelein, IL 60060. Shades of Blue is © 2000 by James S. Harris and Rachel Nacion. ALL RIGHTS RESERVED. Any similarity to actual persons living or dead is purely coincidental. No reproduction permitted except for the purpose of review. Printed in the U.S.A.

The Definition of 'Amok' and Other Time-Killing Activities

words:

Rachel Nacion
Jim Harris

pictures:

Greg Grucel

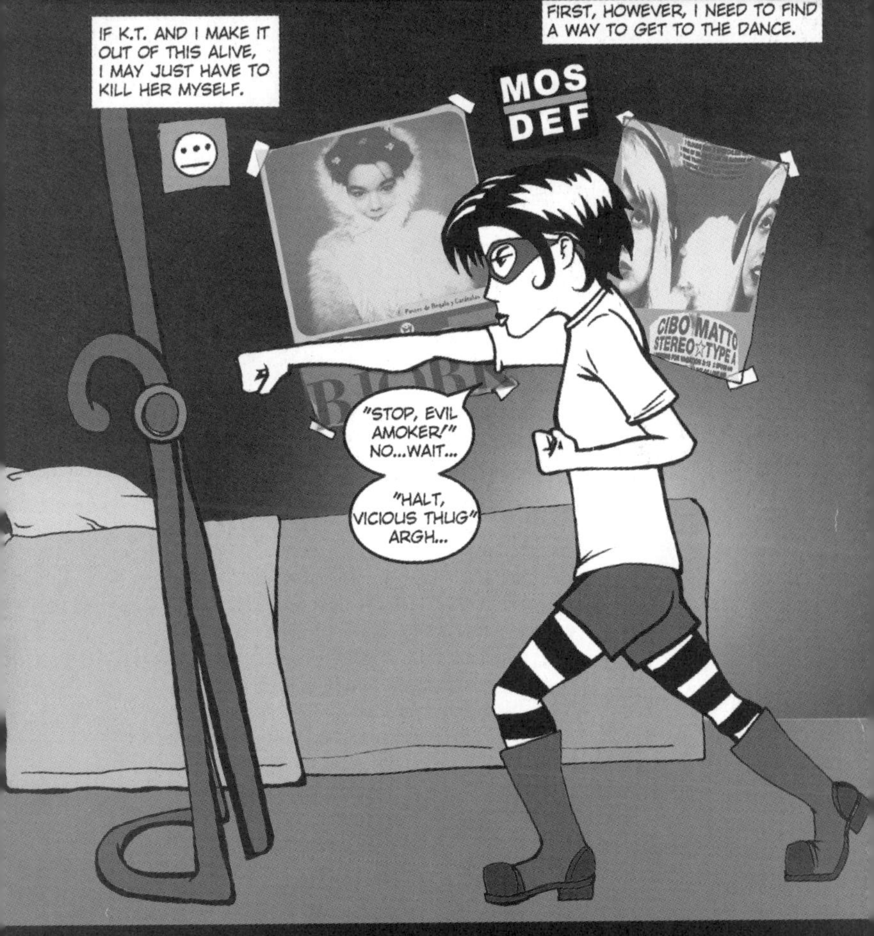
IF K.T. AND I MAKE IT OUT OF THIS ALIVE, I MAY JUST HAVE TO KILL HER MYSELF.
FIRST, HOWEVER, I NEED TO FIND A WAY TO GET TO THE DANCE.
MOS DEF
CIBO MATTO
STEREO☆TYPE A
"STOP, EVIL AMOKER!" NO...WAIT...
"HALT, VICIOUS THUG" ARGH...

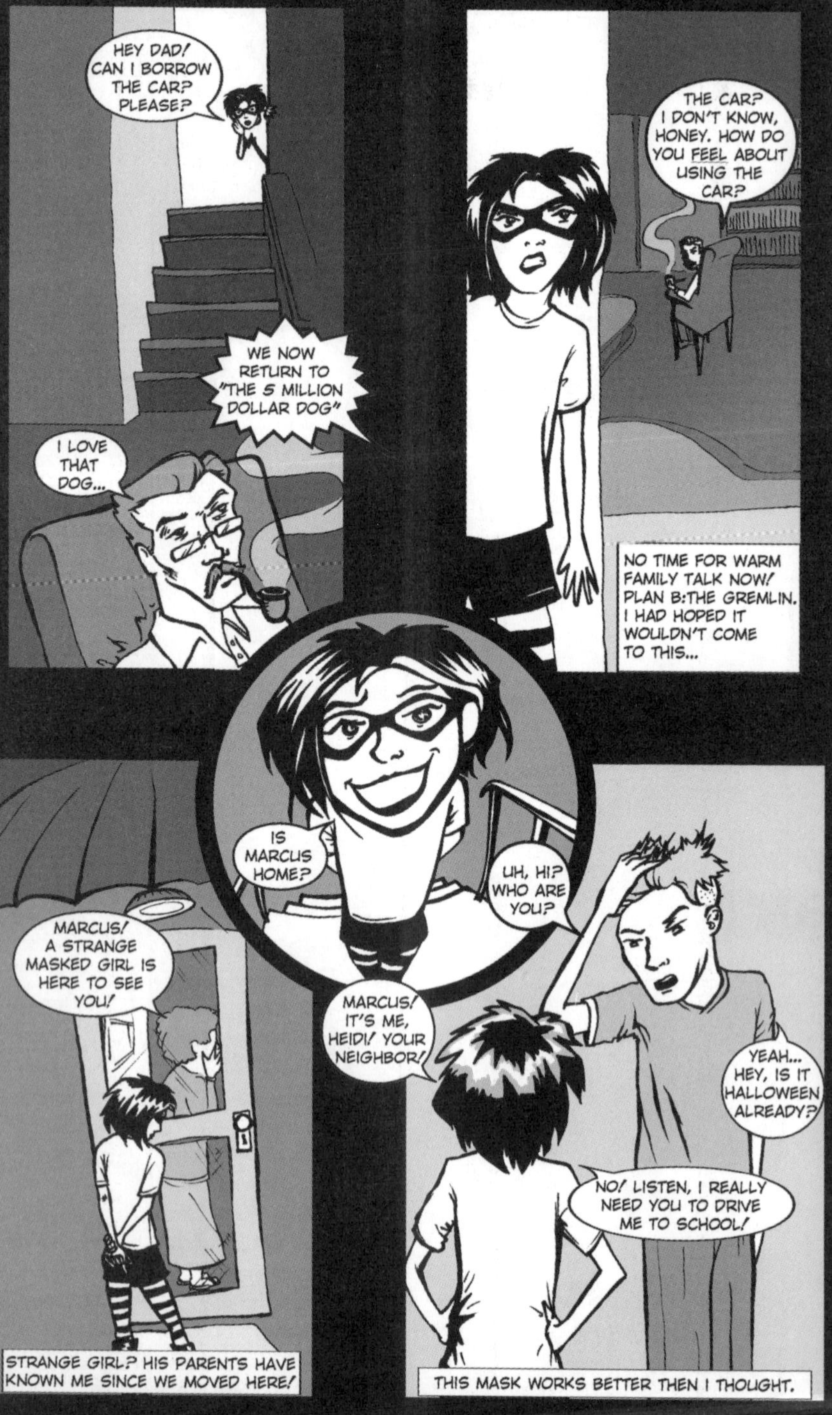
HEY DAD! CAN I BORROW THE CAR? PLEASE?
WE NOW RETURN TO "THE 5 MILLION DOLLAR DOG"
I LOVE THAT DOG...
THE CAR? I DON'T KNOW, HONEY. HOW DO YOU FEEL ABOUT USING THE CAR?
NO TIME FOR WARM FAMILY TALK NOW! PLAN B:THE GREMLIN. I HAD HOPED IT WOULDN'T COME TO THIS...
IS MARCUS HOME?
MARCUS! A STRANGE MASKED GIRL IS HERE TO SEE YOU!
STRANGE GIRL? HIS PARENTS HAVE KNOWN ME SINCE WE MOVED HERE!
UH, HI? WHO ARE YOU?
MARCUS! IT'S ME, HEIDI! YOUR NEIGHBOR!
YEAH... HEY, IS IT HALLOWEEN ALREADY?
NO! LISTEN, I REALLY NEED YOU TO DRIVE ME TO SCHOOL!
THIS MASK WORKS BETTER THEN I THOUGHT.

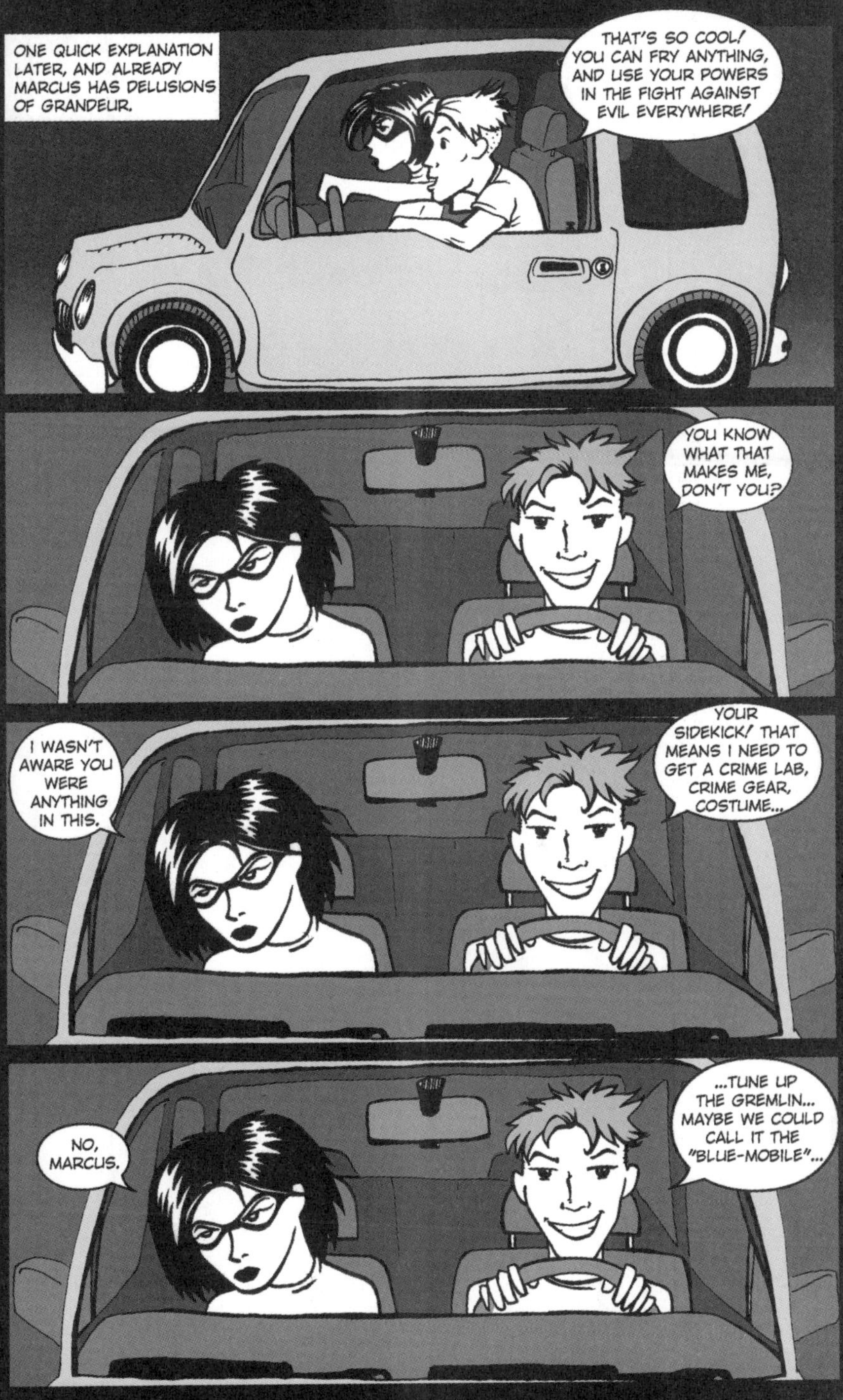
ONE QUICK EXPLANATION LATER, AND ALREADY MARCUS HAS DELUSIONS OF GRANDEUR.
THAT'S SO COOL! YOU CAN FRY ANYTHING, AND USE YOUR POWERS IN THE FIGHT AGAINST EVIL EVERYWHERE!
YOU KNOW WHAT THAT MAKES ME, DON'T YOU?
YOUR SIDEKICK! THAT MEANS I NEED TO GET A CRIME LAB, CRIME GEAR, COSTUME...
I WASN'T AWARE YOU WERE ANYTHING IN THIS.
...TUNE UP THE GREMLIN... MAYBE WE COULD CALL IT THE "BLUE-MOBILE"...
NO, MARCUS.

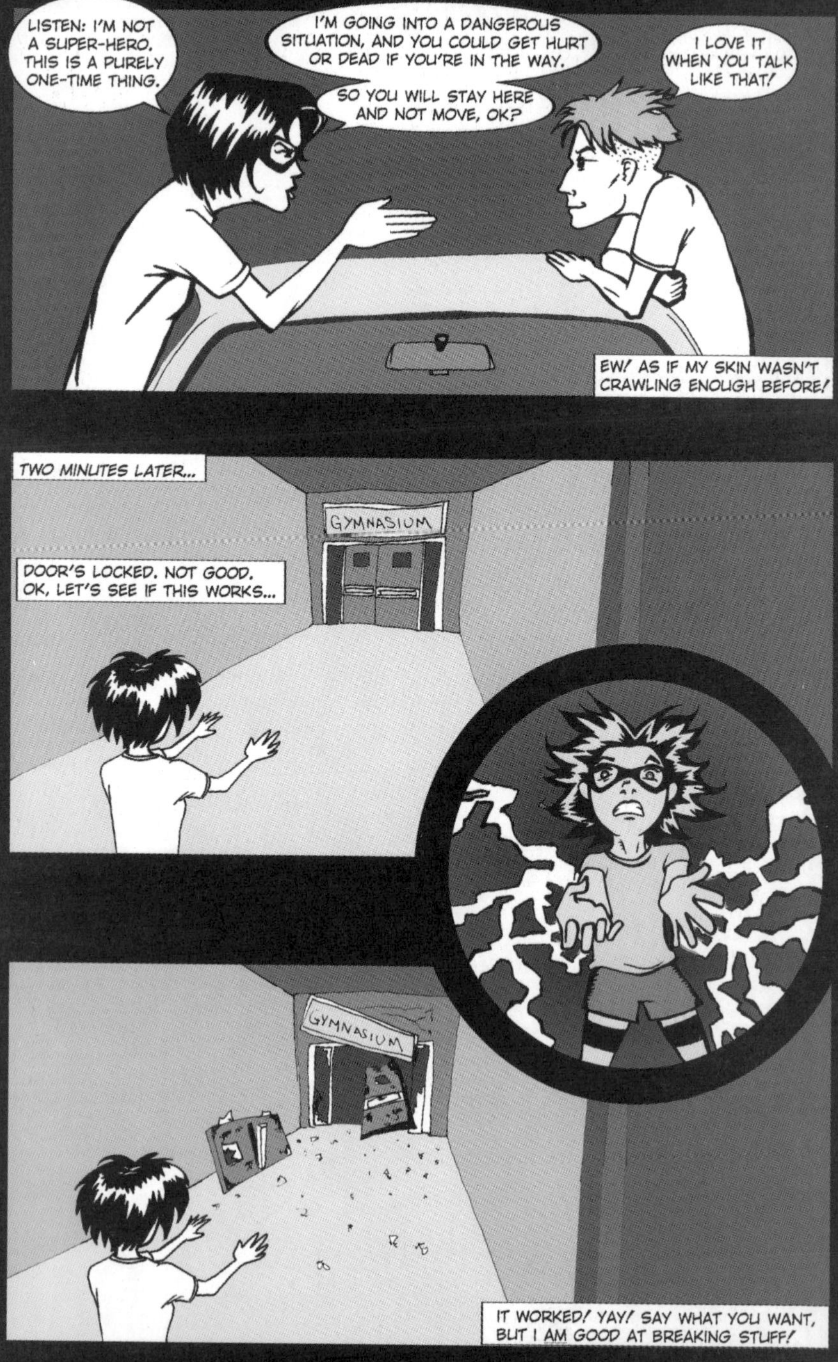
LISTEN: I'M NOT A SUPER-HERO. THIS IS A PURELY ONE-TIME THING.
I'M GOING INTO A DANGEROUS SITUATION, AND YOU COULD GET HURT OR DEAD IF YOU'RE IN THE WAY.
SO YOU WILL STAY HERE AND NOT MOVE, OK?
I LOVE IT WHEN YOU TALK LIKE THAT!
EW! AS IF MY SKIN WASN'T CRAWLING ENOUGH BEFORE!
TWO MINUTES LATER...
GYMNASIUM
DOOR'S LOCKED. NOT GOOD. OK, LET'S SEE IF THIS WORKS...
GYMNASIUM
IT WORKED! YAY! SAY WHAT YOU WANT, BUT I AM GOOD AT BREAKING STUFF!

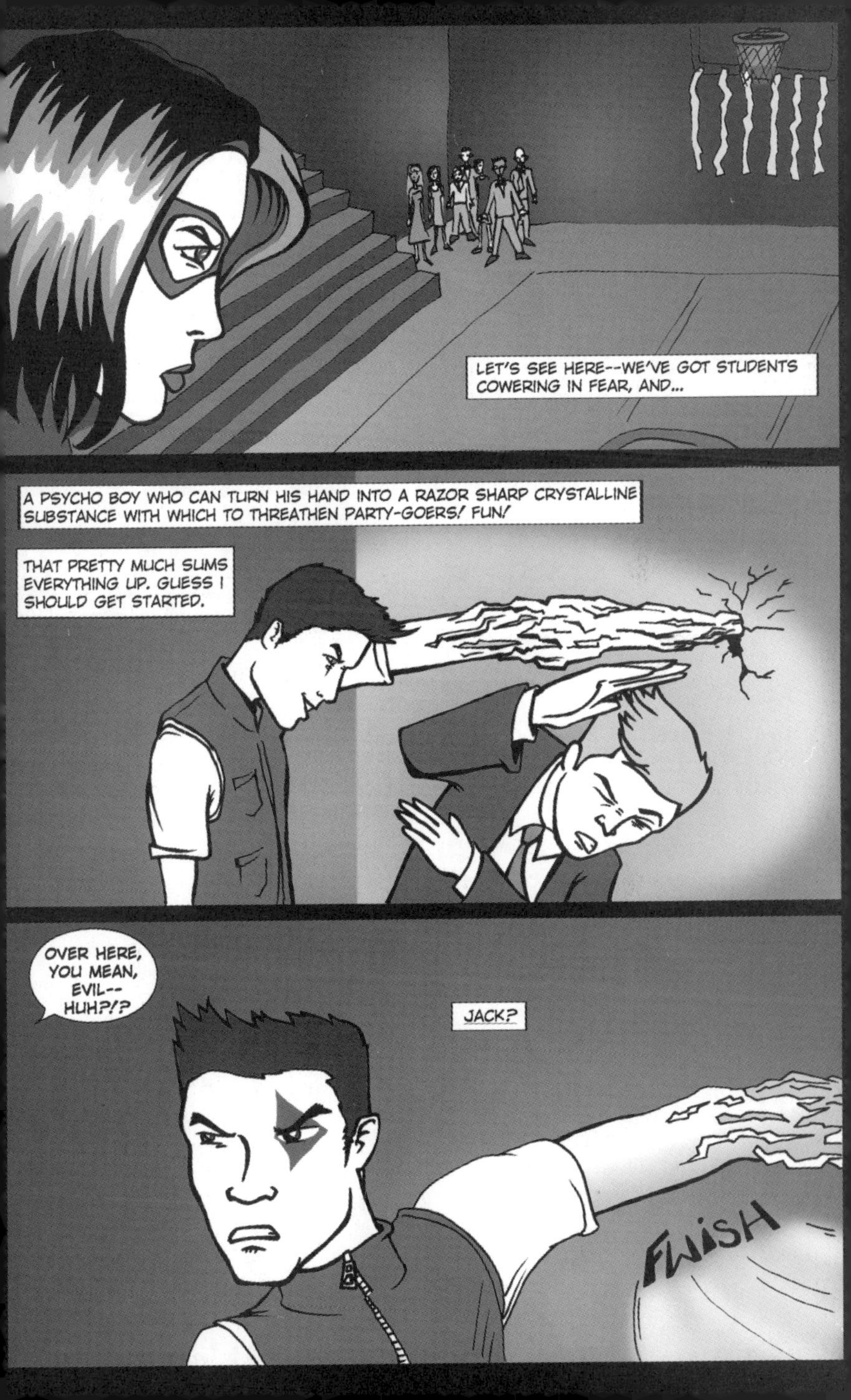
LET'S SEE HERE--WE'VE GOT STUDENTS COWERING IN FEAR, AND...
A PSYCHO BOY WHO CAN TURN HIS HAND INTO A RAZOR SHARP CRYSTALLINE SUBSTANCE WITH WHICH TO THREATHEN PARTY-GOERS! FUN!
THAT PRETTY MUCH SUMS EVERYTHING UP. GUESS I SHOULD GET STARTED.
OVER HERE, YOU MEAN, EVIL-- HUH?!?
JACK?
FWISH

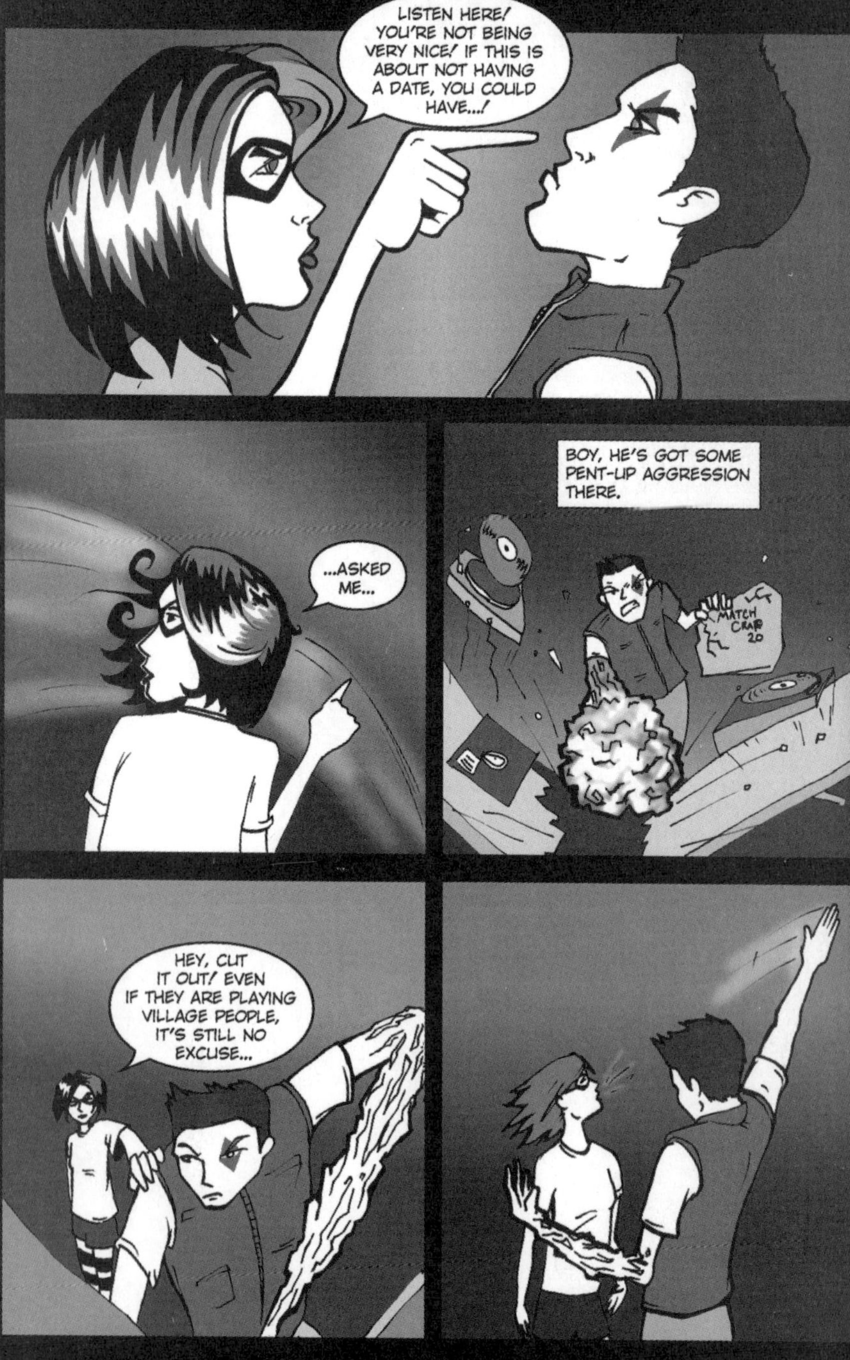
LISTEN HERE! YOU'RE NOT BEING VERY NICE! IF THIS IS ABOUT NOT HAVING A DATE, YOU COULD HAVE...!
...ASKED ME...
BOY, HE'S GOT SOME PENT-UP AGGRESSION THERE.
HEY, CUT IT OUT! EVEN IF THEY ARE PLAYING VILLAGE PEOPLE, IT'S STILL NO EXCUSE...

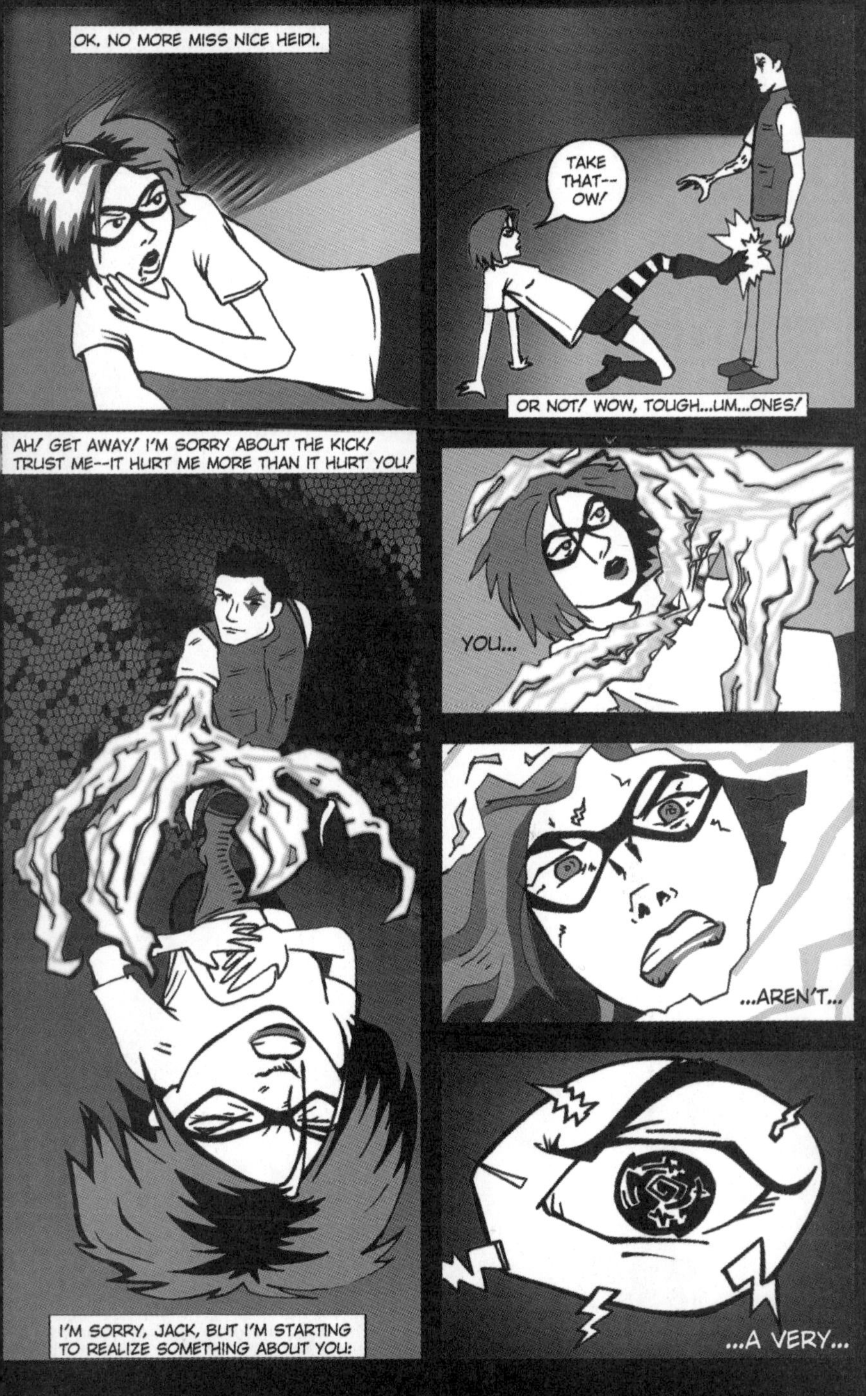
OK. NO MORE MISS NICE HEIDI.
TAKE THAT-- OW!
OR NOT! WOW, TOUGH...UM...ONES!
AH! GET AWAY! I'M SORRY ABOUT THE KICK! TRUST ME--IT HURT ME MORE THAN IT HURT YOU!
I'M SORRY, JACK, BUT I'M STARTING TO REALIZE SOMETHING ABOUT YOU:
YOU...
...AREN'T...
...A VERY...

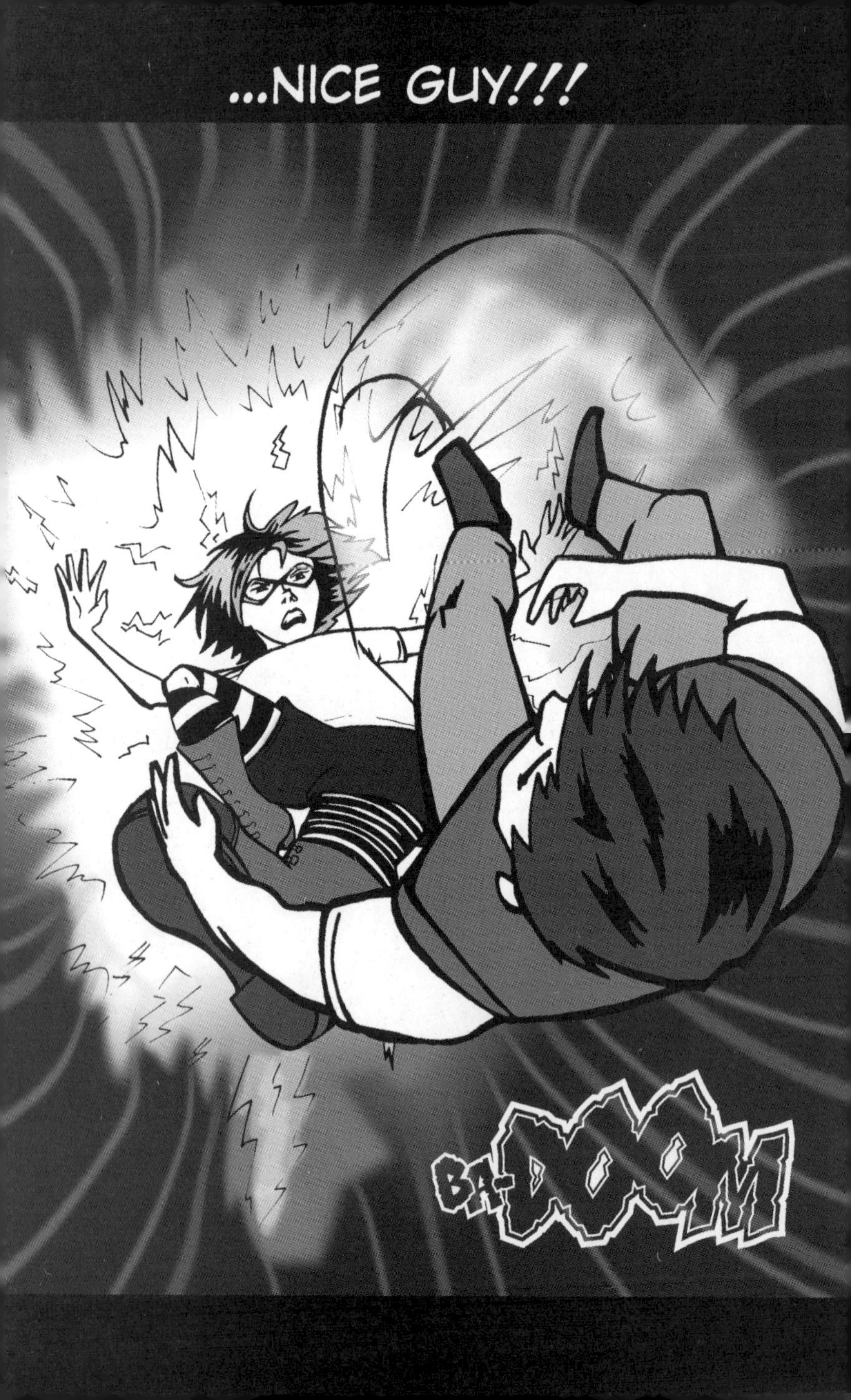
...NICE GUY!!!
BA-DOOM

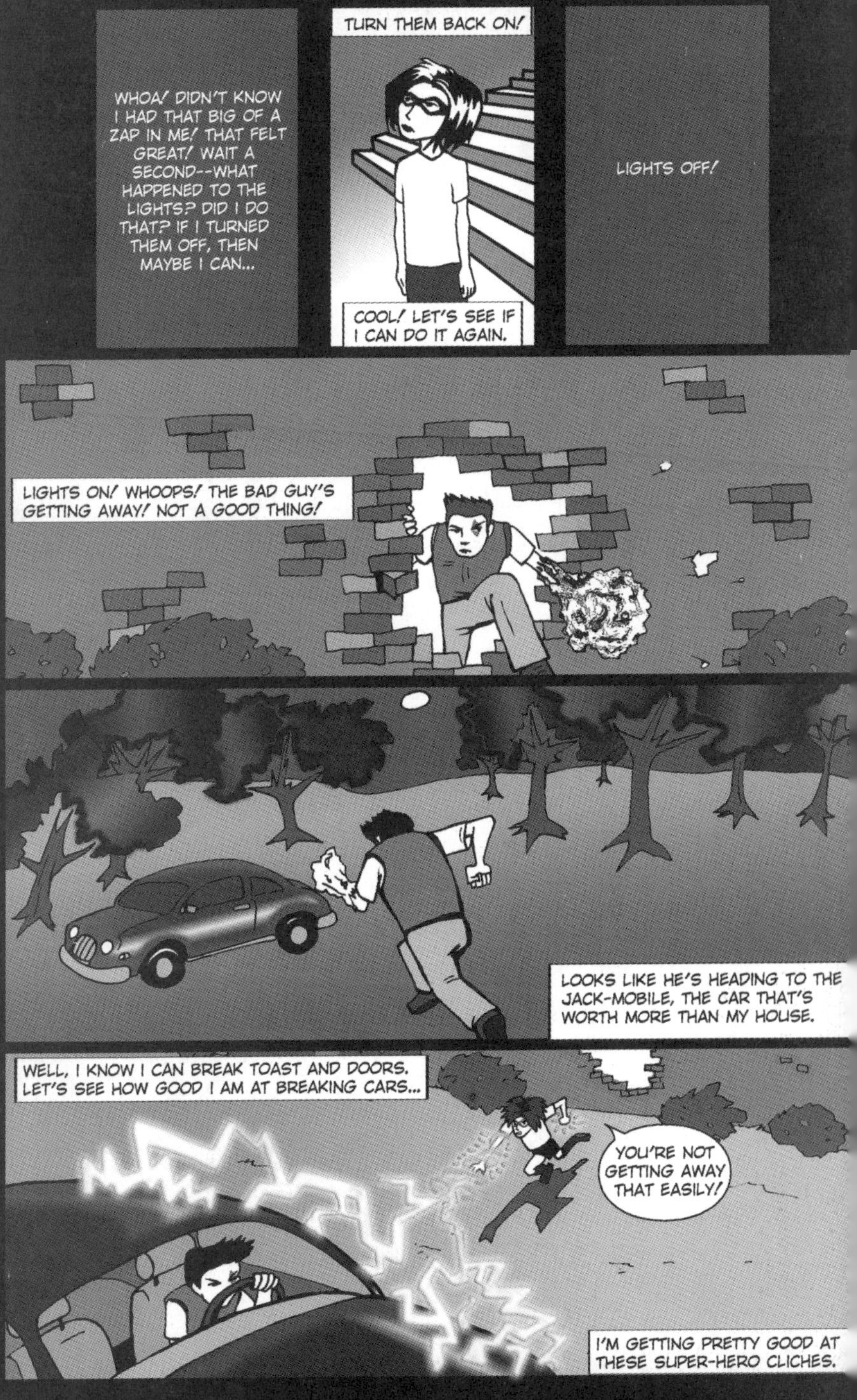
WHOA! DIDN'T KNOW I HAD THAT BIG OF A ZAP IN ME! THAT FELT GREAT! WAIT A SECOND--WHAT HAPPENED TO THE LIGHTS? DID I DO THAT? IF I TURNED THEM OFF, THEN MAYBE I CAN...
TURN THEM BACK ON!
COOL! LET'S SEE IF I CAN DO IT AGAIN.
LIGHTS OFF!
LIGHTS ON! WHOOPS! THE BAD GUY'S GETTING AWAY! NOT A GOOD THING!
LOOKS LIKE HE'S HEADING TO THE JACK-MOBILE, THE CAR THAT'S WORTH MORE THAN MY HOUSE.
WELL, I KNOW I CAN BREAK TOAST AND DOORS. LET'S SEE HOW GOOD I AM AT BREAKING CARS...
YOU'RE NOT GETTING AWAY THAT EASILY!
I'M GETTING PRETTY GOOD AT THESE SUPER-HERO CLICHES.

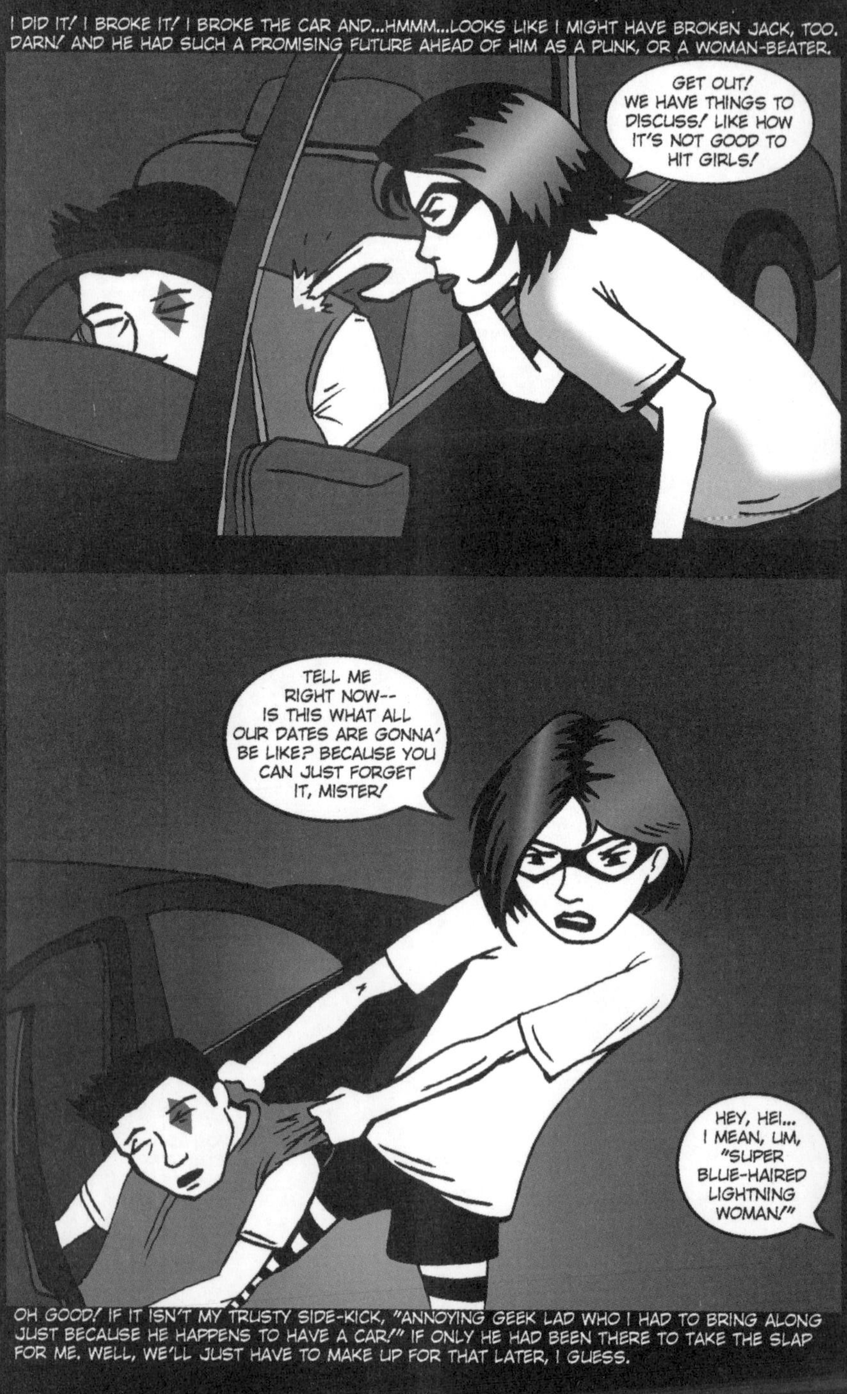
I DID IT! I BROKE IT! I BROKE THE CAR AND...HMMM...LOOKS LIKE I MIGHT HAVE BROKEN JACK, TOO. DARN! AND HE HAD SUCH A PROMISING FUTURE AHEAD OF HIM AS A PUNK, OR A WOMAN-BEATER.
GET OUT! WE HAVE THINGS TO DISCUSS! LIKE HOW IT'S NOT GOOD TO HIT GIRLS!
TELL ME RIGHT NOW-- IS THIS WHAT ALL OUR DATES ARE GONNA' BE LIKE? BECAUSE YOU CAN JUST FORGET IT, MISTER!
HEY, HEI... I MEAN, UM, "SUPER BLUE-HAIRED LIGHTNING WOMAN!"
OH GOOD! IF IT ISN'T MY TRUSTY SIDE-KICK, "ANNOYING GEEK LAD WHO I HAD TO BRING ALONG JUST BECAUSE HE HAPPENS TO HAVE A CAR!" IF ONLY HE HAD BEEN THERE TO TAKE THE SLAP FOR ME. WELL, WE'LL JUST HAVE TO MAKE UP FOR THAT LATER, I GUESS.

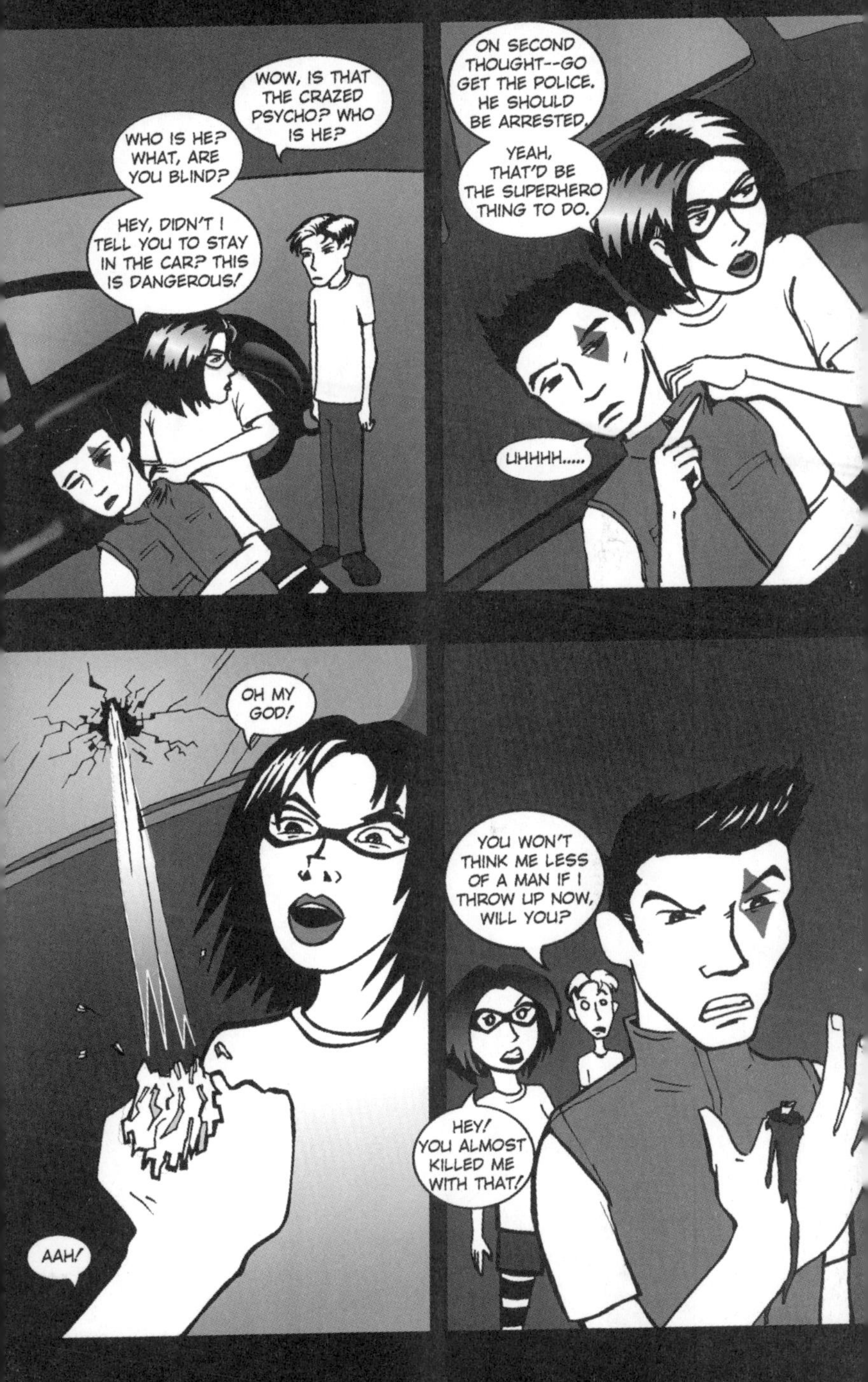
WOW, IS THAT THE CRAZED PSYCHO? WHO IS HE?
WHO IS HE? WHAT, ARE YOU BLIND?
HEY, DIDN'T I TELL YOU TO STAY IN THE CAR? THIS IS DANGEROUS!
ON SECOND THOUGHT--GO GET THE POLICE. HE SHOULD BE ARRESTED.
YEAH, THAT'D BE THE SUPERHERO THING TO DO.
UHHHH.....
OH MY GOD!
AAH!
YOU WON'T THINK ME LESS OF A MAN IF I THROW UP NOW, WILL YOU?
HEY! YOU ALMOST KILLED ME WITH THAT!

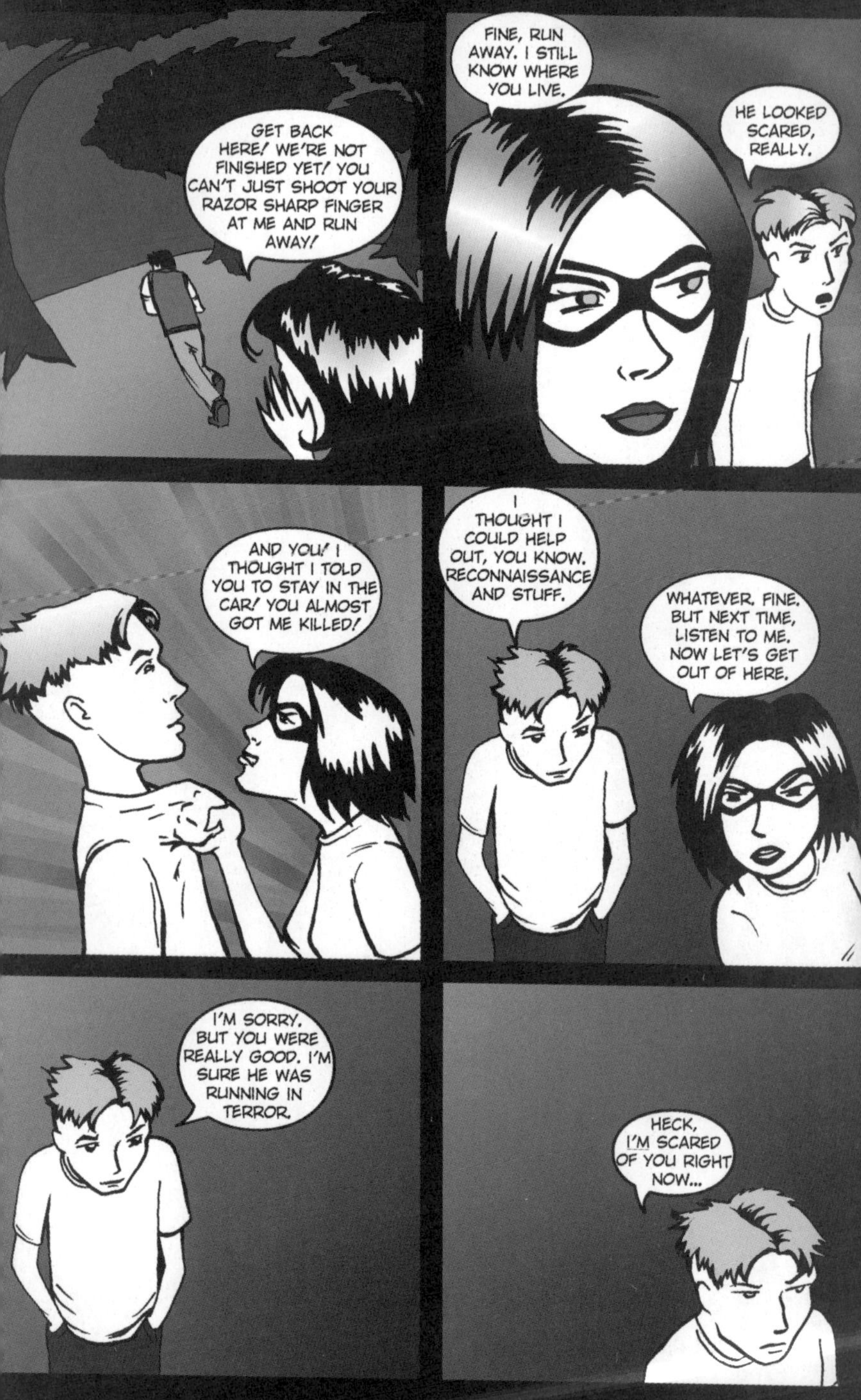
GET BACK HERE! WE'RE NOT FINISHED YET! YOU CAN'T JUST SHOOT YOUR RAZOR SHARP FINGER AT ME AND RUN AWAY!
FINE, RUN AWAY. I STILL KNOW WHERE YOU LIVE.
HE LOOKED SCARED, REALLY.
AND YOU! I THOUGHT I TOLD YOU TO STAY IN THE CAR! YOU ALMOST GOT ME KILLED!
I THOUGHT I COULD HELP OUT, YOU KNOW. RECONNAISSANCE AND STUFF.
WHATEVER. FINE. BUT NEXT TIME, LISTEN TO ME. NOW LET'S GET OUT OF HERE.
I'M SORRY. BUT YOU WERE REALLY GOOD. I'M SURE HE WAS RUNNING IN TERROR.
HECK, I'M SCARED OF YOU RIGHT NOW...

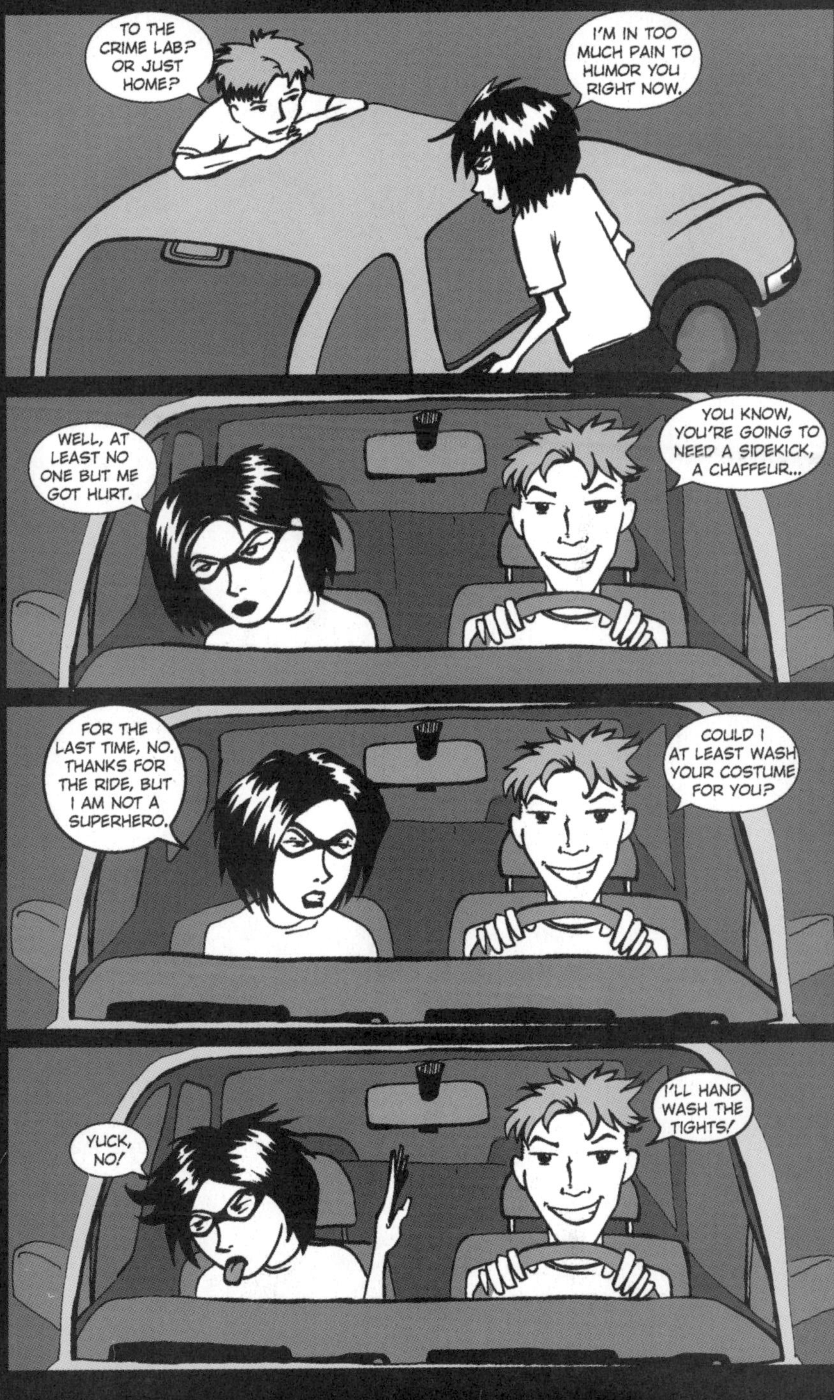
TO THE CRIME LAB? OR JUST HOME?
I'M IN TOO MUCH PAIN TO HUMOR YOU RIGHT NOW.
WELL, AT LEAST NO ONE BUT ME GOT HURT.
YOU KNOW, YOU'RE GOING TO NEED A SIDEKICK, A CHAFFEUR...
FOR THE LAST TIME, NO. THANKS FOR THE RIDE, BUT I AM NOT A SUPERHERO.
COULD I AT LEAST WASH YOUR COSTUME FOR YOU?
YUCK, NO!
I'LL HAND WASH THE TIGHTS!

MONDAY MORNING...

FZZ...
CRACKLE...
HARRINGTON...
CRAZED PSYCHO...
AMOK...SCHOOL
GYM DAMAGED...
FZZ...

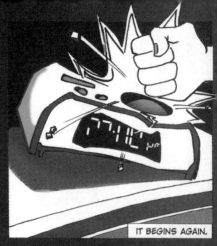

IT BEGINS AGAIN.

HEIDI!
ARE YOU
UP YET?!?

HEIDI!
GET UP!

I HATE RHETORICAL QUESTIONS IN THE MORNING.

I'M ALMOST
AFRAID TO
LOOK...

WOW. WORSE
THAN USUAL.
I GUESS THAT'S
WHAT HAPPENS
WHEN SOME
SUPER-VILLAINOUS
JERK SLAPS YOU
ACROSS THE FACE.
AND TO THINK I
USED TO HAVE A
CRUSH ON HIM...
2 WHOLE
DAYS AGO.

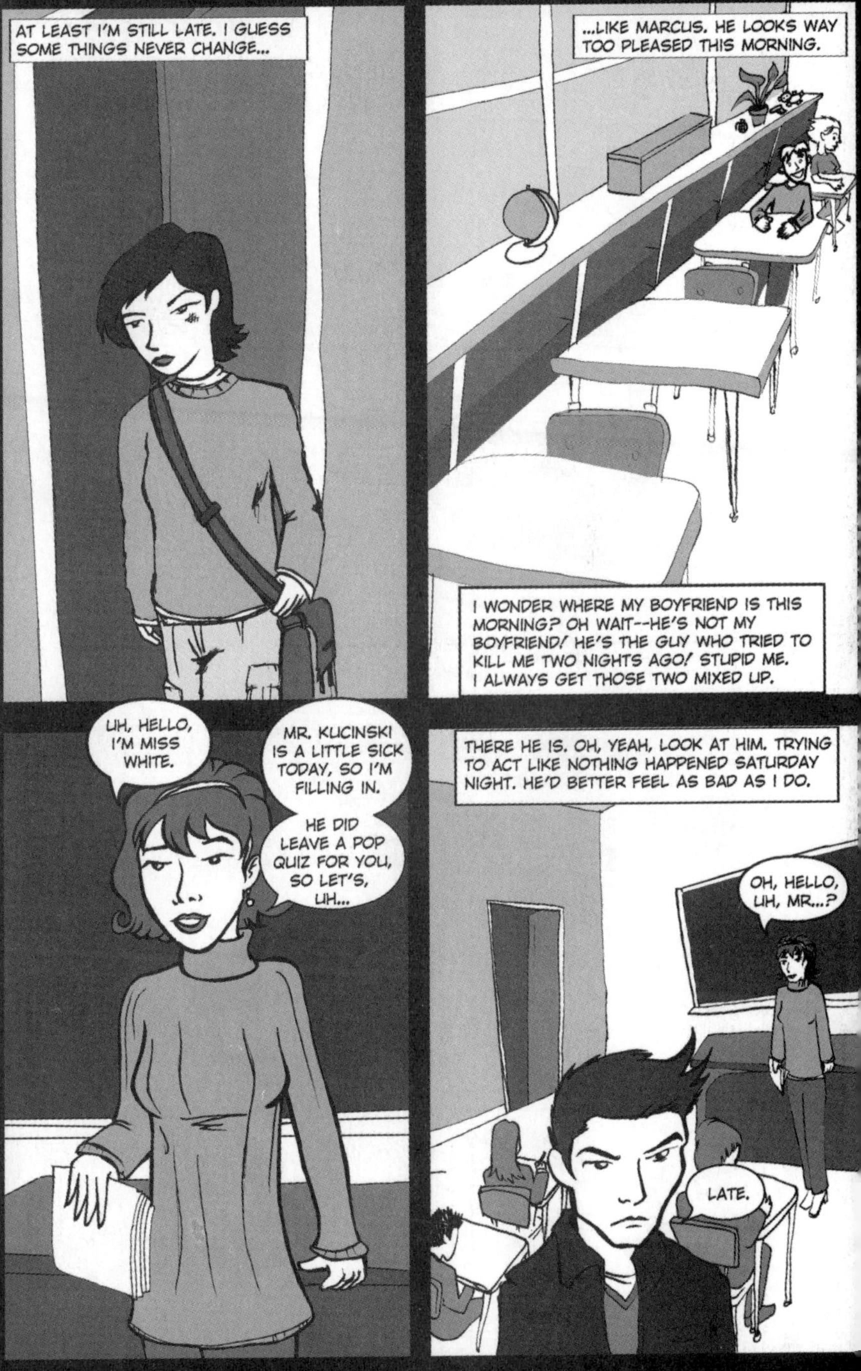
AT LEAST I'M STILL LATE. I GUESS SOME THINGS NEVER CHANGE...
...LIKE MARCUS. HE LOOKS WAY TOO PLEASED THIS MORNING.
I WONDER WHERE MY BOYFRIEND IS THIS MORNING? OH WAIT--HE'S NOT MY BOYFRIEND! HE'S THE GUY WHO TRIED TO KILL ME TWO NIGHTS AGO! STUPID ME. I ALWAYS GET THOSE TWO MIXED UP.
UH, HELLO, I'M MISS WHITE.
MR. KUCINSKI IS A LITTLE SICK TODAY, SO I'M FILLING IN.
HE DID LEAVE A POP QUIZ FOR YOU, SO LET'S, UH...
THERE HE IS. OH, YEAH, LOOK AT HIM. TRYING TO ACT LIKE NOTHING HAPPENED SATURDAY NIGHT. HE'D BETTER FEEL AS BAD AS I DO.
OH, HELLO, UH, MR...?
LATE.

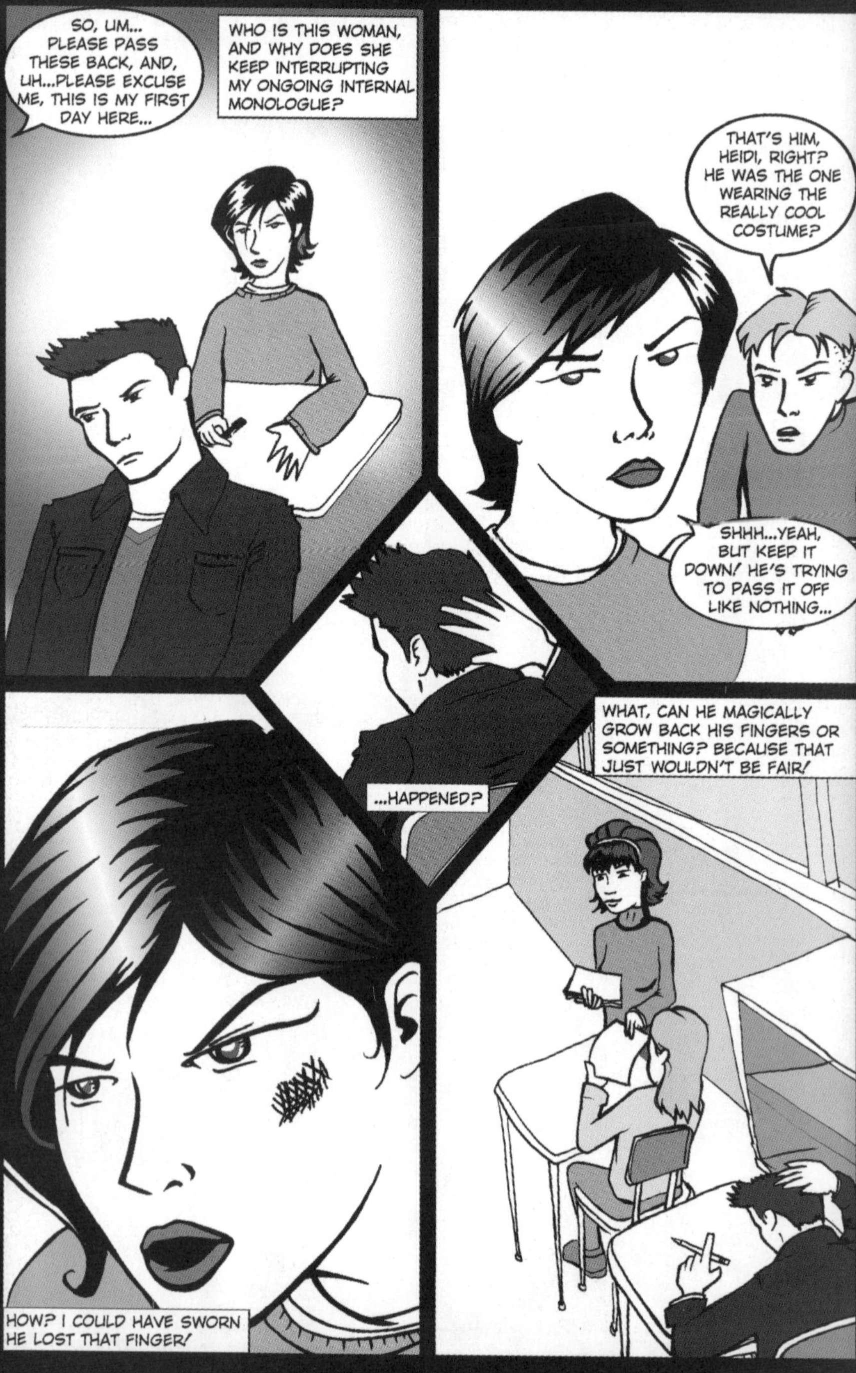
SO, UM... PLEASE PASS THESE BACK, AND, UH...PLEASE EXCUSE ME, THIS IS MY FIRST DAY HERE...
WHO IS THIS WOMAN, AND WHY DOES SHE KEEP INTERRUPTING MY ONGOING INTERNAL MONOLOGUE?
THAT'S HIM, HEIDI, RIGHT? HE WAS THE ONE WEARING THE REALLY COOL COSTUME?
SHHH...YEAH, BUT KEEP IT DOWN! HE'S TRYING TO PASS IT OFF LIKE NOTHING...
...HAPPENED?
HOW? I COULD HAVE SWORN HE LOST THAT FINGER!
WHAT, CAN HE MAGICALLY GROW BACK HIS FINGERS OR SOMETHING? BECAUSE THAT JUST WOULDN'T BE FAIR!

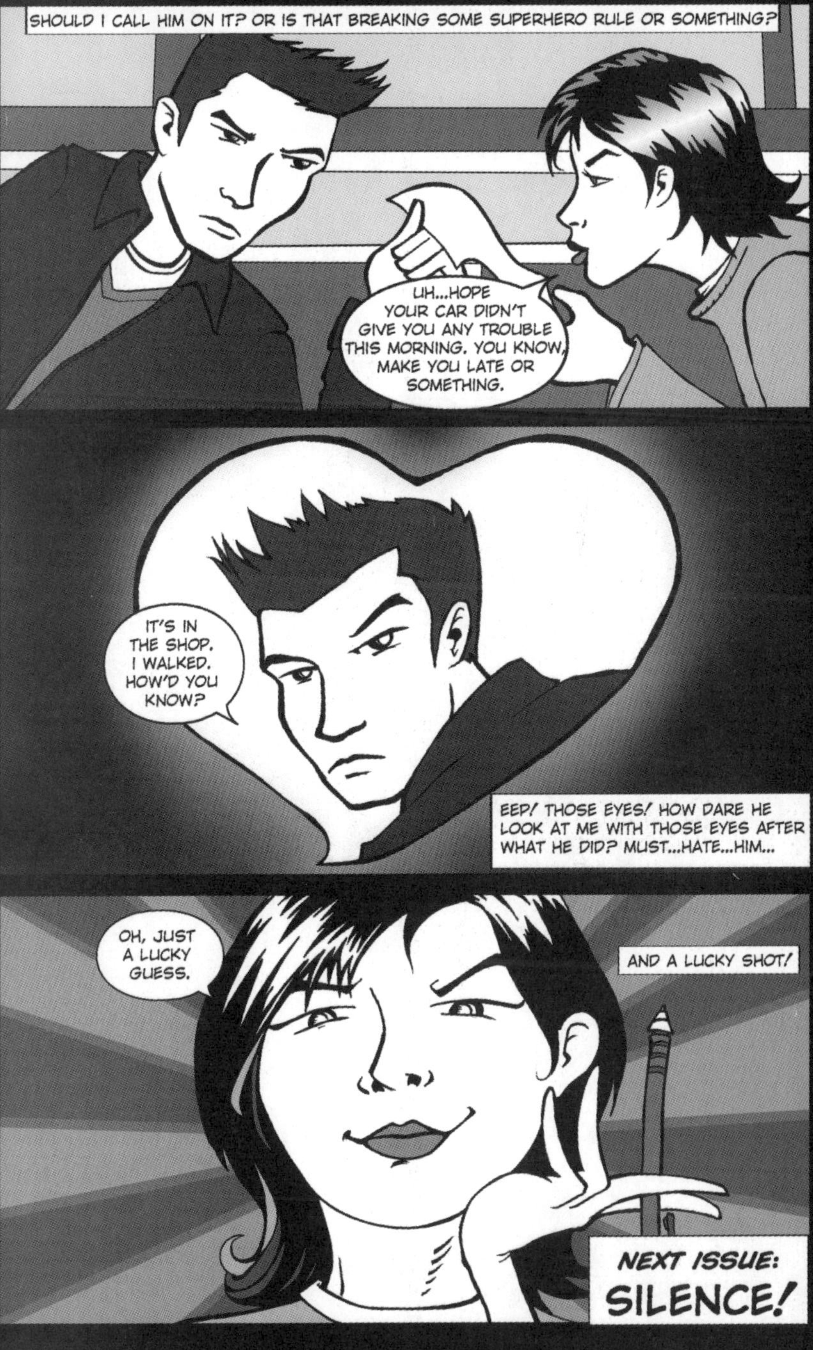
SHOULD I CALL HIM ON IT? OR IS THAT BREAKING SOME SUPERHERO RULE OR SOMETHING?
UH...HOPE YOUR CAR DIDN'T GIVE YOU ANY TROUBLE THIS MORNING. YOU KNOW, MAKE YOU LATE OR SOMETHING.
IT'S IN THE SHOP. I WALKED. HOW'D YOU KNOW?
EEP! THOSE EYES! HOW DARE HE LOOK AT ME WITH THOSE EYES AFTER WHAT HE DID? MUST...HATE...HIM...
OH, JUST A LUCKY GUESS.
AND A LUCKY SHOT!
NEXT ISSUE:
SILENCE!

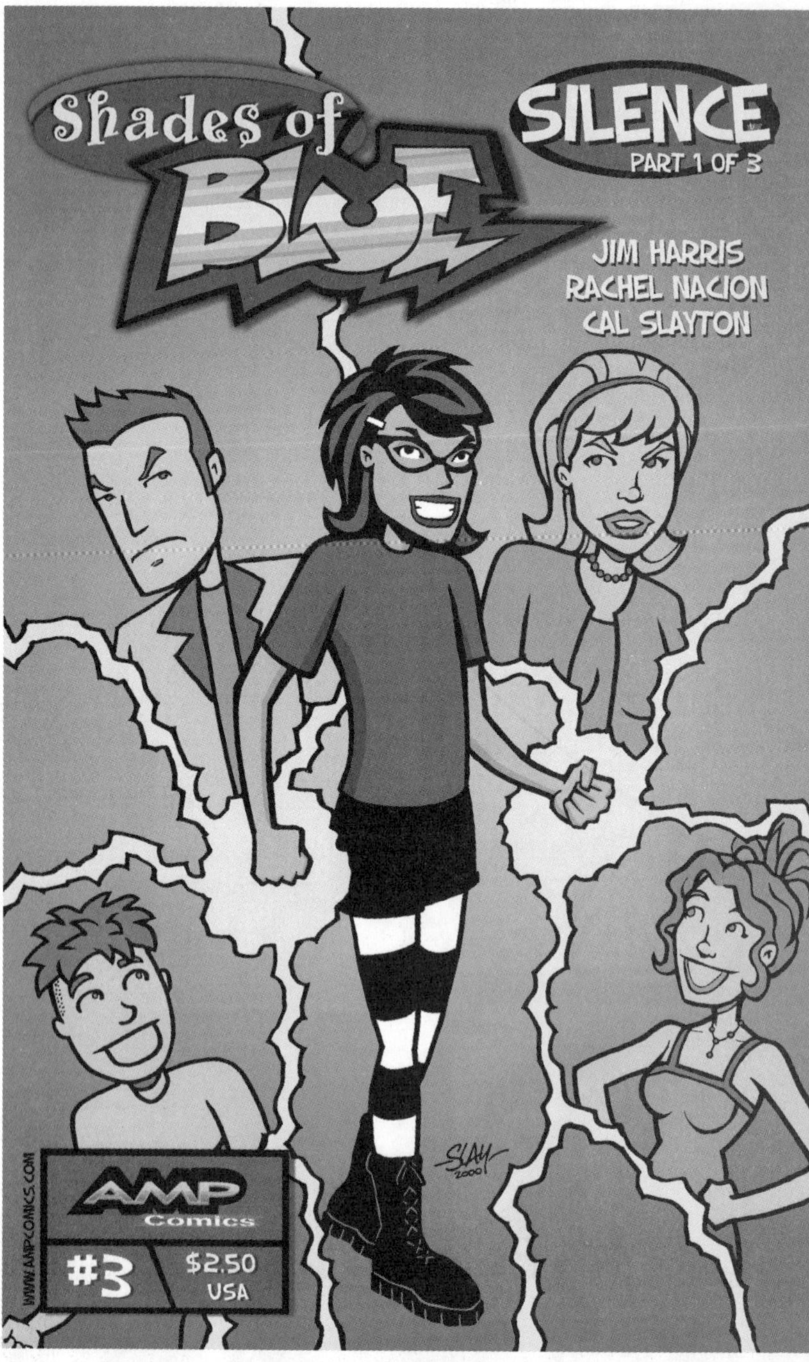
Shades of
BLUE
SILENCE
PART 1 OF 3
JIM HARRIS
RACHEL NACION
CAL SLAYTON
SLAY 2000
AMP Comics
#3
$2.50 USA
WWW.AMPCOMICS.COM

"SILENCE!"

PART 1 OF 3

WORDS:

JAMES S. HARRIS & RACHEL NACION

ALL ART:

CAL SLAYTON

Yearbook Snapshots:

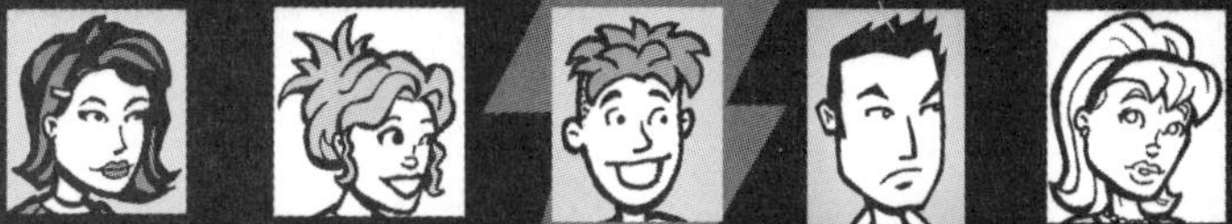

HEIDI PAIGE:
SUPERHERO
LIKES: JACK

K.T. O'HARA
HEIDI'S BEST FRIEND
LIKES: THE MALL

MARCUS:
NERD WITH A CAR
LIKES: HEIDI

JACK:
SUPER-VILLAIN?
LIKES: ?

MISS WHITE:
SUBSTITUTE TEACH
LIKES: SILENCE

The Story Thus Far: One day, Heidi woke up with blue hair and superpowers. So, naturally, she became a superhero. In her first mission, Heidi defeated a villain who looked a whole lot like Jack at the Harrington High Homecoming Dance. Meanwhile, the mysterious Miss Dessa White arrived in Harrington and was offered a substitute teaching job at Heidi's school. Conveniently enough, Heidi's English teacher Mr. Kucinski has disappeared. But Miss White may have more in store for Heidi than a pop quiz on Chaucer...

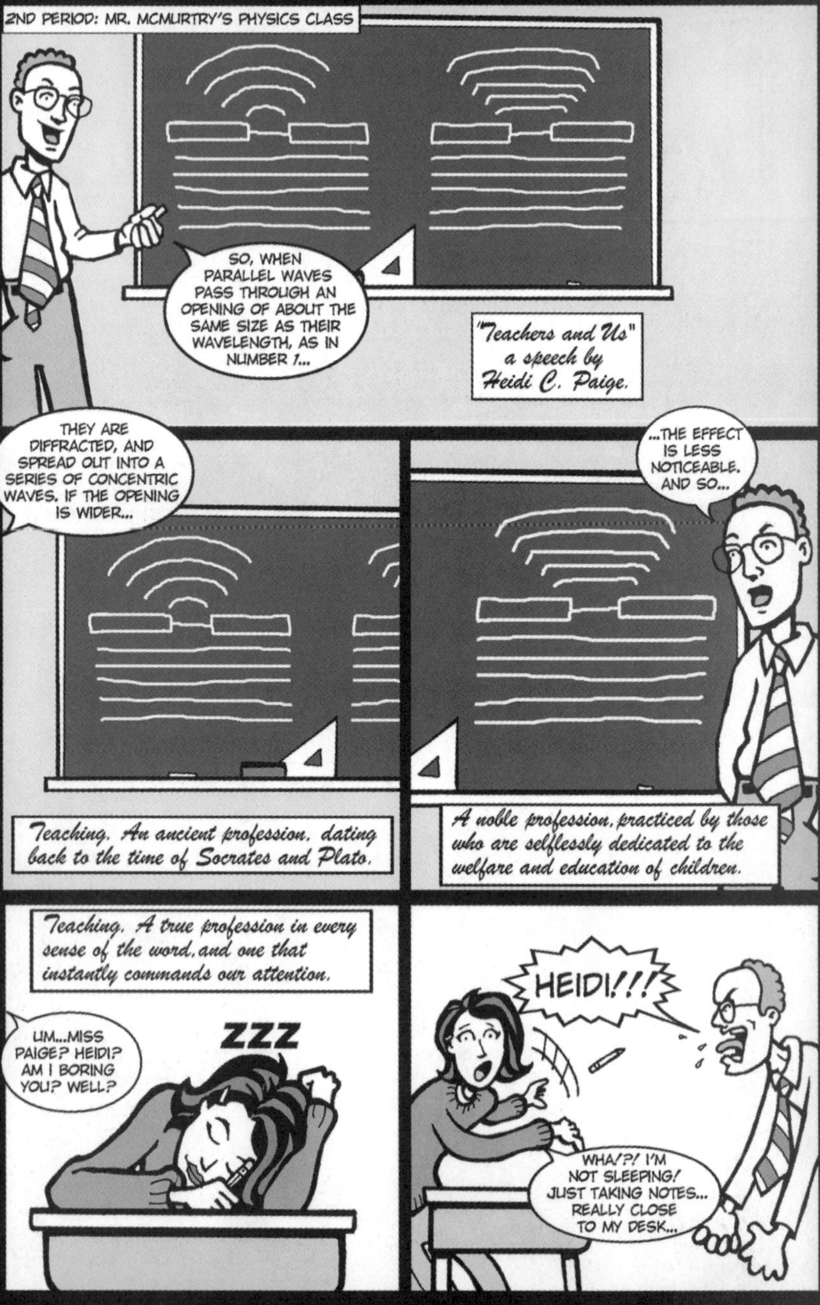

2ND PERIOD: MR. MCMURTRY'S PHYSICS CLASS
SO, WHEN PARALLEL WAVES PASS THROUGH AN OPENING OF ABOUT THE SAME SIZE AS THEIR WAVELENGTH, AS IN NUMBER 1...
"Teachers and Us" a speech by Heidi C. Paige.
THEY ARE DIFFRACTED, AND SPREAD OUT INTO A SERIES OF CONCENTRIC WAVES. IF THE OPENING IS WIDER...
Teaching. An ancient profession, dating back to the time of Socrates and Plato.
...THE EFFECT IS LESS NOTICEABLE. AND SO...
A noble profession, practiced by those who are selflessly dedicated to the welfare and education of children.
Teaching. A true profession in every sense of the word, and one that instantly commands our attention.
UM...MISS PAIGE? HEIDI? AM I BORING YOU? WELL?
ZZZ
HEIDI!!!
WHA!?! I'M NOT SLEEPING! JUST TAKING NOTES... REALLY CLOSE TO MY DESK...

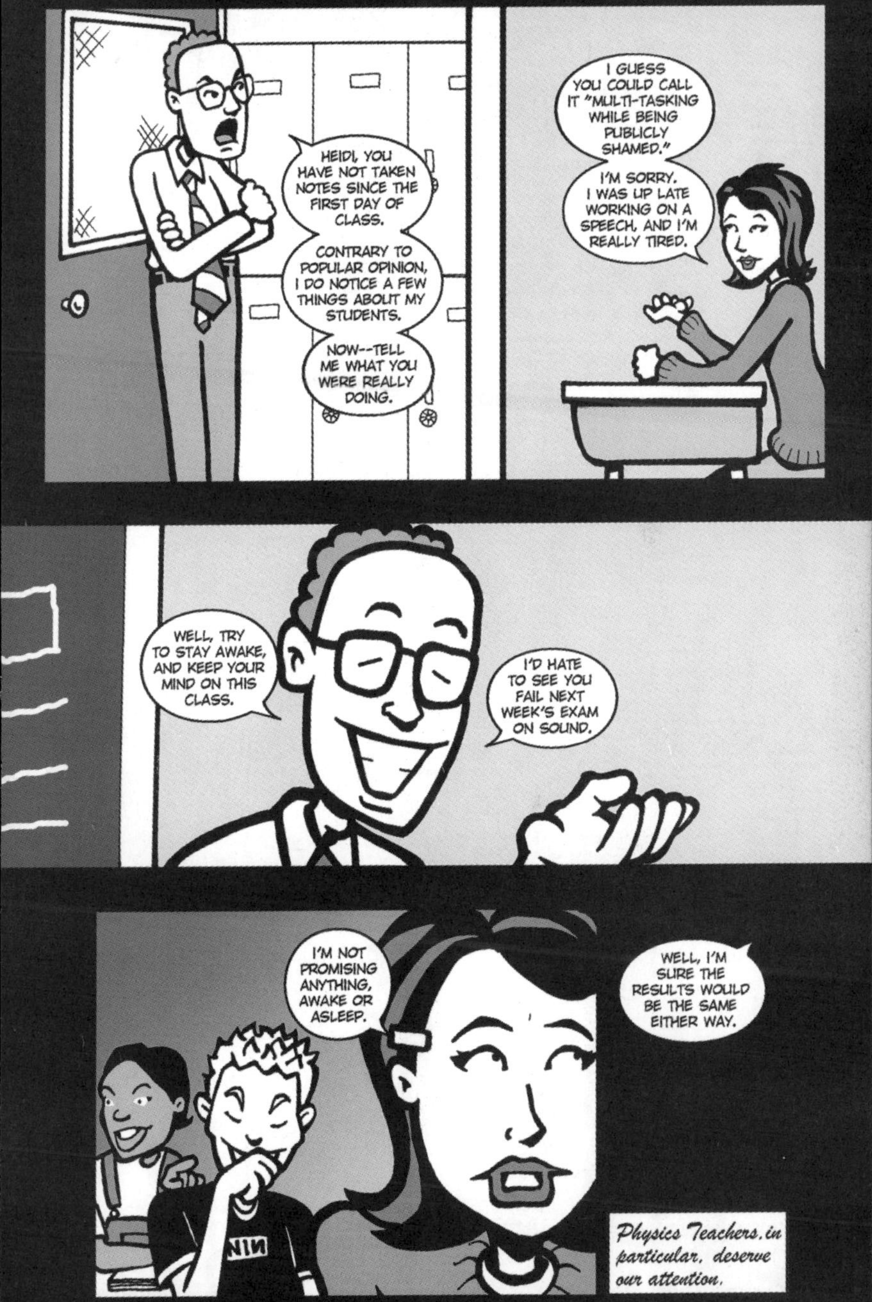
HEIDI, YOU HAVE NOT TAKEN NOTES SINCE THE FIRST DAY OF CLASS.
CONTRARY TO POPULAR OPINION, I DO NOTICE A FEW THINGS ABOUT MY STUDENTS.
NOW--TELL ME WHAT YOU WERE REALLY DOING.
I GUESS YOU COULD CALL IT "MULTI-TASKING WHILE BEING PUBLICLY SHAMED."
I'M SORRY. I WAS UP LATE WORKING ON A SPEECH, AND I'M REALLY TIRED.
WELL, TRY TO STAY AWAKE, AND KEEP YOUR MIND ON THIS CLASS.
I'D HATE TO SEE YOU FAIL NEXT WEEK'S EXAM ON SOUND.
I'M NOT PROMISING ANYTHING, AWAKE OR ASLEEP.
WELL, I'M SURE THE RESULTS WOULD BE THE SAME EITHER WAY.
NIN
Physics Teachers, in particular, deserve our attention.

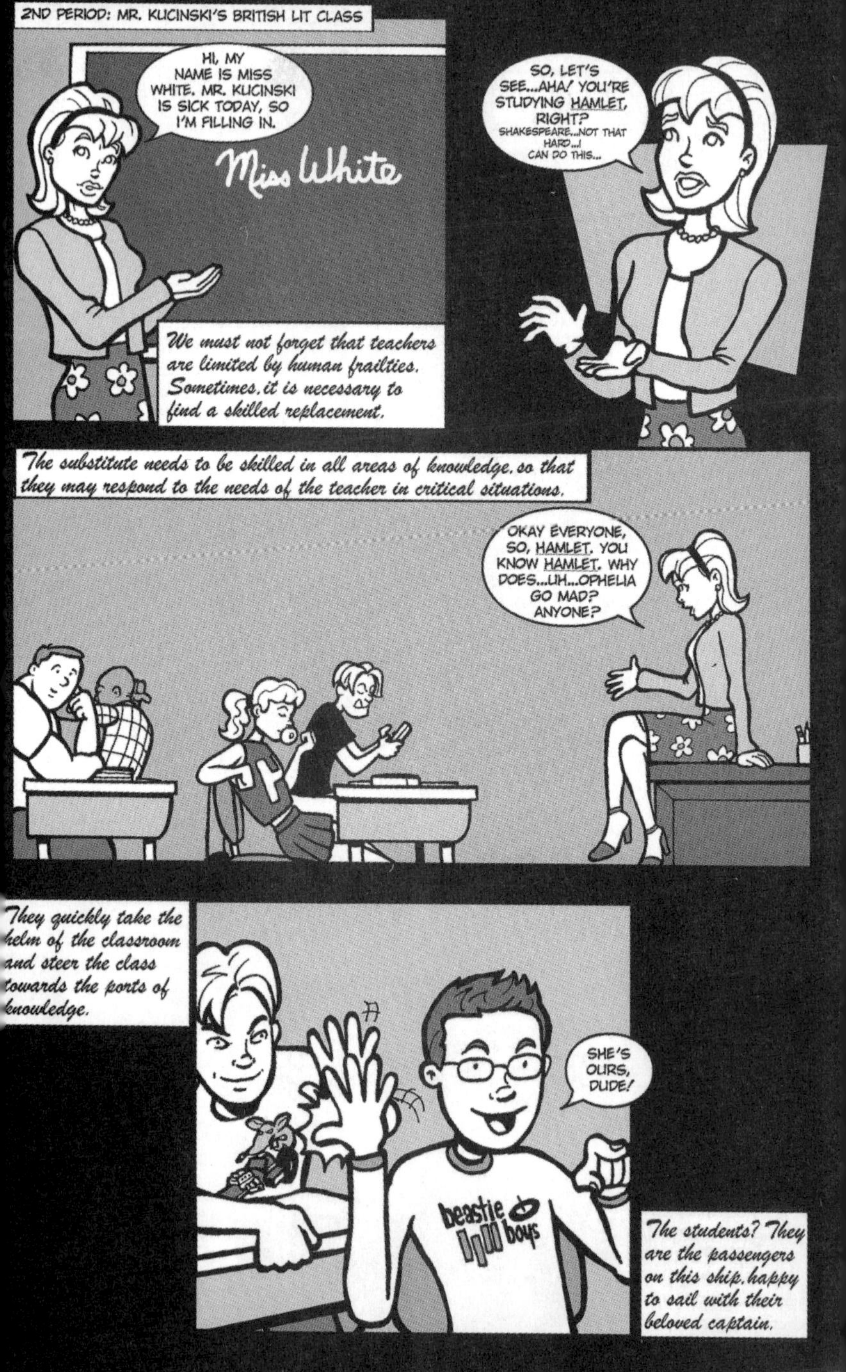
2ND PERIOD: MR. KUCINSKI'S BRITISH LIT CLASS
HI, MY NAME IS MISS WHITE. MR. KUCINSKI IS SICK TODAY, SO I'M FILLING IN.
Miss White
We must not forget that teachers are limited by human frailties. Sometimes, it is necessary to find a skilled replacement.
SO, LET'S SEE...AHA! YOU'RE STUDYING HAMLET, RIGHT? SHAKESPEARE...NOT THAT HARD...I CAN DO THIS...
The substitute needs to be skilled in all areas of knowledge, so that they may respond to the needs of the teacher in critical situations.
OKAY EVERYONE, SO, HAMLET. YOU KNOW HAMLET. WHY DOES...UH...OPHELIA GO MAD? ANYONE?
They quickly take the helm of the classroom and steer the class towards the ports of knowledge.
SHE'S OURS, DUDE!
beastie boys
The students? They are the passengers on this ship, happy to sail with their beloved captain.

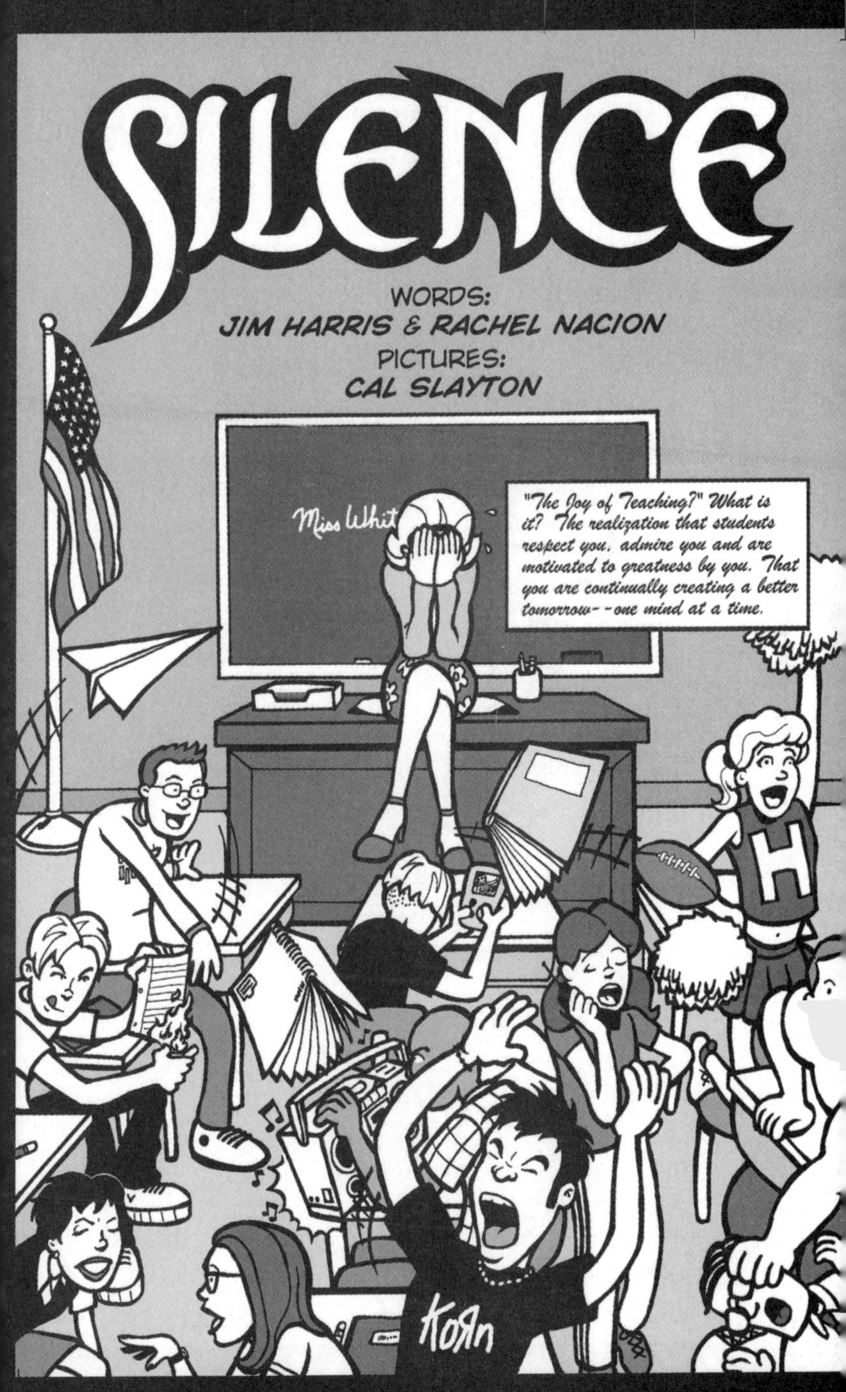
SILENCE
WORDS:
JIM HARRIS & RACHEL NACION
PICTURES:
CAL SLAYTON
Miss Whit
"The Joy of Teaching?" What is it? The realization that students respect you, admire you and are motivated to greatness by you. That you are continually creating a better tomorrow--one mind at a time.
H
KoRn

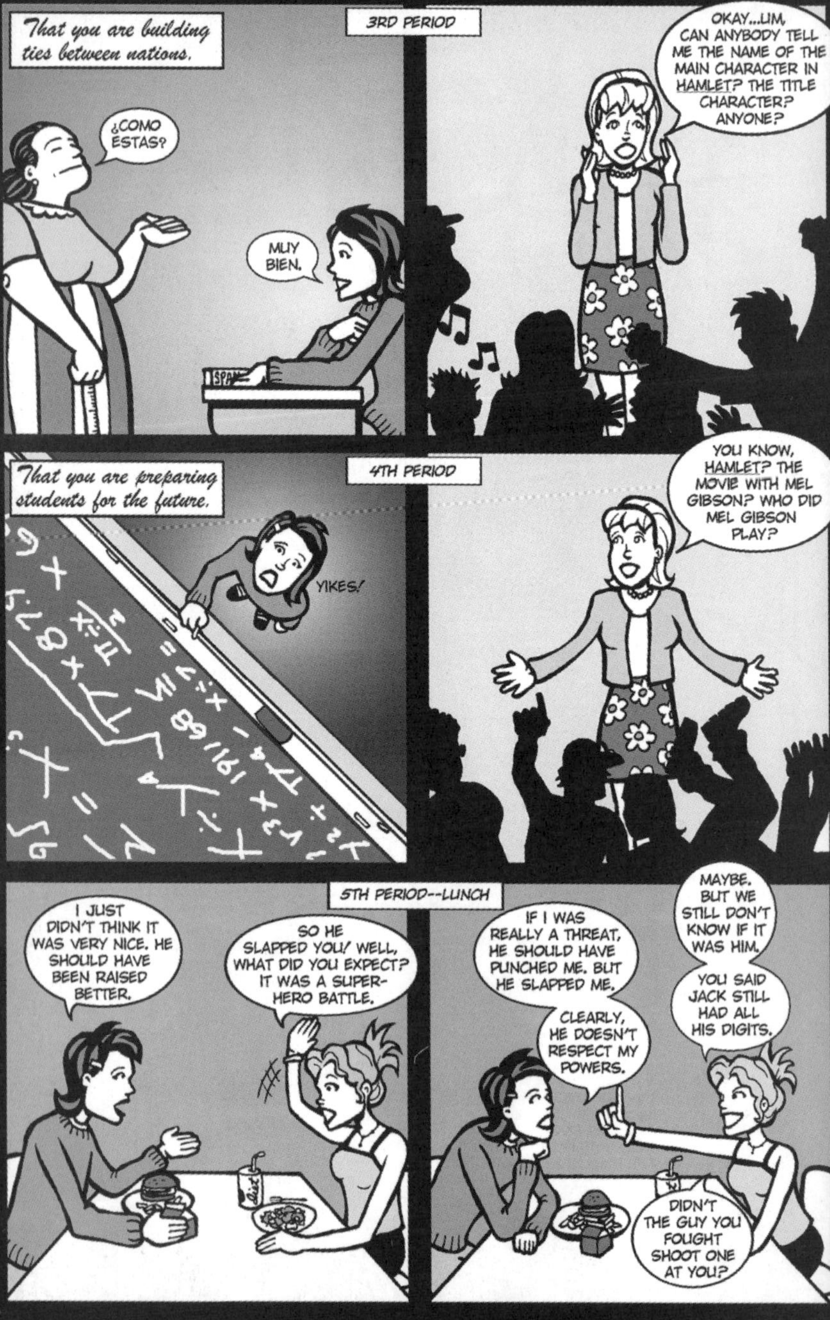
That you are building ties between nations.
3RD PERIOD
¿COMO ESTAS?
MUY BIEN.
OKAY...UM, CAN ANYBODY TELL ME THE NAME OF THE MAIN CHARACTER IN HAMLET? THE TITLE CHARACTER? ANYONE?
That you are preparing students for the future.
4TH PERIOD
YIKES!
YOU KNOW, HAMLET? THE MOVIE WITH MEL GIBSON? WHO DID MEL GIBSON PLAY?
5TH PERIOD--LUNCH
I JUST DIDN'T THINK IT WAS VERY NICE. HE SHOULD HAVE BEEN RAISED BETTER.
SO HE SLAPPED YOU! WELL, WHAT DID YOU EXPECT? IT WAS A SUPER-HERO BATTLE.
IF I WAS REALLY A THREAT, HE SHOULD HAVE PUNCHED ME. BUT HE SLAPPED ME.
CLEARLY, HE DOESN'T RESPECT MY POWERS.
MAYBE. BUT WE STILL DON'T KNOW IF IT WAS HIM.
YOU SAID JACK STILL HAD ALL HIS DIGITS.
DIDN'T THE GUY YOU FOUGHT SHOOT ONE AT YOU?

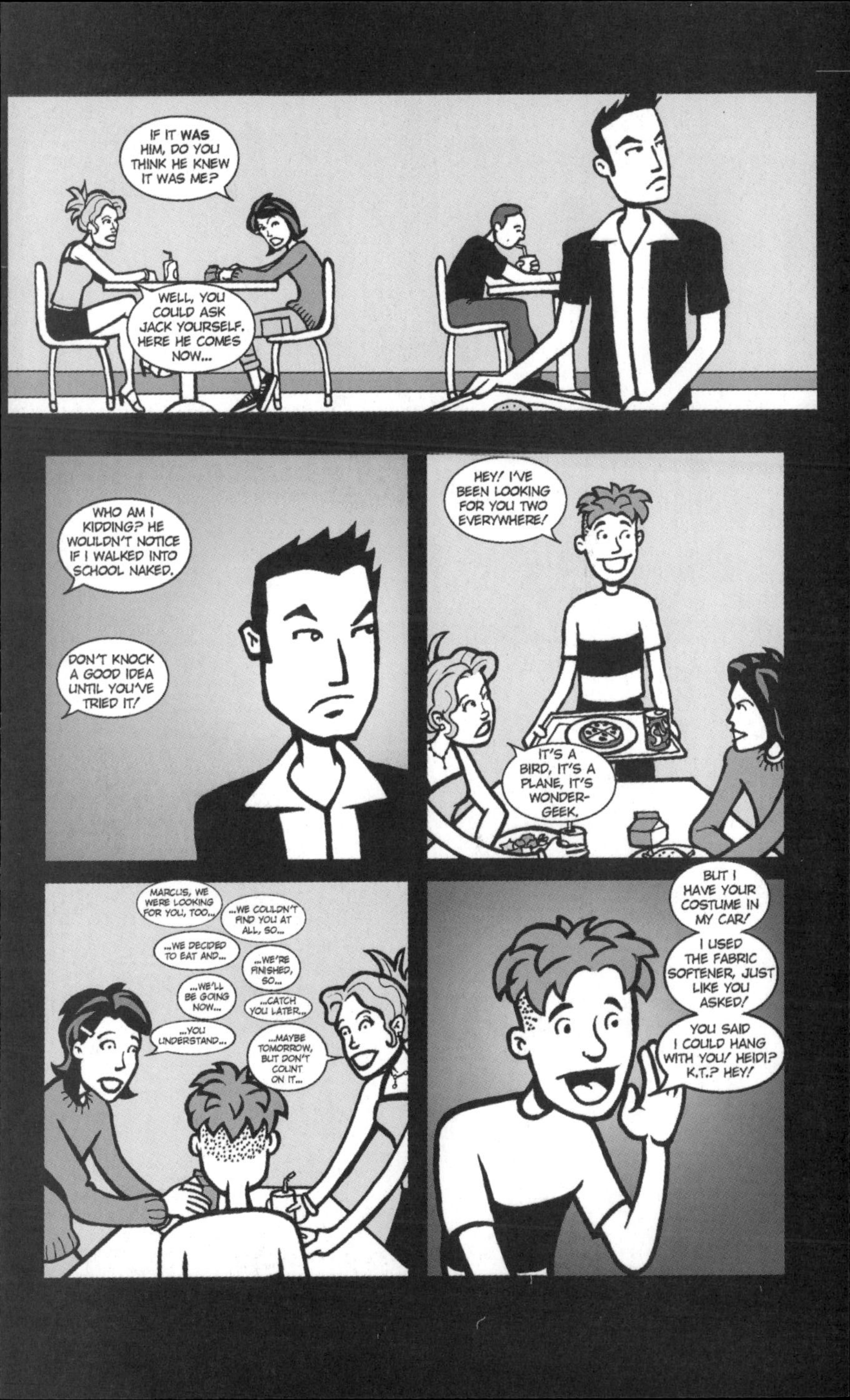
IF IT WAS HIM, DO YOU THINK HE KNEW IT WAS ME?
WELL, YOU COULD ASK JACK YOURSELF. HERE HE COMES NOW...
WHO AM I KIDDING? HE WOULDN'T NOTICE IF I WALKED INTO SCHOOL NAKED.
DON'T KNOCK A GOOD IDEA UNTIL YOU'VE TRIED IT!
HEY! I'VE BEEN LOOKING FOR YOU TWO EVERYWHERE!
IT'S A BIRD, IT'S A PLANE, IT'S WONDER-GEEK.
MARCUS, WE WERE LOOKING FOR YOU, TOO...
...WE COULDN'T FIND YOU AT ALL, SO...
...WE DECIDED TO EAT AND...
...WE'RE FINISHED, SO...
...WE'LL BE GOING NOW...
...CATCH YOU LATER...
...YOU UNDERSTAND...
...MAYBE TOMORROW, BUT DON'T COUNT ON IT...
BUT I HAVE YOUR COSTUME IN MY CAR!
I USED THE FABRIC SOFTENER, JUST LIKE YOU ASKED!
YOU SAID I COULD HANG WITH YOU! HEIDI? K.T.? HEY!

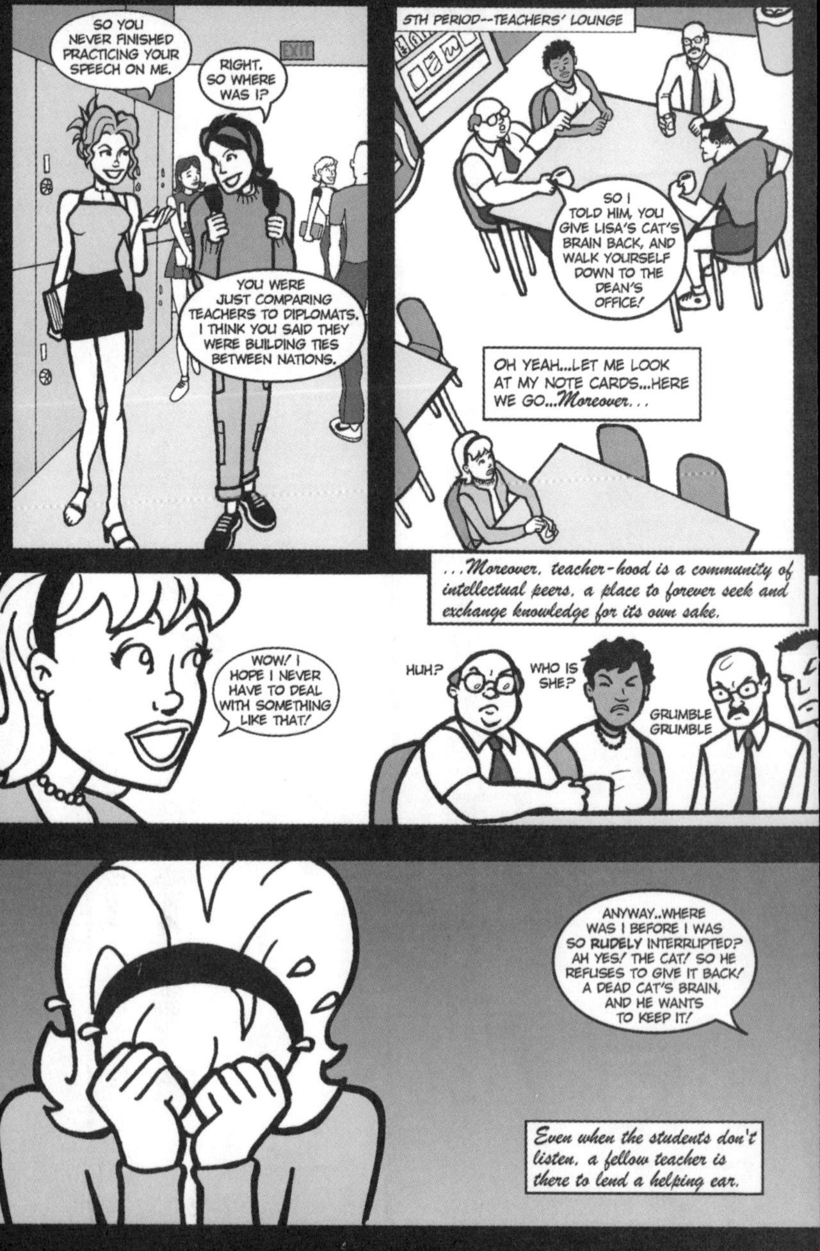

SO YOU NEVER FINISHED PRACTICING YOUR SPEECH ON ME.
EXIT
RIGHT. SO WHERE WAS I?
YOU WERE JUST COMPARING TEACHERS TO DIPLOMATS. I THINK YOU SAID THEY WERE BUILDING TIES BETWEEN NATIONS.
5TH PERIOD--TEACHERS' LOUNGE
SO I TOLD HIM, YOU GIVE LISA'S CAT'S BRAIN BACK, AND WALK YOURSELF DOWN TO THE DEAN'S OFFICE!
OH YEAH...LET ME LOOK AT MY NOTE CARDS...HERE WE GO...*Moreover...*
...Moreover, teacher-hood is a community of intellectual peers, a place to forever seek and exchange knowledge for its own sake.
WOW! I HOPE I NEVER HAVE TO DEAL WITH SOMETHING LIKE THAT!
HUH?
WHO IS SHE?
GRUMBLE GRUMBLE
ANYWAY..WHERE WAS I BEFORE I WAS SO **RUDELY** INTERRUPTED? AH YES! THE CAT! SO HE REFUSES TO GIVE IT BACK! A DEAD CAT'S BRAIN, AND HE WANTS TO KEEP IT!
Even when the students don't listen, a fellow teacher is there to lend a helping ear.

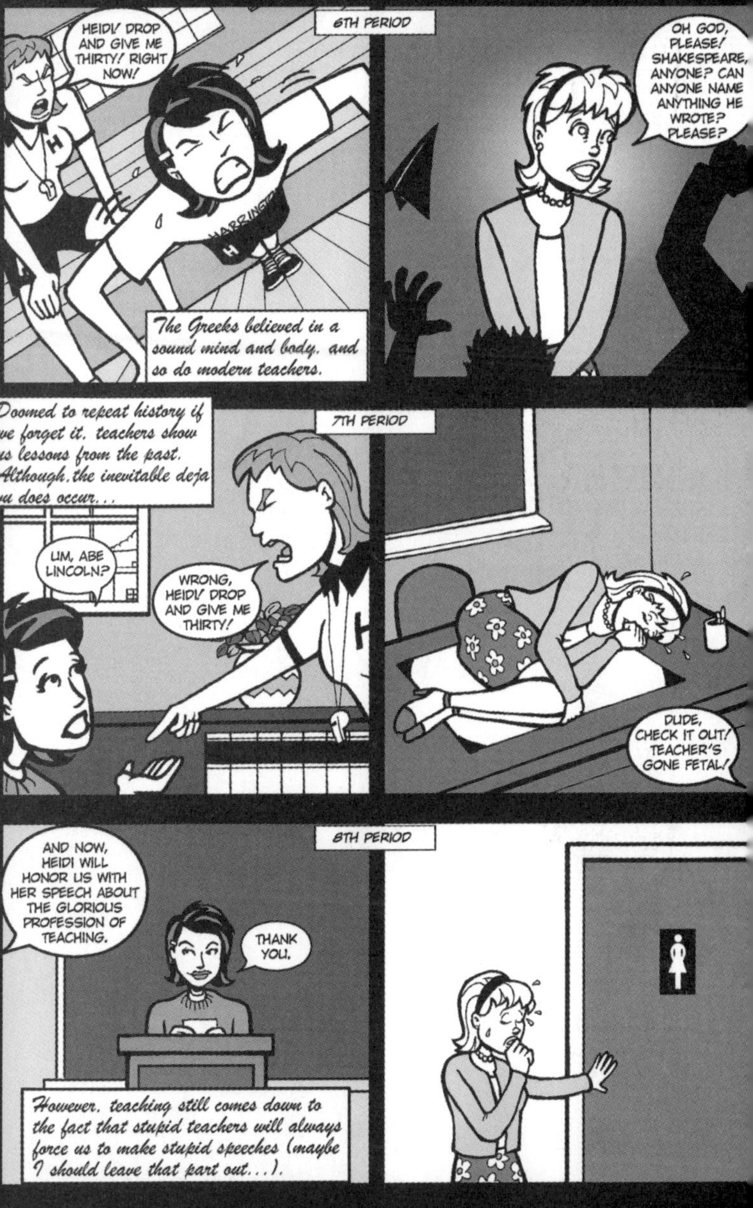
6TH PERIOD
HEIDI! DROP AND GIVE ME THIRTY! RIGHT NOW!
The Greeks believed in a sound mind and body, and so do modern teachers.
OH GOD, PLEASE! SHAKESPEARE, ANYONE? CAN ANYONE NAME ANYTHING HE WROTE? PLEASE?
Doomed to repeat history if we forget it, teachers show us lessons from the past. Although, the inevitable deja vu does occur...
7TH PERIOD
UM, ABE LINCOLN?
WRONG, HEIDI! DROP AND GIVE ME THIRTY!
DUDE, CHECK IT OUT! TEACHER'S GONE FETAL!
8TH PERIOD
AND NOW, HEIDI WILL HONOR US WITH HER SPEECH ABOUT THE GLORIOUS PROFESSION OF TEACHING.
THANK YOU.
However, teaching still comes down to the fact that stupid teachers will always force us to make stupid speeches (maybe I should leave that part out...).

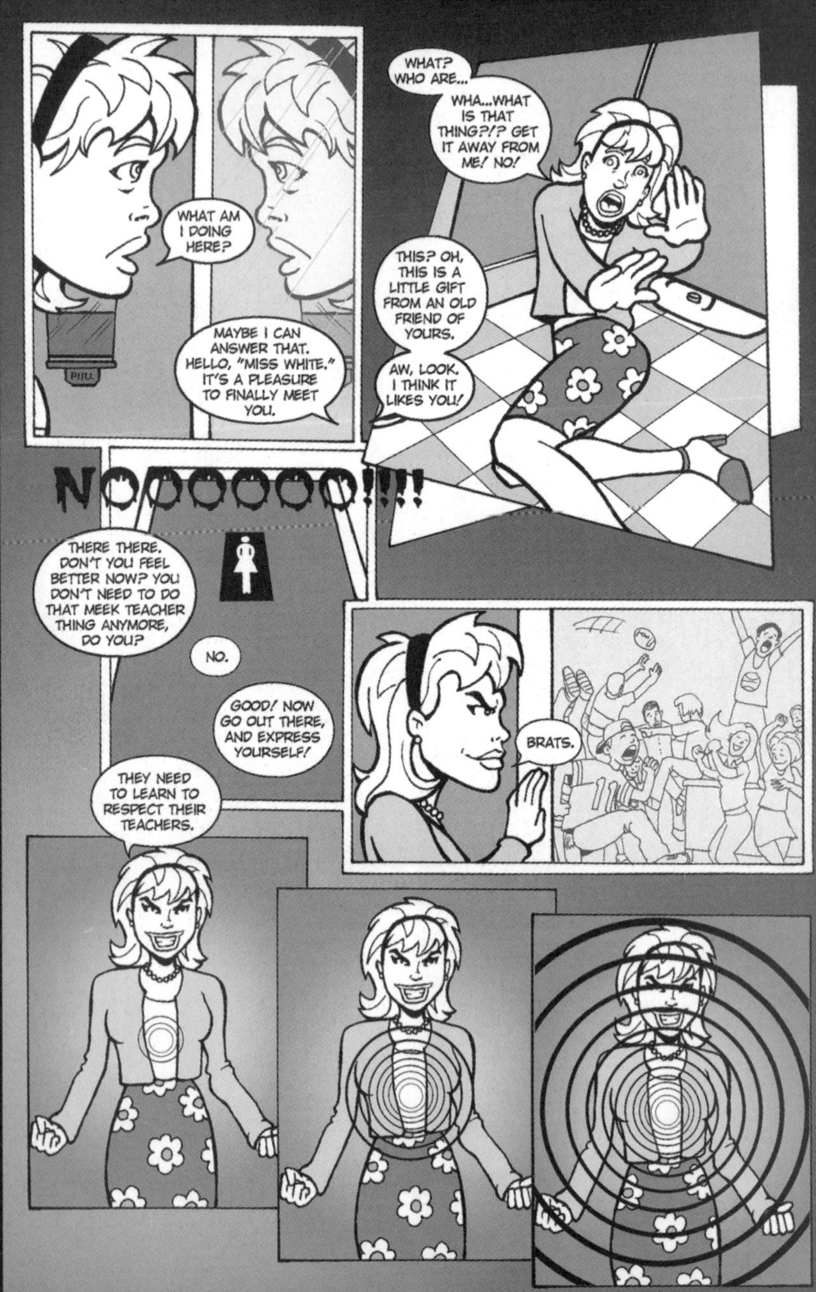
WHAT AM I DOING HERE?
MAYBE I CAN ANSWER THAT. HELLO, "MISS WHITE." IT'S A PLEASURE TO FINALLY MEET YOU.
WHAT? WHO ARE...
WHA...WHAT IS THAT THING?!? GET IT AWAY FROM ME! NO!
THIS? OH, THIS IS A LITTLE GIFT FROM AN OLD FRIEND OF YOURS.
AW, LOOK. I THINK IT LIKES YOU!
NOOOOOO!!!!
THERE THERE. DON'T YOU FEEL BETTER NOW? YOU DON'T NEED TO DO THAT MEEK TEACHER THING ANYMORE, DO YOU?
NO.
GOOD! NOW GO OUT THERE, AND EXPRESS YOURSELF!
BRATS.
THEY NEED TO LEARN TO RESPECT THEIR TEACHERS.

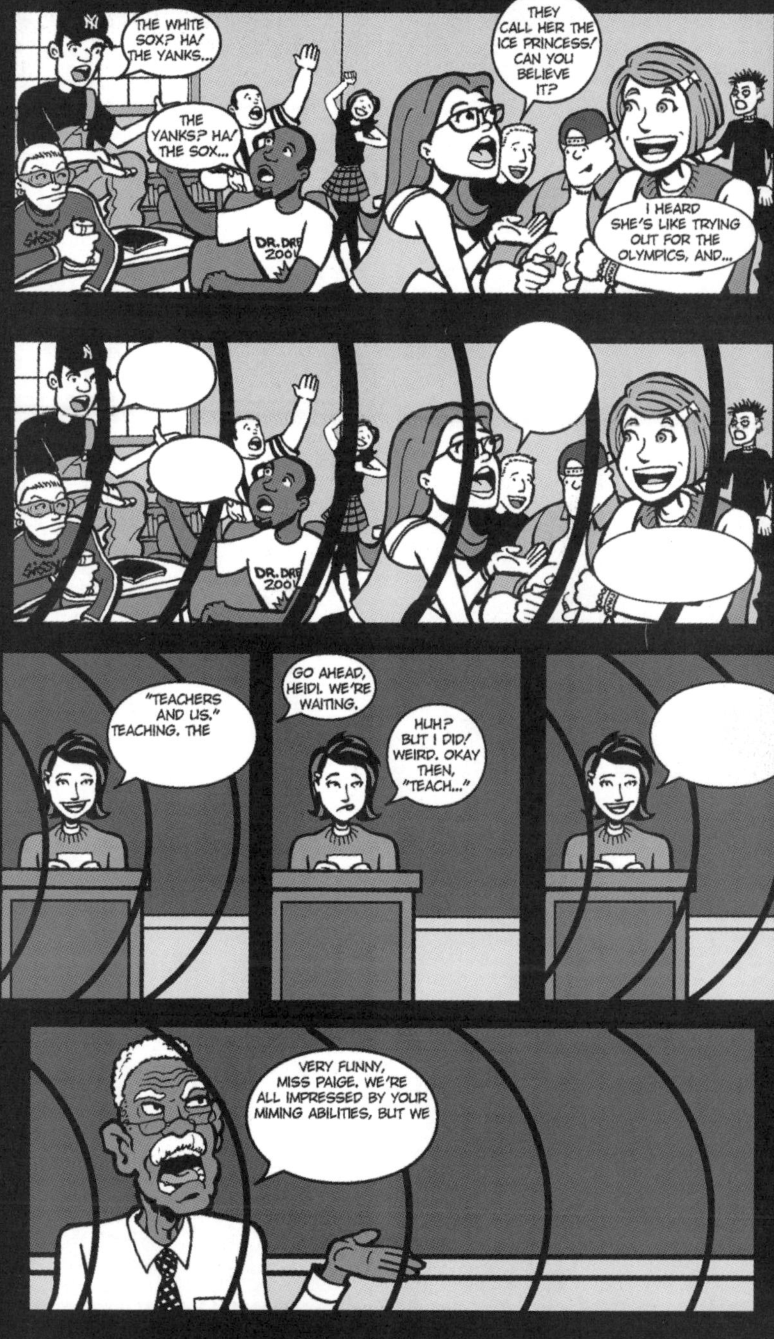
THE WHITE SOX? HA! THE YANKS...
THE YANKS? HA! THE SOX...
THEY CALL HER THE ICE PRINCESS! CAN YOU BELIEVE IT?
I HEARD SHE'S LIKE TRYING OUT FOR THE OLYMPICS, AND...
DR. DRE 2001
"TEACHERS AND US." TEACHING. THE
GO AHEAD, HEIDI. WE'RE WAITING.
HUH? BUT I DID! WEIRD. OKAY THEN, "TEACH..."
VERY FUNNY, MISS PAIGE. WE'RE ALL IMPRESSED BY YOUR MIMING ABILITIES, BUT WE

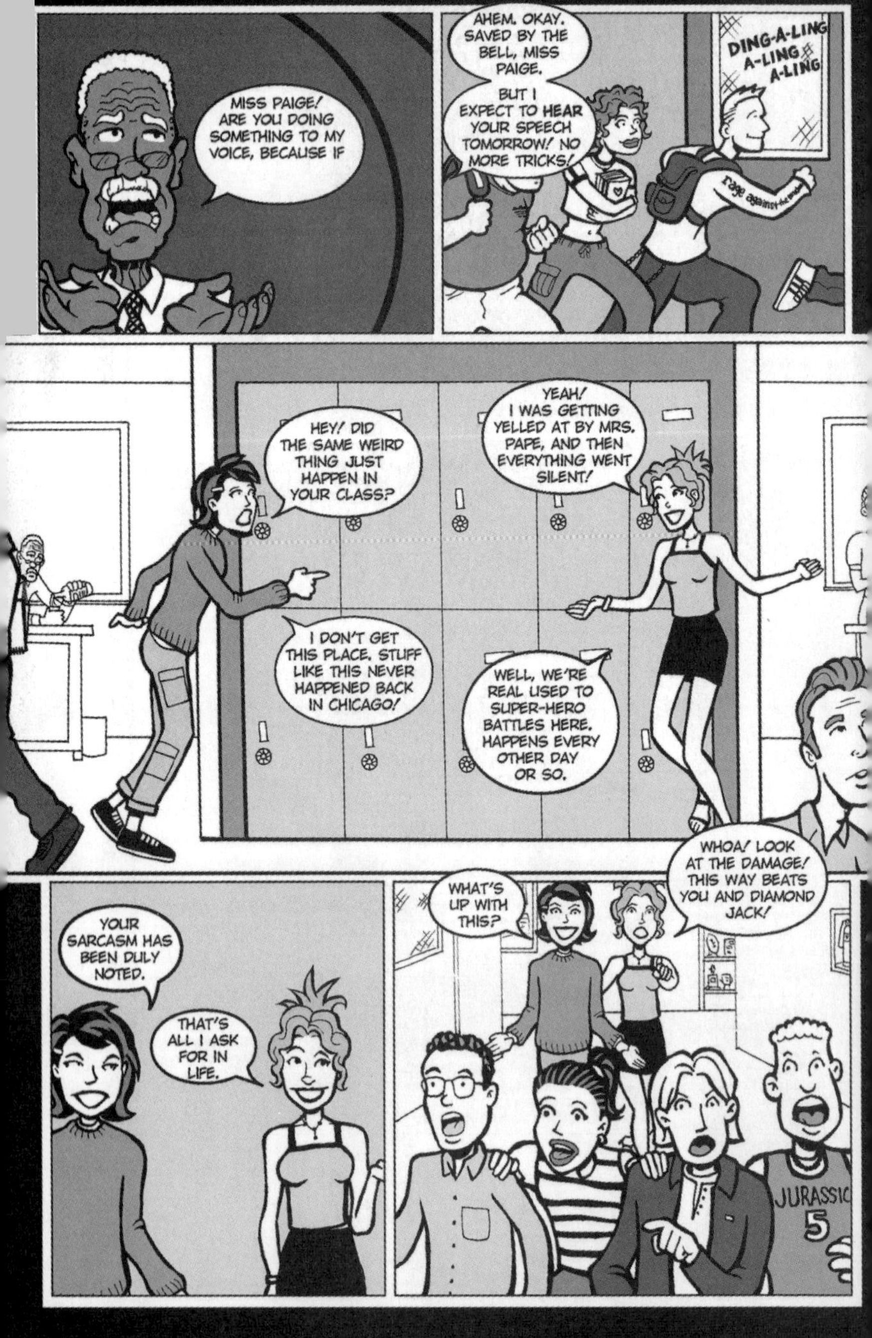
MISS PAIGE! ARE YOU DOING SOMETHING TO MY VOICE, BECAUSE IF
AHEM. OKAY. SAVED BY THE BELL, MISS PAIGE.
BUT I EXPECT TO HEAR YOUR SPEECH TOMORROW! NO MORE TRICKS!
DING-A-LING A-LING A-LING
rage against the machine
HEY! DID THE SAME WEIRD THING JUST HAPPEN IN YOUR CLASS?
YEAH! I WAS GETTING YELLED AT BY MRS. PAPE, AND THEN EVERYTHING WENT SILENT!
I DON'T GET THIS PLACE. STUFF LIKE THIS NEVER HAPPENED BACK IN CHICAGO!
WELL, WE'RE REAL USED TO SUPER-HERO BATTLES HERE. HAPPENS EVERY OTHER DAY OR SO.
YOUR SARCASM HAS BEEN DULY NOTED.
THAT'S ALL I ASK FOR IN LIFE.
WHAT'S UP WITH THIS?
WHOA! LOOK AT THE DAMAGE! THIS WAY BEATS YOU AND DIAMOND JACK!
JURASSIC 5

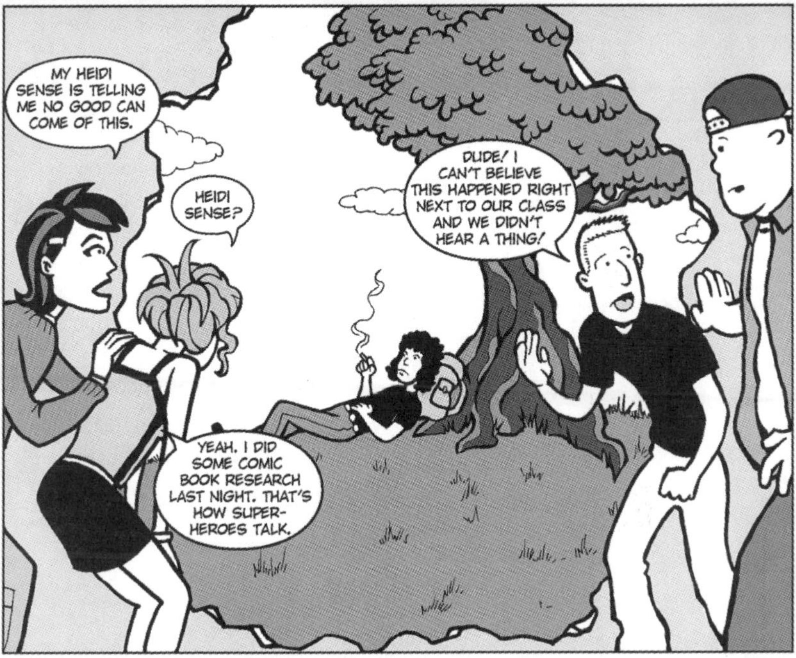
MY HEIDI SENSE IS TELLING ME NO GOOD CAN COME OF THIS.
HEIDI SENSE?
DUDE! I CAN'T BELIEVE THIS HAPPENED RIGHT NEXT TO OUR CLASS AND WE DIDN'T HEAR A THING!
YEAH. I DID SOME COMIC BOOK RESEARCH LAST NIGHT. THAT'S HOW SUPER-HEROES TALK.

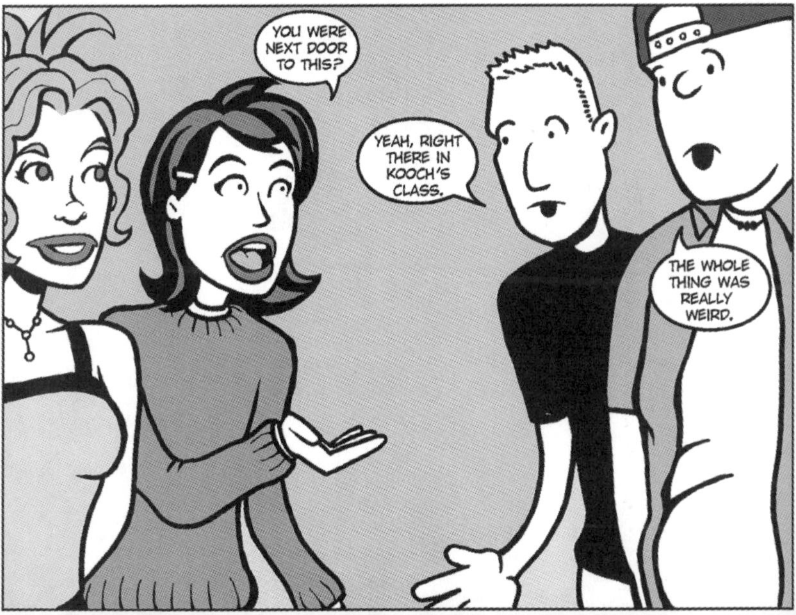
YOU WERE NEXT DOOR TO THIS?
YEAH, RIGHT THERE IN KOOCH'S CLASS.
THE WHOLE THING WAS REALLY WEIRD.

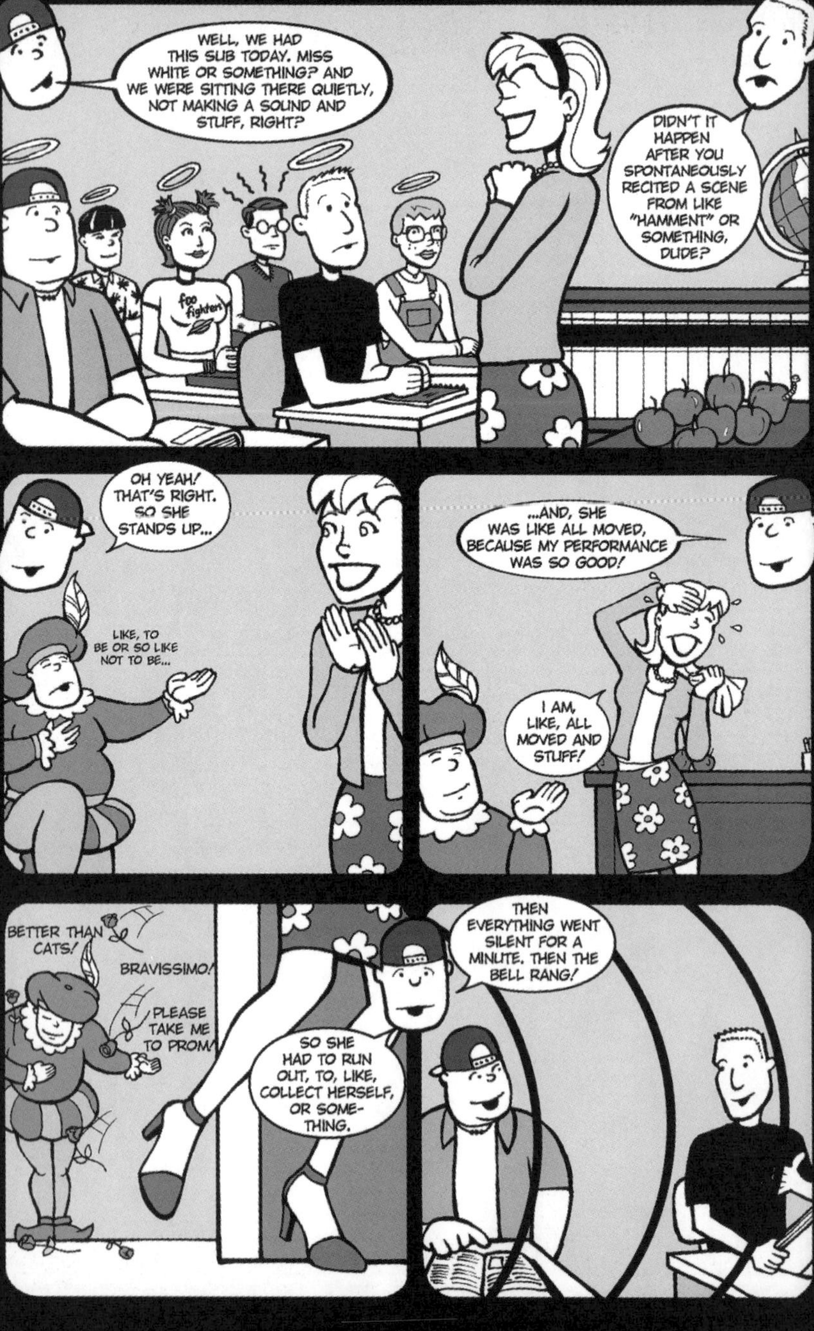
WELL, WE HAD THIS SUB TODAY. MISS WHITE OR SOMETHING? AND WE WERE SITTING THERE QUIETLY, NOT MAKING A SOUND AND STUFF, RIGHT?
DIDN'T IT HAPPEN AFTER YOU SPONTANEOUSLY RECITED A SCENE FROM LIKE "HAMMENT" OR SOMETHING, DUDE?
foo fighters
OH YEAH! THAT'S RIGHT. SO SHE STANDS UP...
LIKE, TO BE OR SO LIKE NOT TO BE...
...AND, SHE WAS LIKE ALL MOVED, BECAUSE MY PERFORMANCE WAS SO GOOD!
I AM, LIKE, ALL MOVED AND STUFF!
BETTER THAN CATS!
BRAVISSIMO!
PLEASE TAKE ME TO PROM!
SO SHE HAD TO RUN OUT, TO, LIKE, COLLECT HERSELF, OR SOMETHING.
THEN EVERYTHING WENT SILENT FOR A MINUTE. THEN THE BELL RANG!

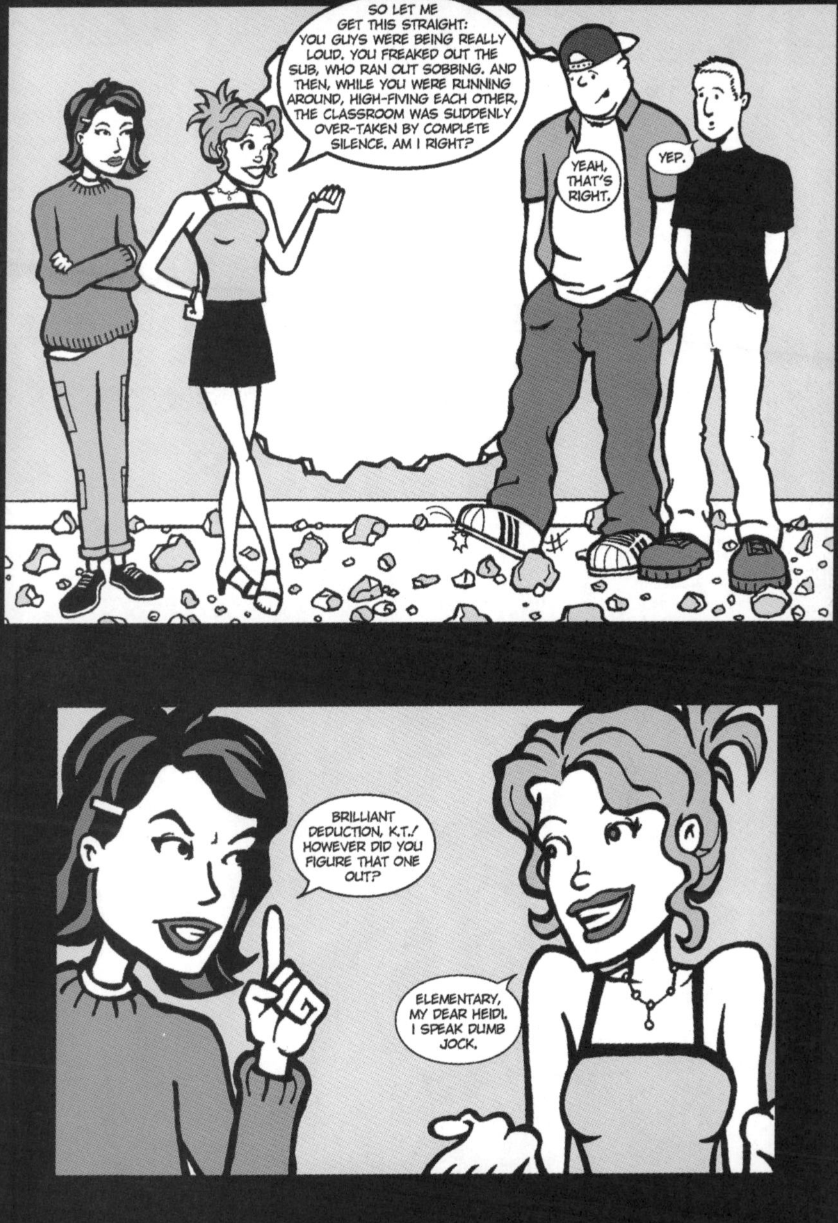
SO LET ME GET THIS STRAIGHT: YOU GUYS WERE BEING REALLY LOUD. YOU FREAKED OUT THE SUB, WHO RAN OUT SOBBING. AND THEN, WHILE YOU WERE RUNNING AROUND, HIGH-FIVING EACH OTHER, THE CLASSROOM WAS SUDDENLY OVER-TAKEN BY COMPLETE SILENCE. AM I RIGHT?
YEAH, THAT'S RIGHT.
YEP.
BRILLIANT DEDUCTION, K.T.! HOWEVER DID YOU FIGURE THAT ONE OUT?
ELEMENTARY, MY DEAR HEIDI. I SPEAK DUMB JOCK.

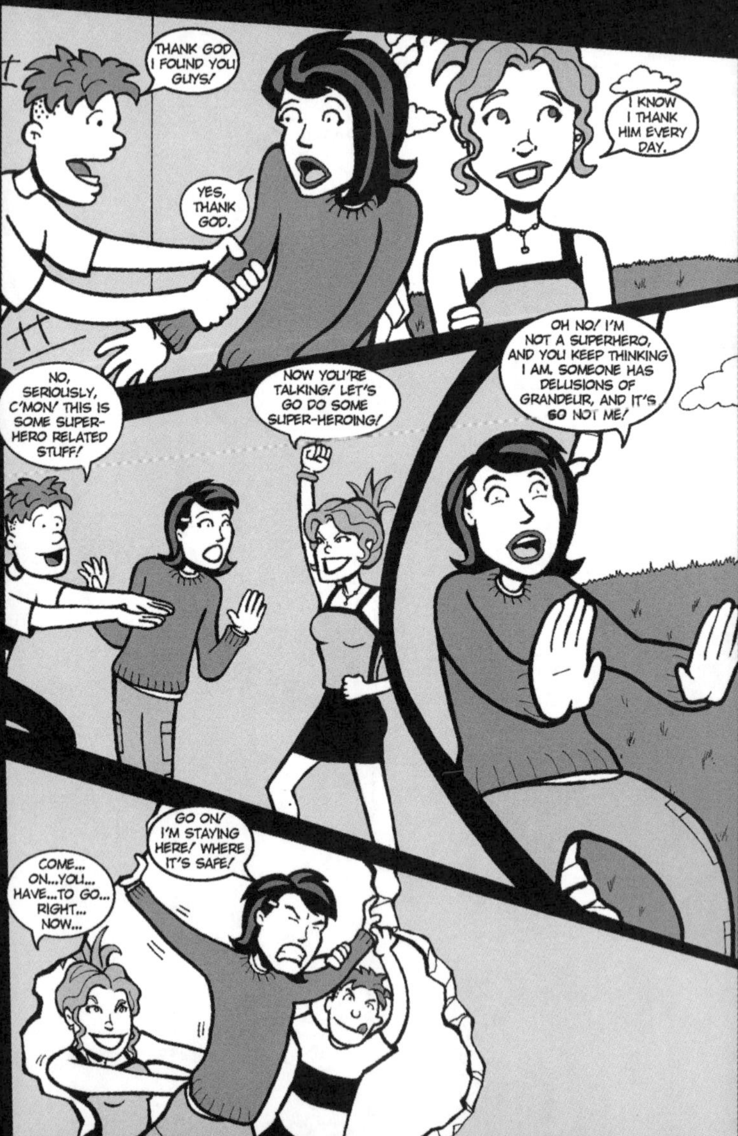
THANK GOD I FOUND YOU GUYS!
YES, THANK GOD.
I KNOW I THANK HIM EVERY DAY.
NO, SERIOUSLY, C'MON! THIS IS SOME SUPER-HERO RELATED STUFF!
NOW YOU'RE TALKING! LET'S GO DO SOME SUPER-HEROING!
OH NO! I'M NOT A SUPERHERO, AND YOU KEEP THINKING I AM. SOMEONE HAS DELUSIONS OF GRANDEUR, AND IT'S SO NOT ME!
COME... ON...YOU... HAVE...TO GO... RIGHT... NOW...
GO ON! I'M STAYING HERE! WHERE IT'S SAFE!

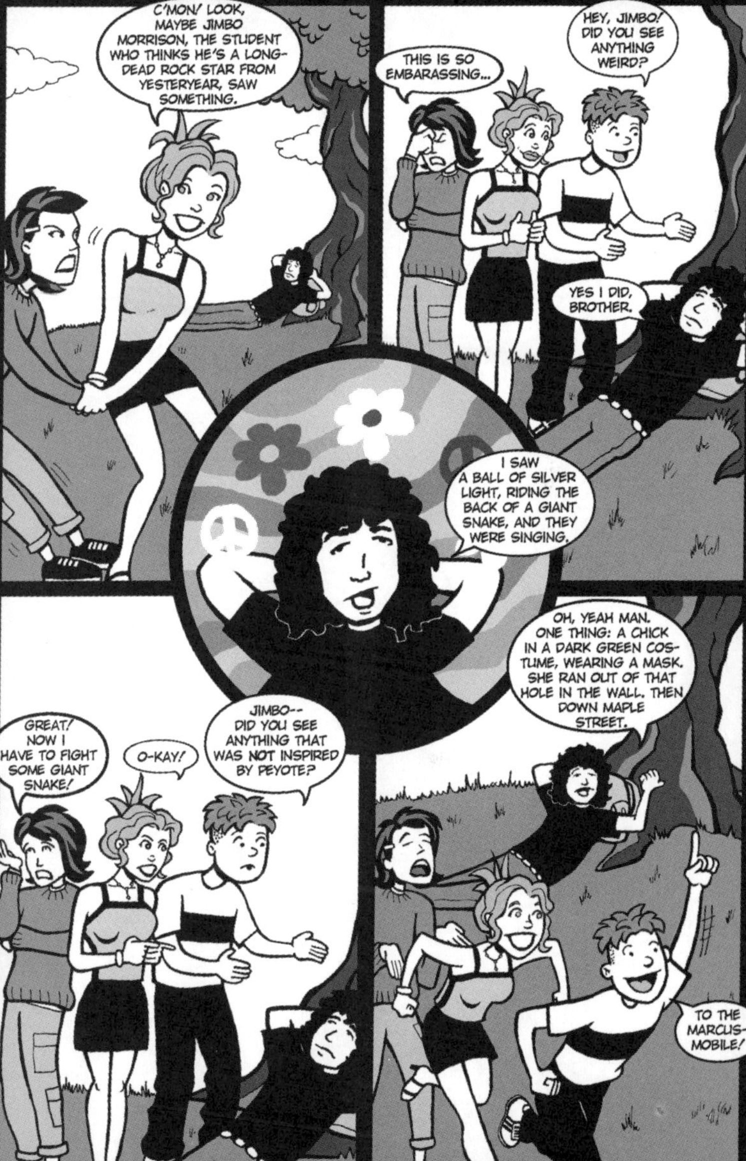

C'MON! LOOK, MAYBE JIMBO MORRISON, THE STUDENT WHO THINKS HE'S A LONG-DEAD ROCK STAR FROM YESTERYEAR, SAW SOMETHING.
THIS IS SO EMBARASSING...
HEY, JIMBO! DID YOU SEE ANYTHING WEIRD?
YES I DID, BROTHER.
I SAW A BALL OF SILVER LIGHT, RIDING THE BACK OF A GIANT SNAKE, AND THEY WERE SINGING.
GREAT! NOW I HAVE TO FIGHT SOME GIANT SNAKE!
O-KAY!
JIMBO-- DID YOU SEE ANYTHING THAT WAS NOT INSPIRED BY PEYOTE?
OH, YEAH MAN. ONE THING: A CHICK IN A DARK GREEN COS-TUME, WEARING A MASK. SHE RAN OUT OF THAT HOLE IN THE WALL. THEN DOWN MAPLE STREET.
TO THE MARCUS-MOBILE!

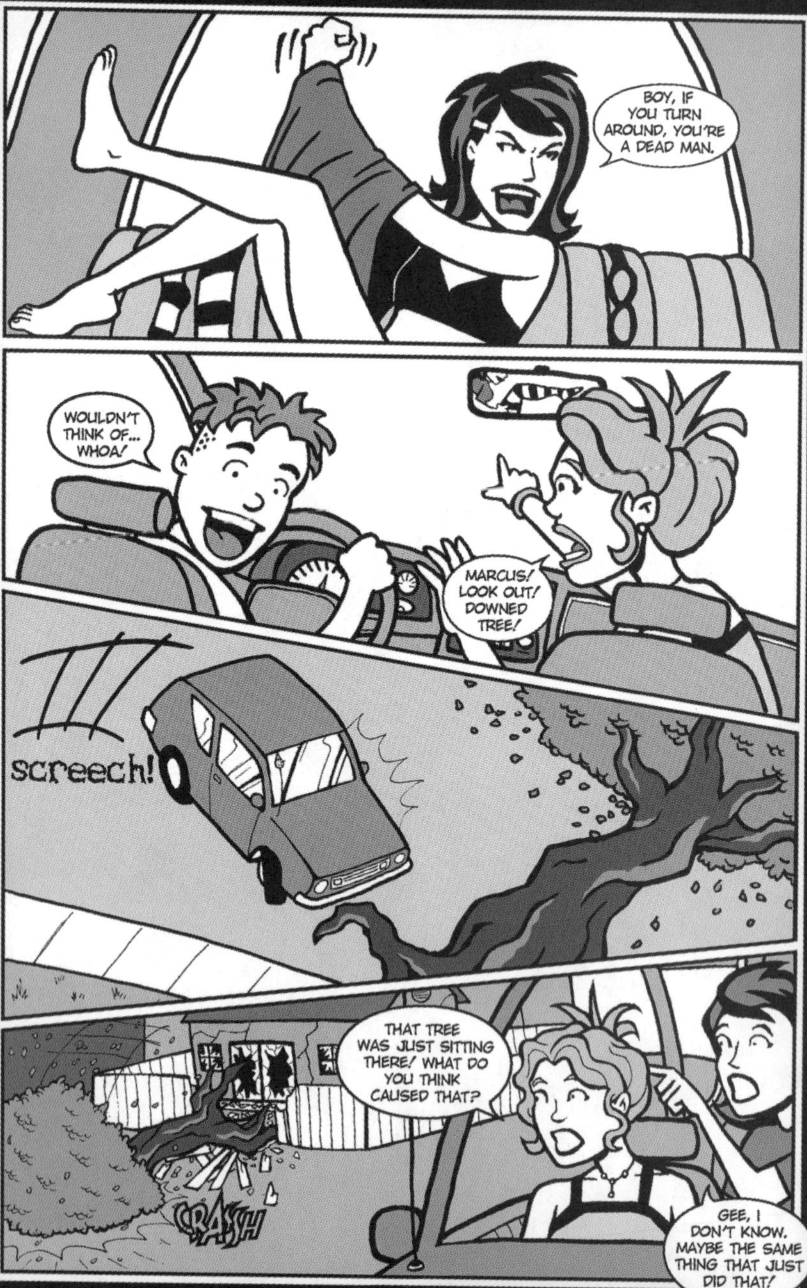
BOY, IF YOU TURN AROUND, YOU'RE A DEAD MAN.
WOULDN'T THINK OF... WHOA!
MARCUS! LOOK OUT! DOWNED TREE!
screech!
CRASH
THAT TREE WAS JUST SITTING THERE! WHAT DO YOU THINK CAUSED THAT?
GEE, I DON'T KNOW. MAYBE THE SAME THING THAT JUST DID THAT!

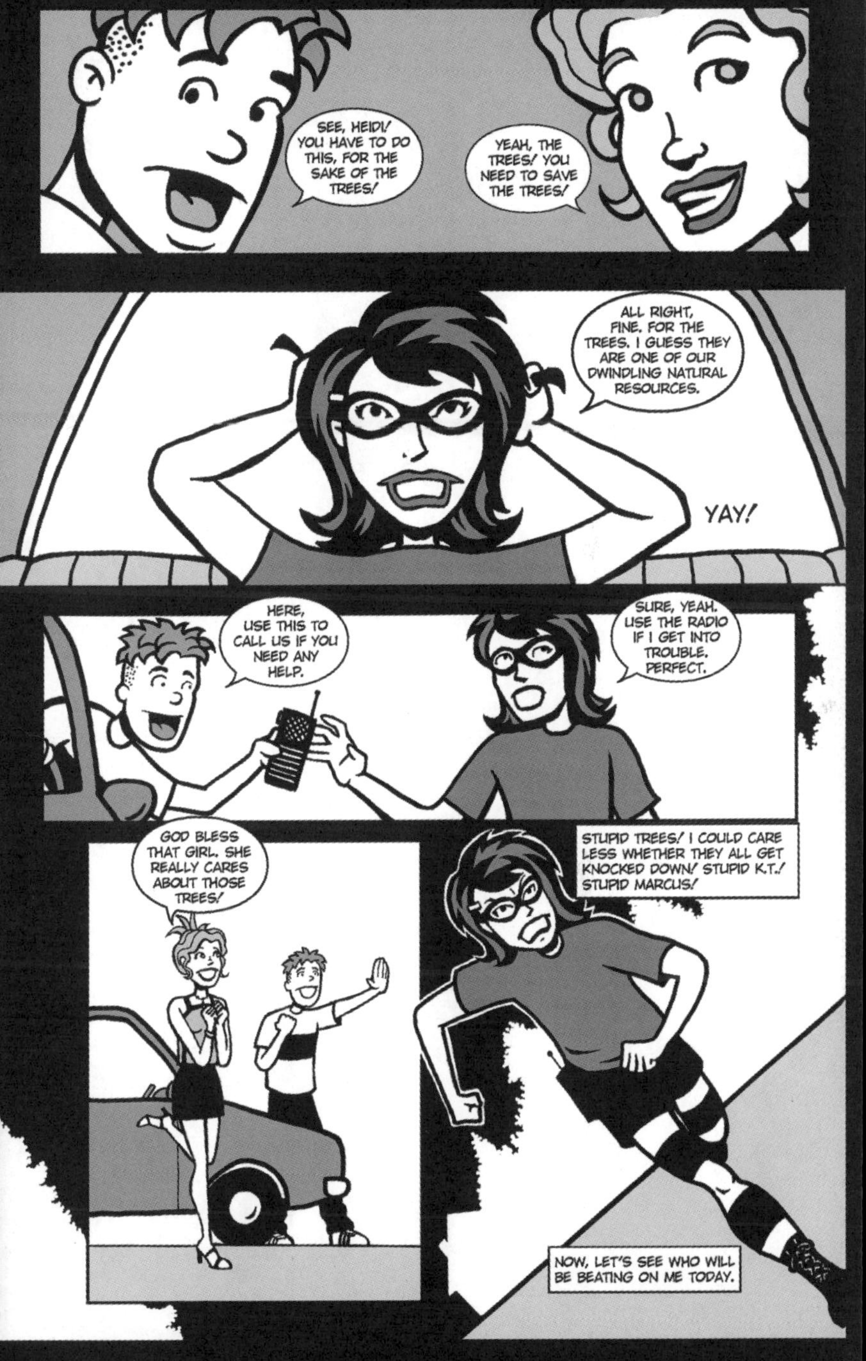
SEE, HEIDI! YOU HAVE TO DO THIS, FOR THE SAKE OF THE TREES!
YEAH, THE TREES! YOU NEED TO SAVE THE TREES!
ALL RIGHT, FINE. FOR THE TREES. I GUESS THEY ARE ONE OF OUR DWINDLING NATURAL RESOURCES.
YAY!
HERE, USE THIS TO CALL US IF YOU NEED ANY HELP.
SURE, YEAH. USE THE RADIO IF I GET INTO TROUBLE. PERFECT.
GOD BLESS THAT GIRL. SHE REALLY CARES ABOUT THOSE TREES!
STUPID TREES! I COULD CARE LESS WHETHER THEY ALL GET KNOCKED DOWN! STUPID K.T.! STUPID MARCUS!
NOW, LET'S SEE WHO WILL BE BEATING ON ME TODAY.

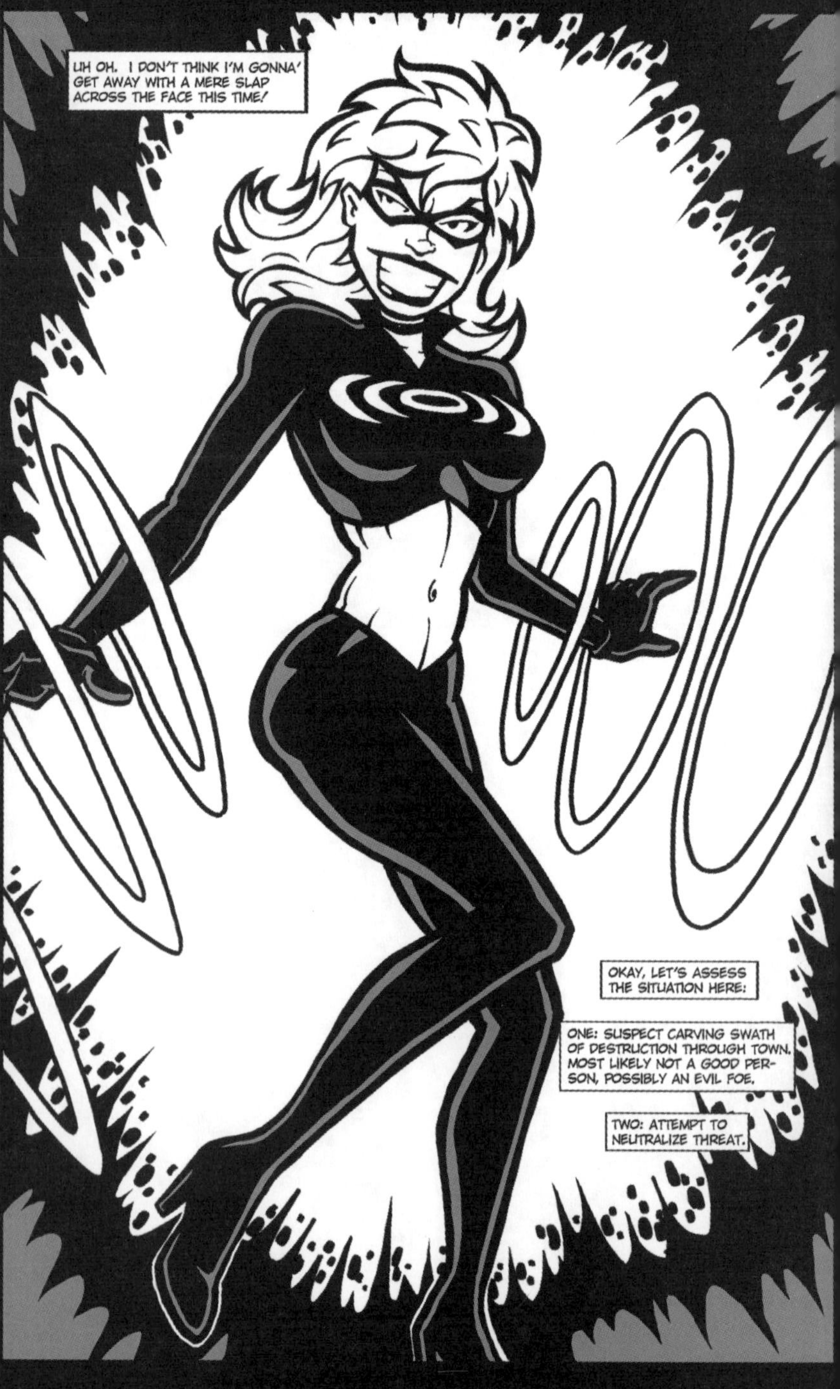
UH OH. I DON'T THINK I'M GONNA' GET AWAY WITH A MERE SLAP ACROSS THE FACE THIS TIME!
OKAY, LET'S ASSESS THE SITUATION HERE:
ONE: SUSPECT CARVING SWATH OF DESTRUCTION THROUGH TOWN. MOST LIKELY NOT A GOOD PERSON, POSSIBLY AN EVIL FOE.
TWO: ATTEMPT TO NEUTRALIZE THREAT.

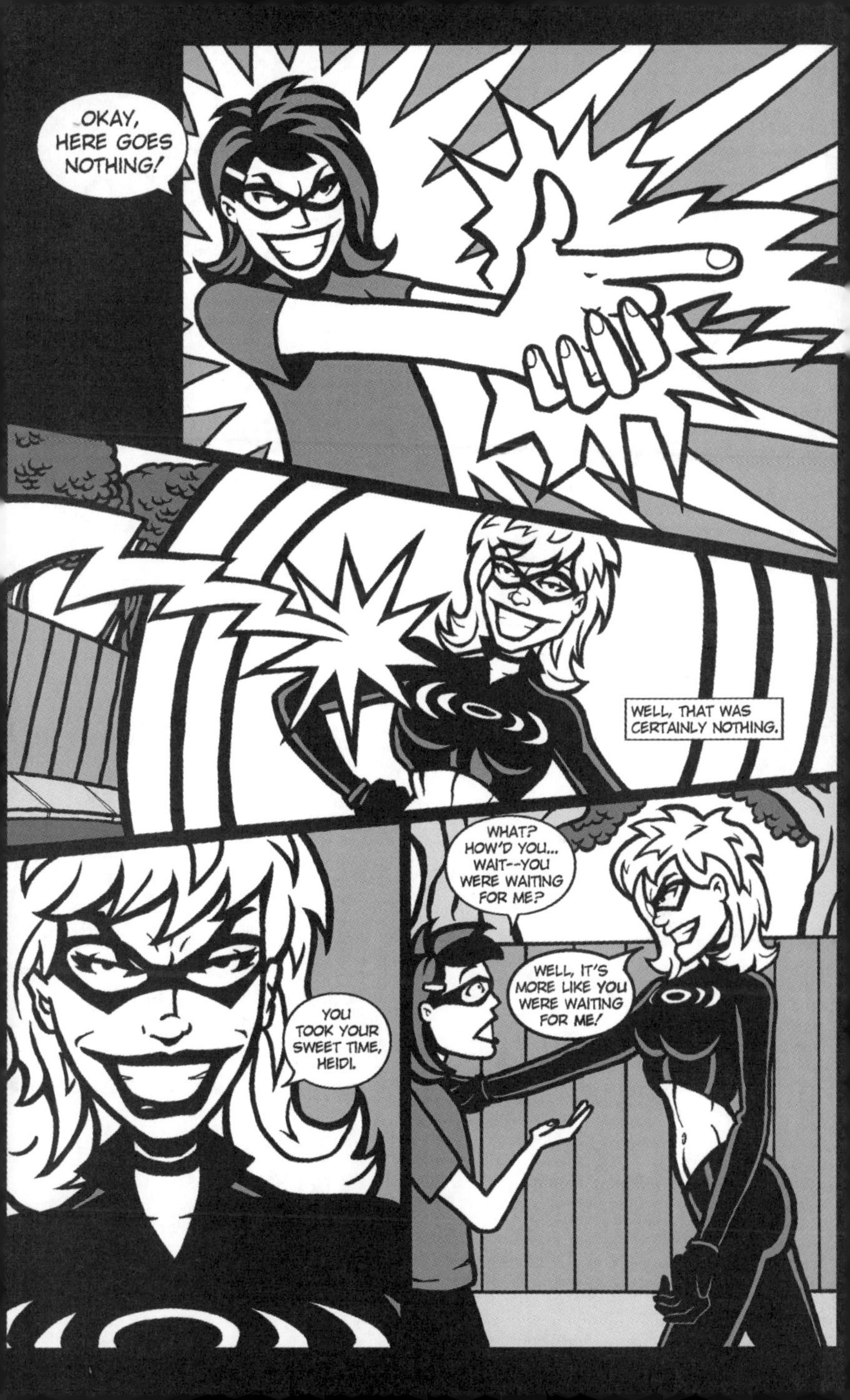
OKAY, HERE GOES NOTHING!
WELL, THAT WAS CERTAINLY NOTHING.
YOU TOOK YOUR SWEET TIME, HEIDI.
WHAT? HOW'D YOU... WAIT--YOU WERE WAITING FOR ME?
WELL, IT'S MORE LIKE YOU WERE WAITING FOR ME!

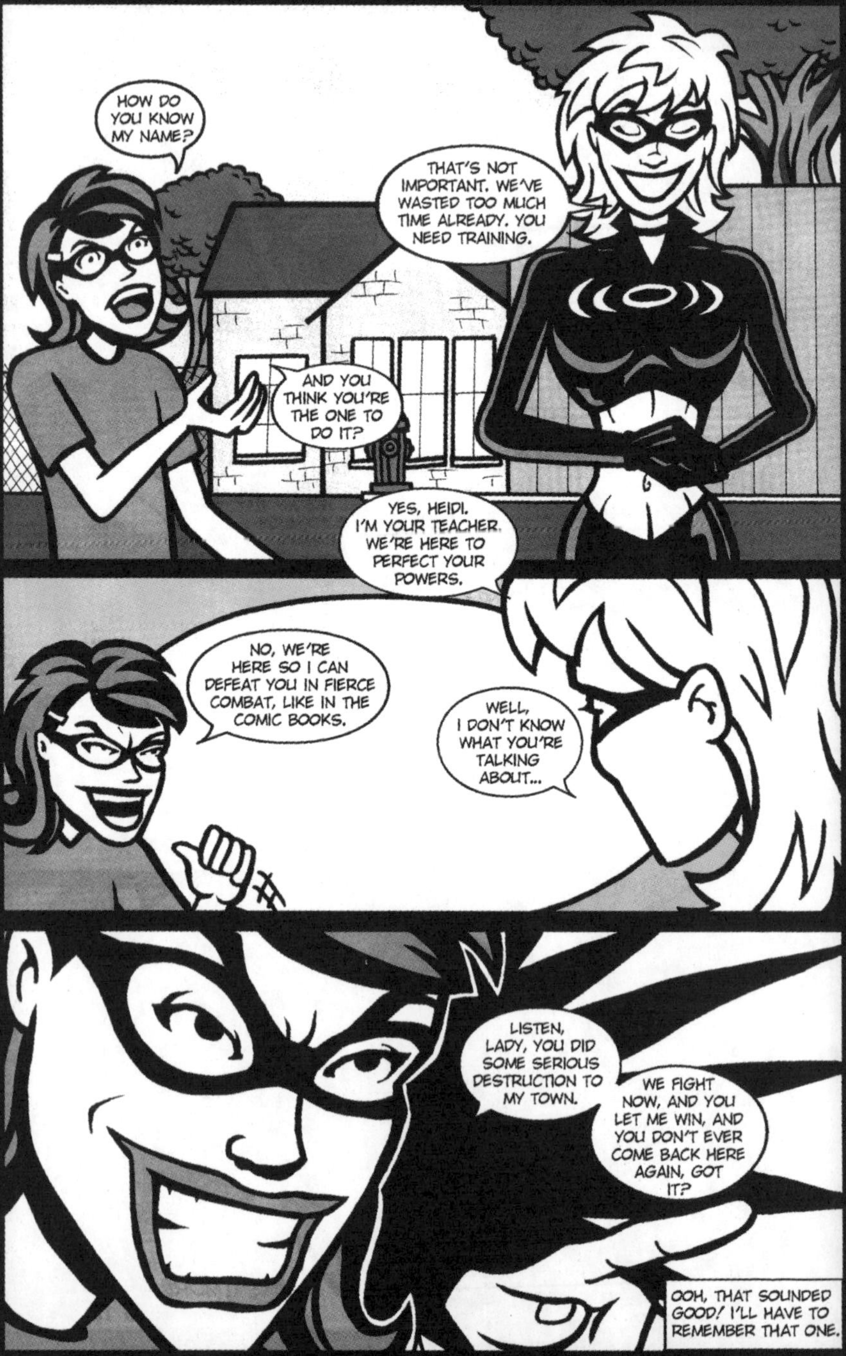
HOW DO YOU KNOW MY NAME?
THAT'S NOT IMPORTANT. WE'VE WASTED TOO MUCH TIME ALREADY. YOU NEED TRAINING.
AND YOU THINK YOU'RE THE ONE TO DO IT?
YES, HEIDI. I'M YOUR TEACHER. WE'RE HERE TO PERFECT YOUR POWERS.
NO, WE'RE HERE SO I CAN DEFEAT YOU IN FIERCE COMBAT, LIKE IN THE COMIC BOOKS.
WELL, I DON'T KNOW WHAT YOU'RE TALKING ABOUT...
LISTEN, LADY, YOU DID SOME SERIOUS DESTRUCTION TO MY TOWN.
WE FIGHT NOW, AND YOU LET ME WIN, AND YOU DON'T EVER COME BACK HERE AGAIN, GOT IT?
OOH, THAT SOUNDED GOOD! I'LL HAVE TO REMEMBER THAT ONE.

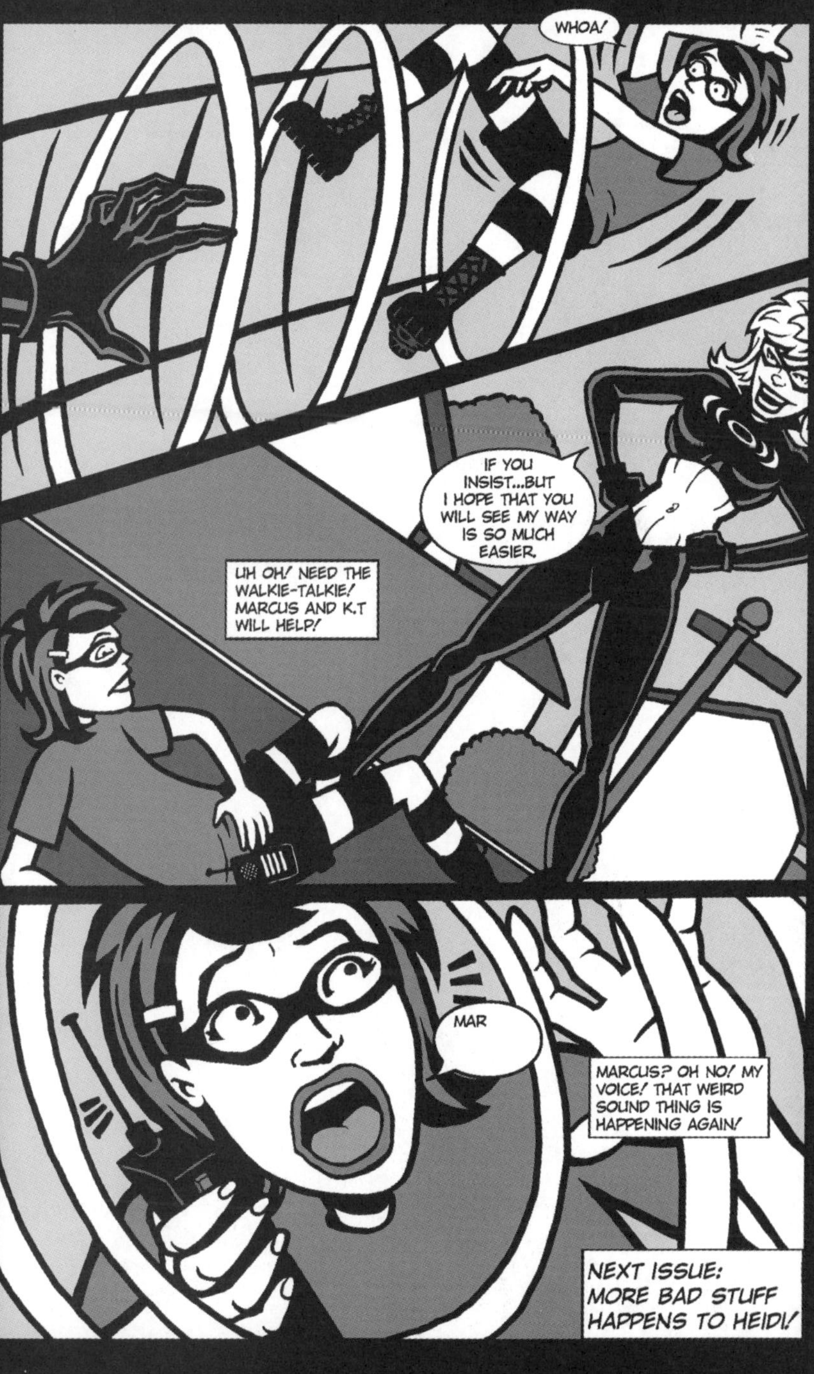
WHOA!
IF YOU INSIST...BUT I HOPE THAT YOU WILL SEE MY WAY IS SO MUCH EASIER.
UH OH! NEED THE WALKIE-TALKIE! MARCUS AND K.T WILL HELP!
MAR
MARCUS? OH NO! MY VOICE! THAT WEIRD SOUND THING IS HAPPENING AGAIN!
NEXT ISSUE: MORE BAD STUFF HAPPENS TO HEIDI!

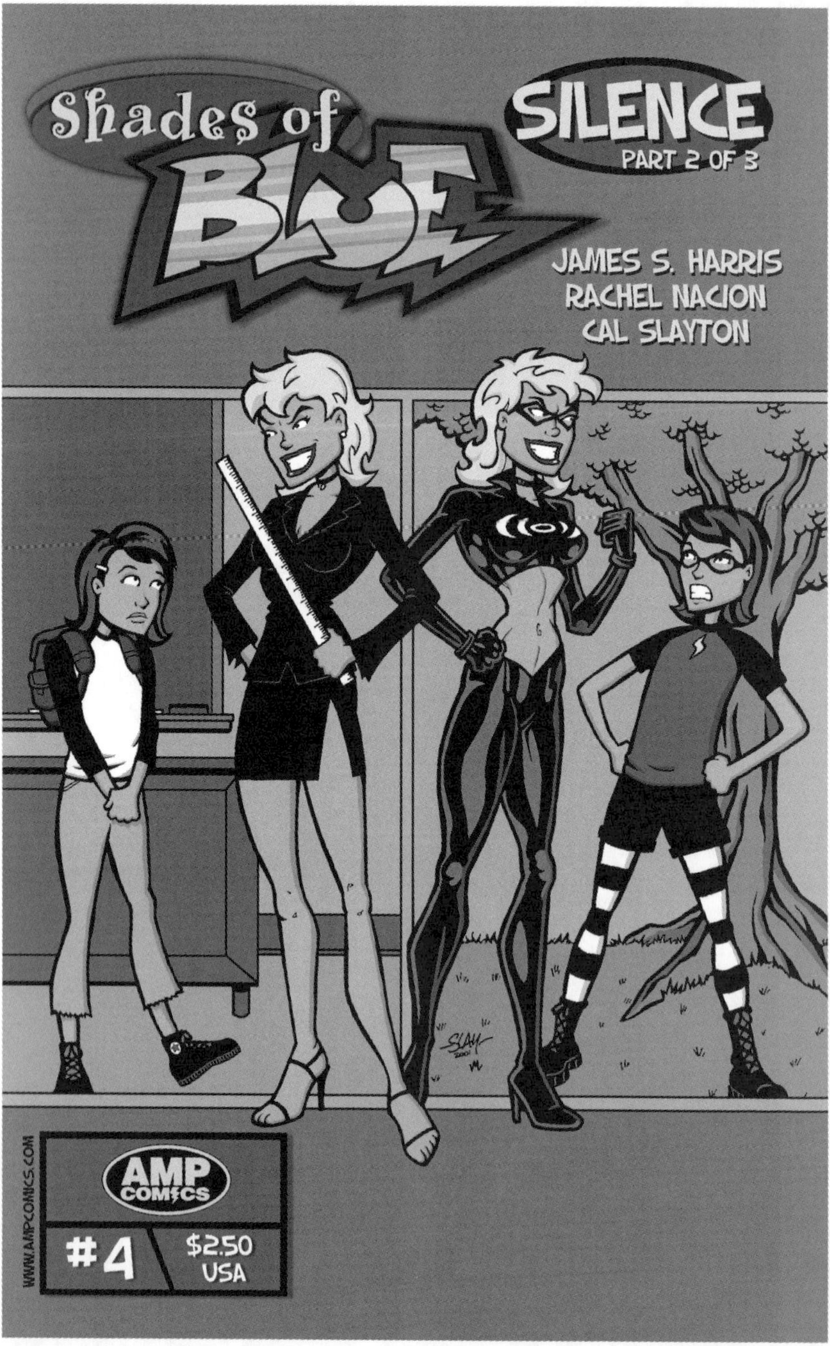
Shades of BLUE
SILENCE
PART 2 OF 3
JAMES S. HARRIS
RACHEL NACION
CAL SLAYTON
WWW.AMPCOMICS.COM
AMP COMICS
#4
$2.50
USA

Shades of BLUE

SILENCE
PART 2 OF 3

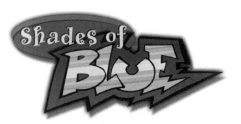

"The Physics Teacher Cometh"

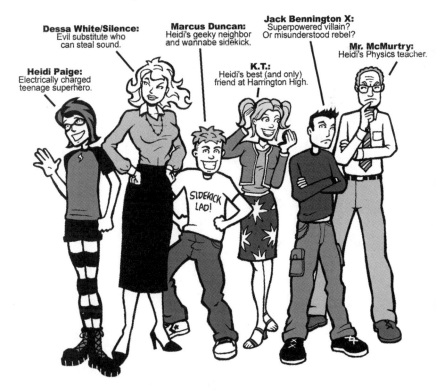

Dessa White/Silence: Evil substitute who can steal sound.
Marcus Duncan: Heidi's geeky neighbor and wannabe sidekick.
Jack Bennington X: Superpowered villain? Or misunderstood rebel?
Mr. McMurtry: Heidi's Physics teacher.
Heidi Paige: Electrically charged teenage superhero.
K.T.: Heidi's best (and only) friend at Harrington High.
SIDEKICK LAD!

Things that happened before now:

HEIDI FACED HER GREATEST CHALLENGE YET - A DERANGED SUBSTITUTE TEACHER NAMED DESSA WHITE, WHO WAS MYSTERIOUSLY GIVEN SUPER POWERS. ACTUALLY, SHE SEEMED MORE MILDLY DISTURBED THAN DERANGED. SLIGHTLY DEMENTED, REALLY.

BUT NO MATTER! HEIDI VALIANTLY SET FORTH TO BRING DOWN THE EVIL VILLAINESS, AND WHEN LAST WE LEFT HER, OUR HERO WAS IN GRAVE DANGER!

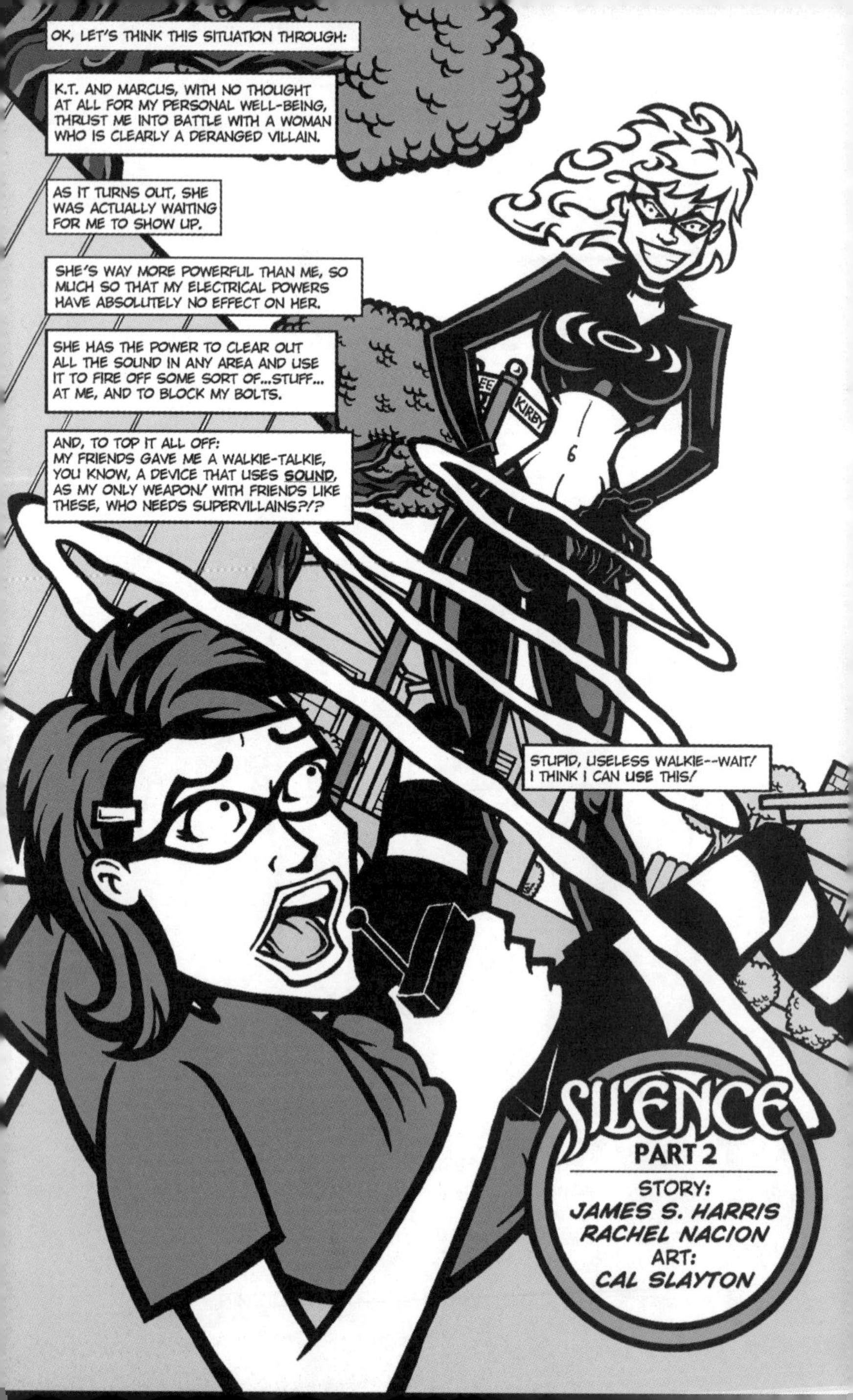
OK, LET'S THINK THIS SITUATION THROUGH:
K.T. AND MARCUS, WITH NO THOUGHT AT ALL FOR MY PERSONAL WELL-BEING, THRUST ME INTO BATTLE WITH A WOMAN WHO IS CLEARLY A DERANGED VILLAIN.
AS IT TURNS OUT, SHE WAS ACTUALLY WAITING FOR ME TO SHOW UP.
SHE'S WAY MORE POWERFUL THAN ME, SO MUCH SO THAT MY ELECTRICAL POWERS HAVE ABSOLUTELY NO EFFECT ON HER.
SHE HAS THE POWER TO CLEAR OUT ALL THE SOUND IN ANY AREA AND USE IT TO FIRE OFF SOME SORT OF...STUFF... AT ME, AND TO BLOCK MY BOLTS.
AND, TO TOP IT ALL OFF: MY FRIENDS GAVE ME A WALKIE-TALKIE, YOU KNOW, A DEVICE THAT USES SOUND, AS MY ONLY WEAPON! WITH FRIENDS LIKE THESE, WHO NEEDS SUPERVILLAINS?!?
KIRBY
6
STUPID, USELESS WALKIE--WAIT! I THINK I CAN USE THIS!
SILENCE
PART 2
STORY:
JAMES S. HARRIS
RACHEL NACION
ART:
CAL SLAYTON

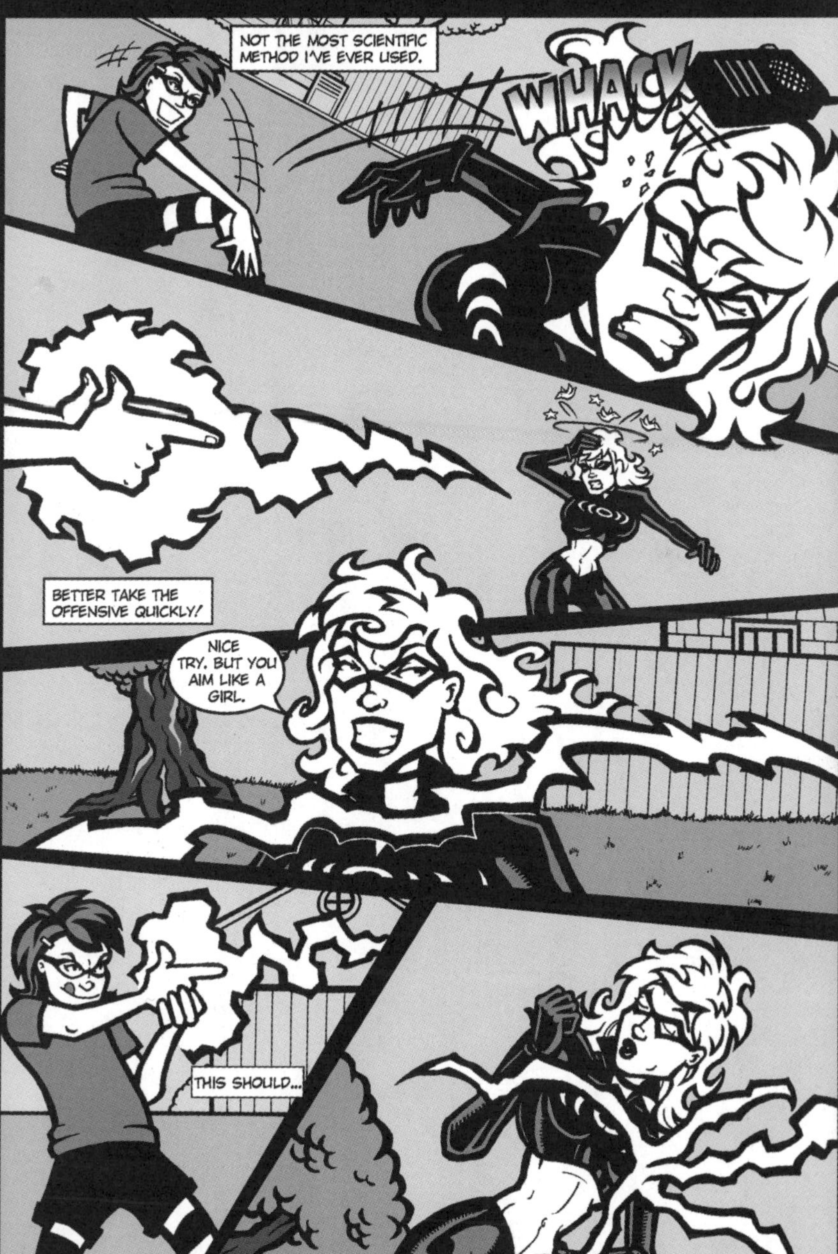
NOT THE MOST SCIENTIFIC METHOD I'VE EVER USED.
WHACK
BETTER TAKE THE OFFENSIVE QUICKLY!
NICE TRY. BUT YOU AIM LIKE A GIRL.
THIS SHOULD...
...HAVE ABSOLUTELY NO EFFECT. STUPID POWERS! WHY CAN'T THEY BE COOL AND USEFUL?!?

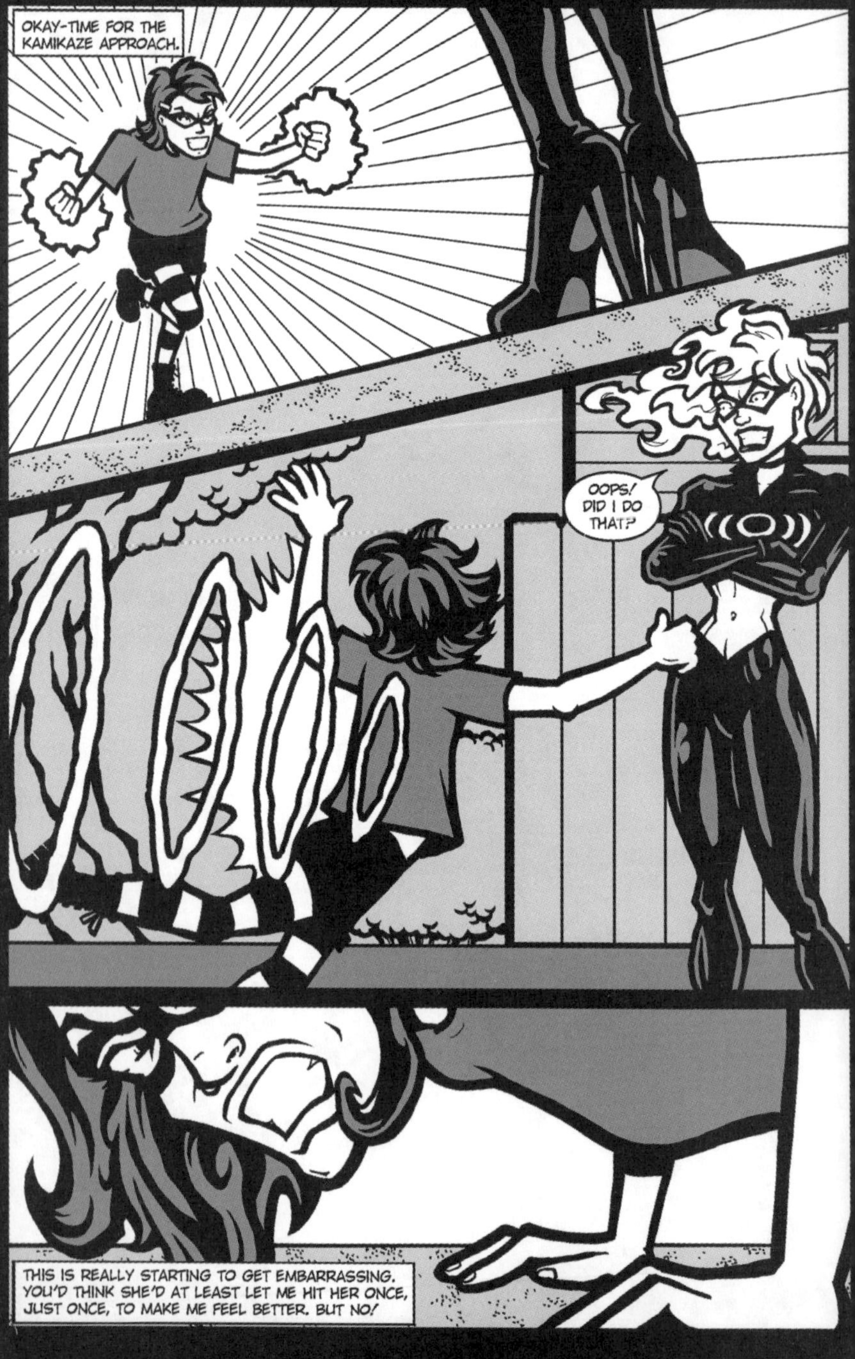
OKAY-TIME FOR THE KAMIKAZE APPROACH.
OOPS! DID I DO THAT?
THIS IS REALLY STARTING TO GET EMBARRASSING. YOU'D THINK SHE'D AT LEAST LET ME HIT HER ONCE, JUST ONCE, TO MAKE ME FEEL BETTER. BUT NO!

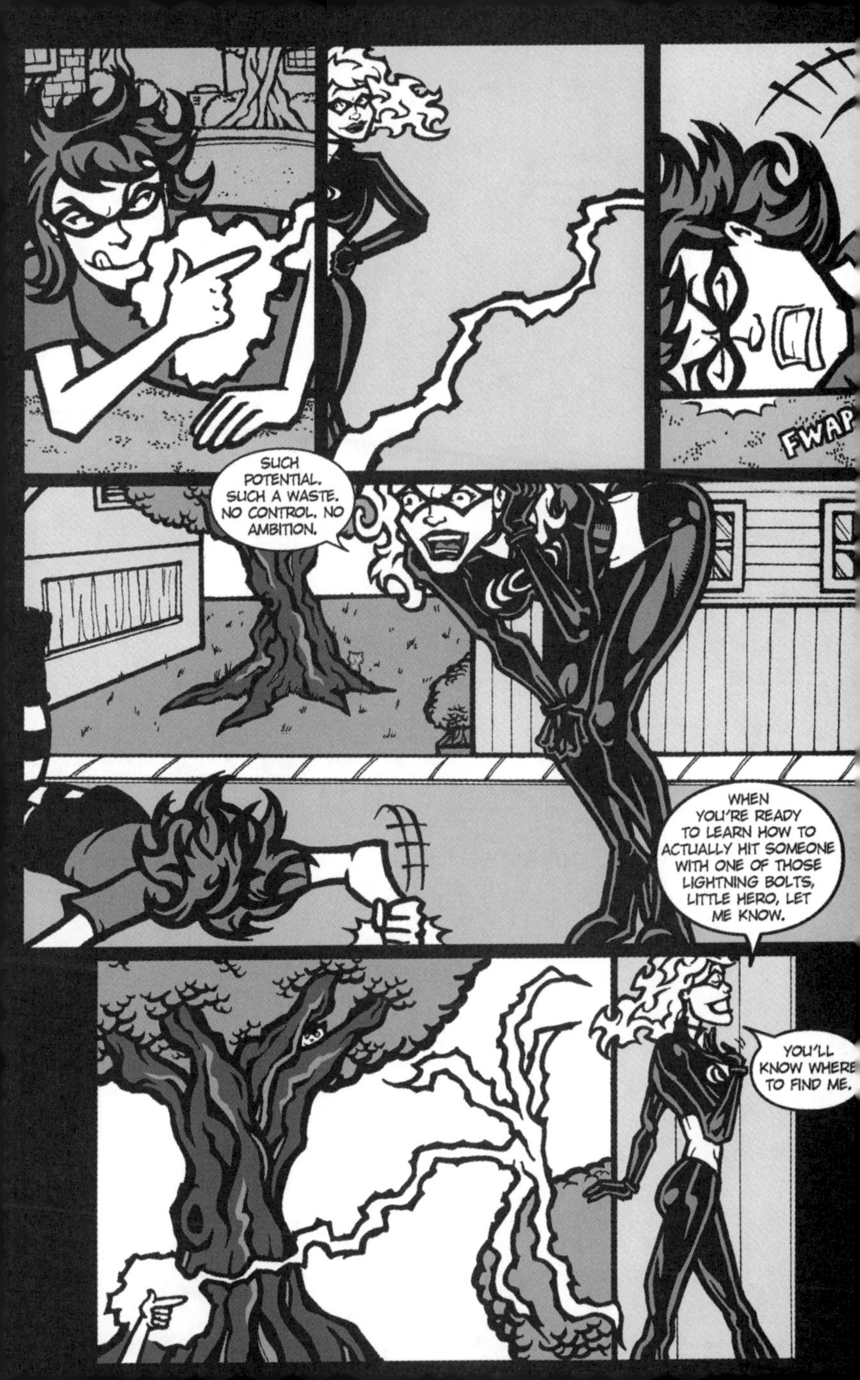
FWAP
SUCH POTENTIAL. SUCH A WASTE. NO CONTROL. NO AMBITION.
WHEN YOU'RE READY TO LEARN HOW TO ACTUALLY HIT SOMEONE WITH ONE OF THOSE LIGHTNING BOLTS, LITTLE HERO, LET ME KNOW.
YOU'LL KNOW WHERE TO FIND ME.

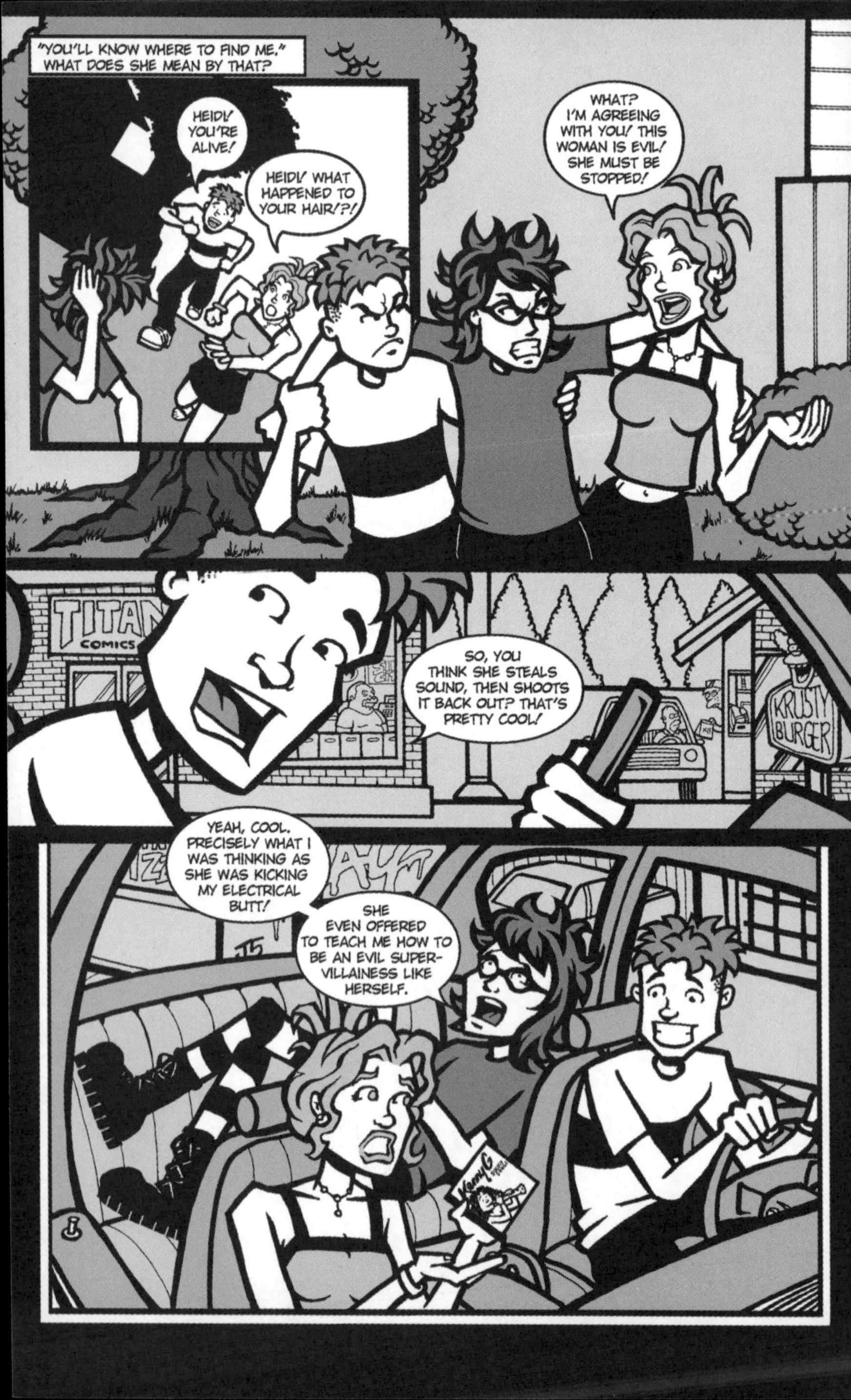
"YOU'LL KNOW WHERE TO FIND ME." WHAT DOES SHE MEAN BY THAT?
HEIDI! YOU'RE ALIVE!
HEIDI! WHAT HAPPENED TO YOUR HAIR!?!
WHAT? I'M AGREEING WITH YOU! THIS WOMAN IS EVIL! SHE MUST BE STOPPED!
TITAN COMICS
SO, YOU THINK SHE STEALS SOUND, THEN SHOOTS IT BACK OUT? THAT'S PRETTY COOL!
KRUSTY BURGER
YEAH, COOL. PRECISELY WHAT I WAS THINKING AS SHE WAS KICKING MY ELECTRICAL BUTT!
SHE EVEN OFFERED TO TEACH ME HOW TO BE AN EVIL SUPER-VILLAINESS LIKE HERSELF.

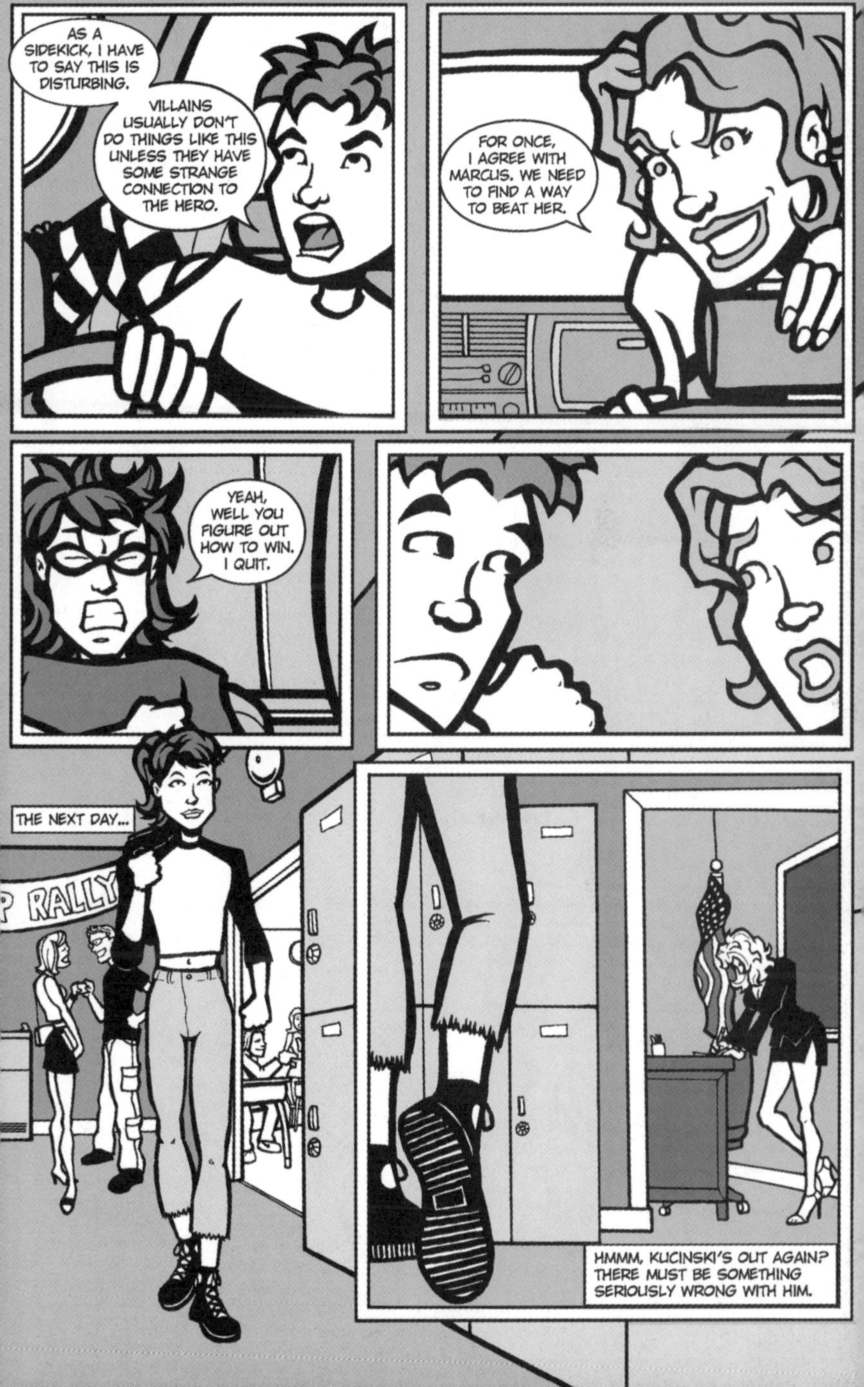
AS A SIDEKICK, I HAVE TO SAY THIS IS DISTURBING.
VILLAINS USUALLY DON'T DO THINGS LIKE THIS UNLESS THEY HAVE SOME STRANGE CONNECTION TO THE HERO.
FOR ONCE, I AGREE WITH MARCUS. WE NEED TO FIND A WAY TO BEAT HER.
YEAH, WELL YOU FIGURE OUT HOW TO WIN. I QUIT.
THE NEXT DAY...
RALLY
HMMM, KUCINSKI'S OUT AGAIN? THERE MUST BE SOMETHING SERIOUSLY WRONG WITH HIM.

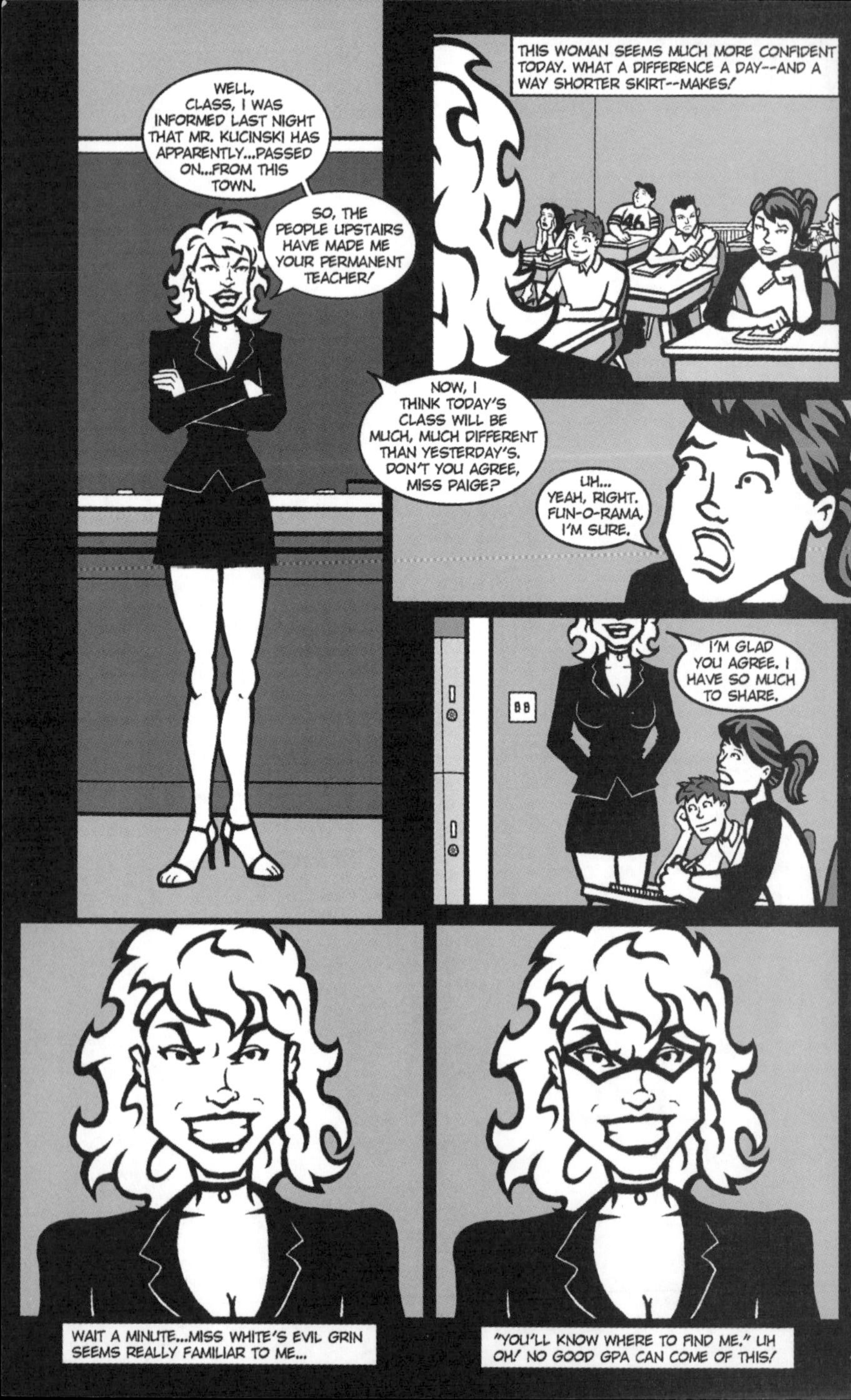

WELL, CLASS, I WAS INFORMED LAST NIGHT THAT MR. KUCINSKI HAS APPARENTLY...PASSED ON...FROM THIS TOWN.
SO, THE PEOPLE UPSTAIRS HAVE MADE ME YOUR PERMANENT TEACHER!
THIS WOMAN SEEMS MUCH MORE CONFIDENT TODAY. WHAT A DIFFERENCE A DAY--AND A WAY SHORTER SKIRT--MAKES!
NOW, I THINK TODAY'S CLASS WILL BE MUCH, MUCH DIFFERENT THAN YESTERDAY'S. DON'T YOU AGREE, MISS PAIGE?
UH... YEAH, RIGHT. FUN-O-RAMA, I'M SURE.
I'M GLAD YOU AGREE. I HAVE SO MUCH TO SHARE.
WAIT A MINUTE...MISS WHITE'S EVIL GRIN SEEMS REALLY FAMILIAR TO ME...
"YOU'LL KNOW WHERE TO FIND ME." UH OH! NO GOOD GPA CAN COME OF THIS!

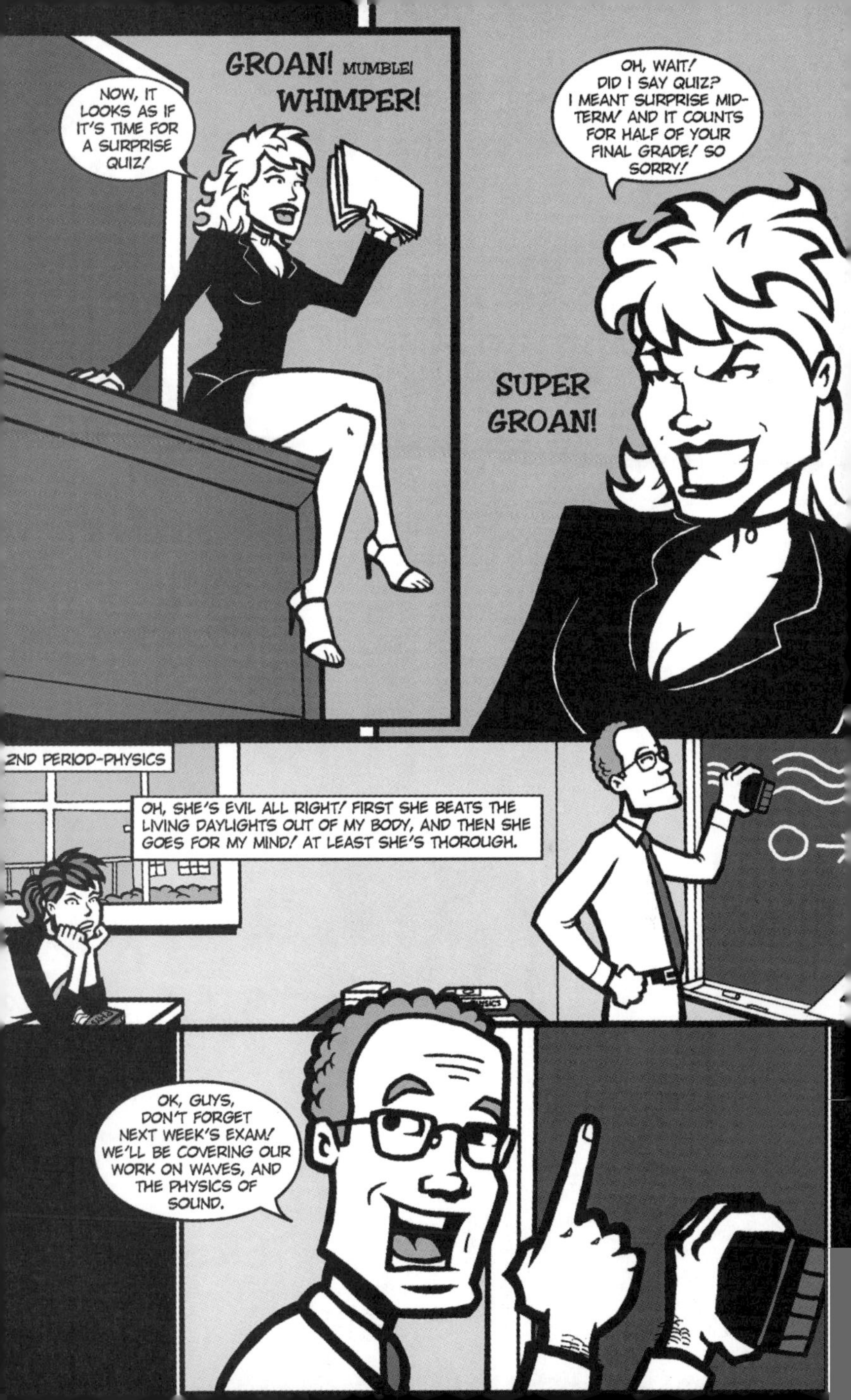
GROAN! MUMBLE! WHIMPER!
NOW, IT LOOKS AS IF IT'S TIME FOR A SURPRISE QUIZ!
OH, WAIT! DID I SAY QUIZ? I MEANT SURPRISE MID-TERM! AND IT COUNTS FOR HALF OF YOUR FINAL GRADE! SO SORRY!
SUPER GROAN!
2ND PERIOD-PHYSICS
OH, SHE'S EVIL ALL RIGHT! FIRST SHE BEATS THE LIVING DAYLIGHTS OUT OF MY BODY, AND THEN SHE GOES FOR MY MIND! AT LEAST SHE'S THOROUGH.
OK, GUYS, DON'T FORGET NEXT WEEK'S EXAM! WE'LL BE COVERING OUR WORK ON WAVES, AND THE PHYSICS OF SOUND.

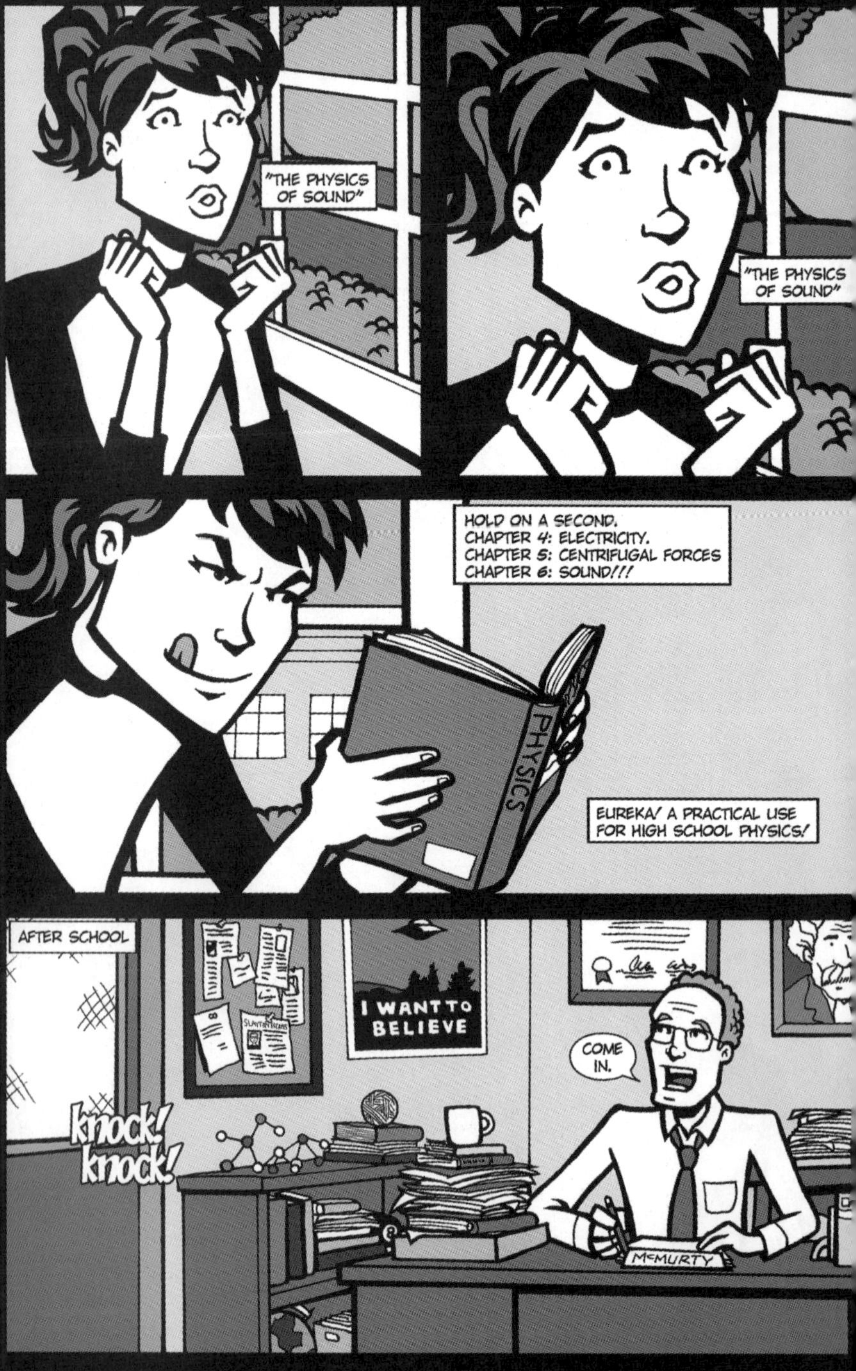
"THE PHYSICS OF SOUND"
"THE PHYSICS OF SOUND"
HOLD ON A SECOND.
CHAPTER 4: ELECTRICITY.
CHAPTER 5: CENTRIFUGAL FORCES
CHAPTER 6: SOUND!!!
PHYSICS
EUREKA! A PRACTICAL USE FOR HIGH SCHOOL PHYSICS!
AFTER SCHOOL
I WANT TO BELIEVE
COME IN.
knock! knock!
McMURTY

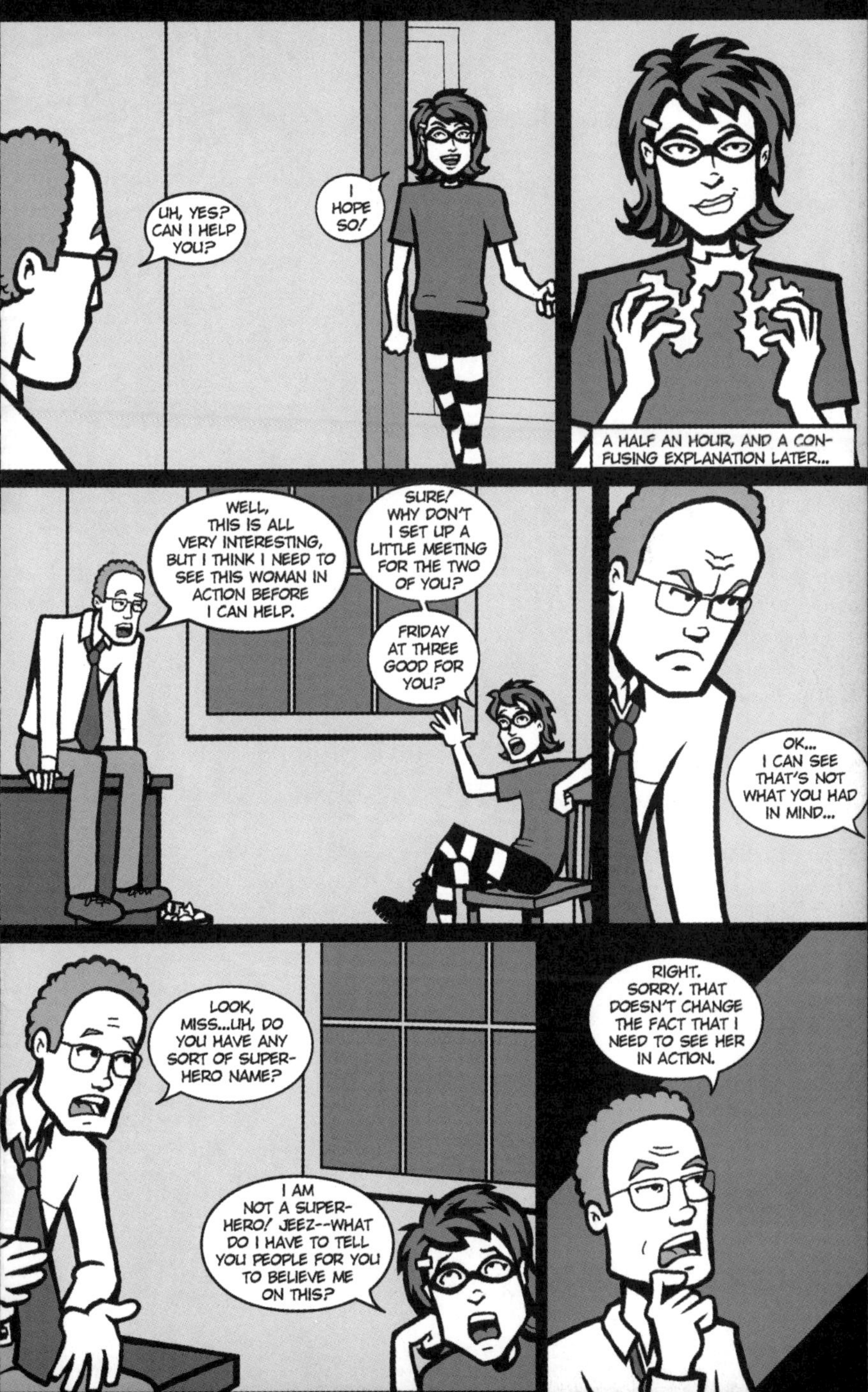
UH, YES? CAN I HELP YOU?
I HOPE SO!
A HALF AN HOUR, AND A CONFUSING EXPLANATION LATER...
WELL, THIS IS ALL VERY INTERESTING, BUT I THINK I NEED TO SEE THIS WOMAN IN ACTION BEFORE I CAN HELP.
SURE! WHY DON'T I SET UP A LITTLE MEETING FOR THE TWO OF YOU?
FRIDAY AT THREE GOOD FOR YOU?
OK... I CAN SEE THAT'S NOT WHAT YOU HAD IN MIND...
LOOK, MISS...UH, DO YOU HAVE ANY SORT OF SUPER-HERO NAME?
I AM NOT A SUPER-HERO! JEEZ--WHAT DO I HAVE TO TELL YOU PEOPLE FOR YOU TO BELIEVE ME ON THIS?
RIGHT. SORRY. THAT DOESN'T CHANGE THE FACT THAT I NEED TO SEE HER IN ACTION.

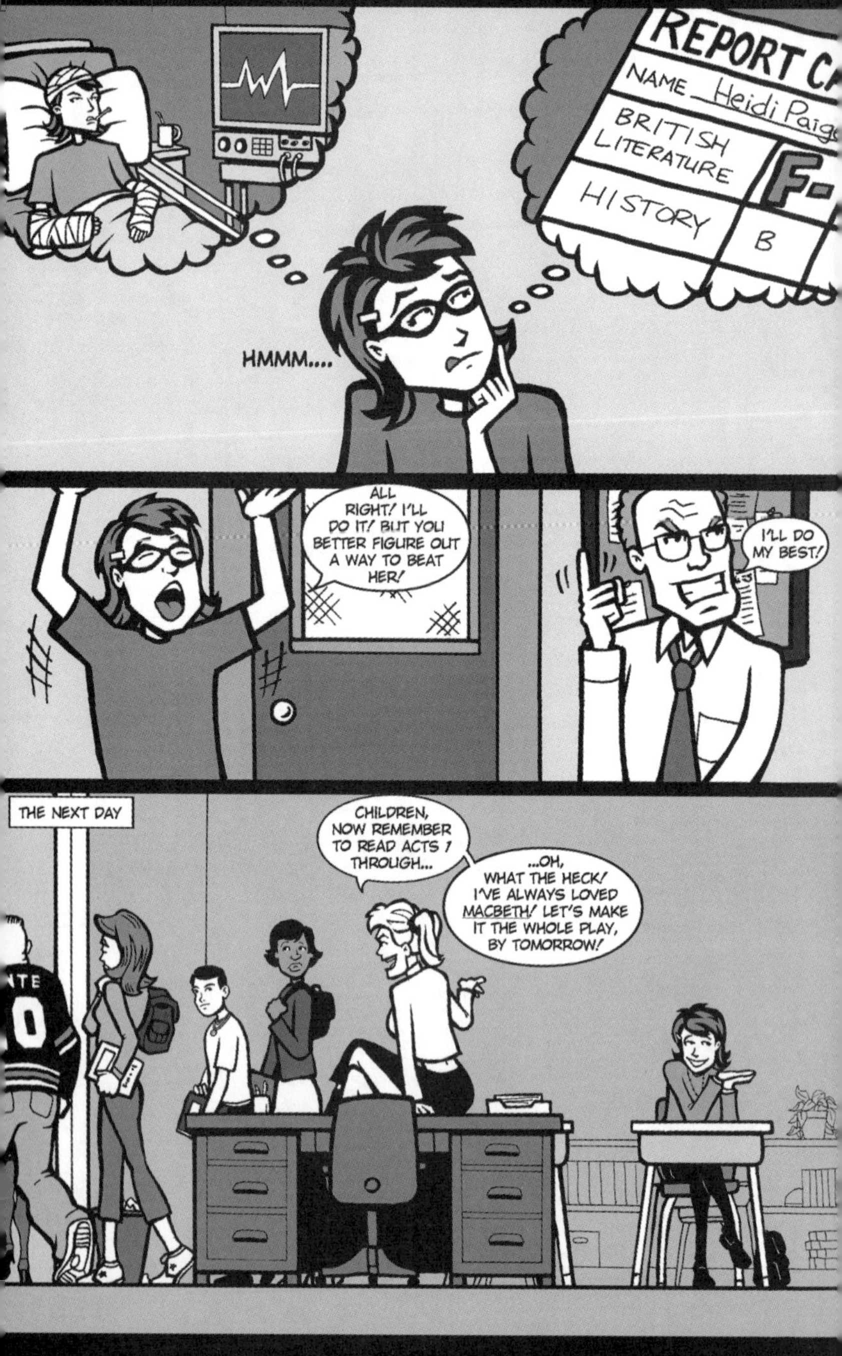

REPORT CA
NAME Heidi Paige
BRITISH LITERATURE
F-
HISTORY
B
HMMM....
ALL RIGHT! I'LL DO IT! BUT YOU BETTER FIGURE OUT A WAY TO BEAT HER!
I'LL DO MY BEST!
THE NEXT DAY
CHILDREN, NOW REMEMBER TO READ ACTS 1 THROUGH...
...OH, WHAT THE HECK! I'VE ALWAYS LOVED MACBETH! LET'S MAKE IT THE WHOLE PLAY, BY TOMORROW!

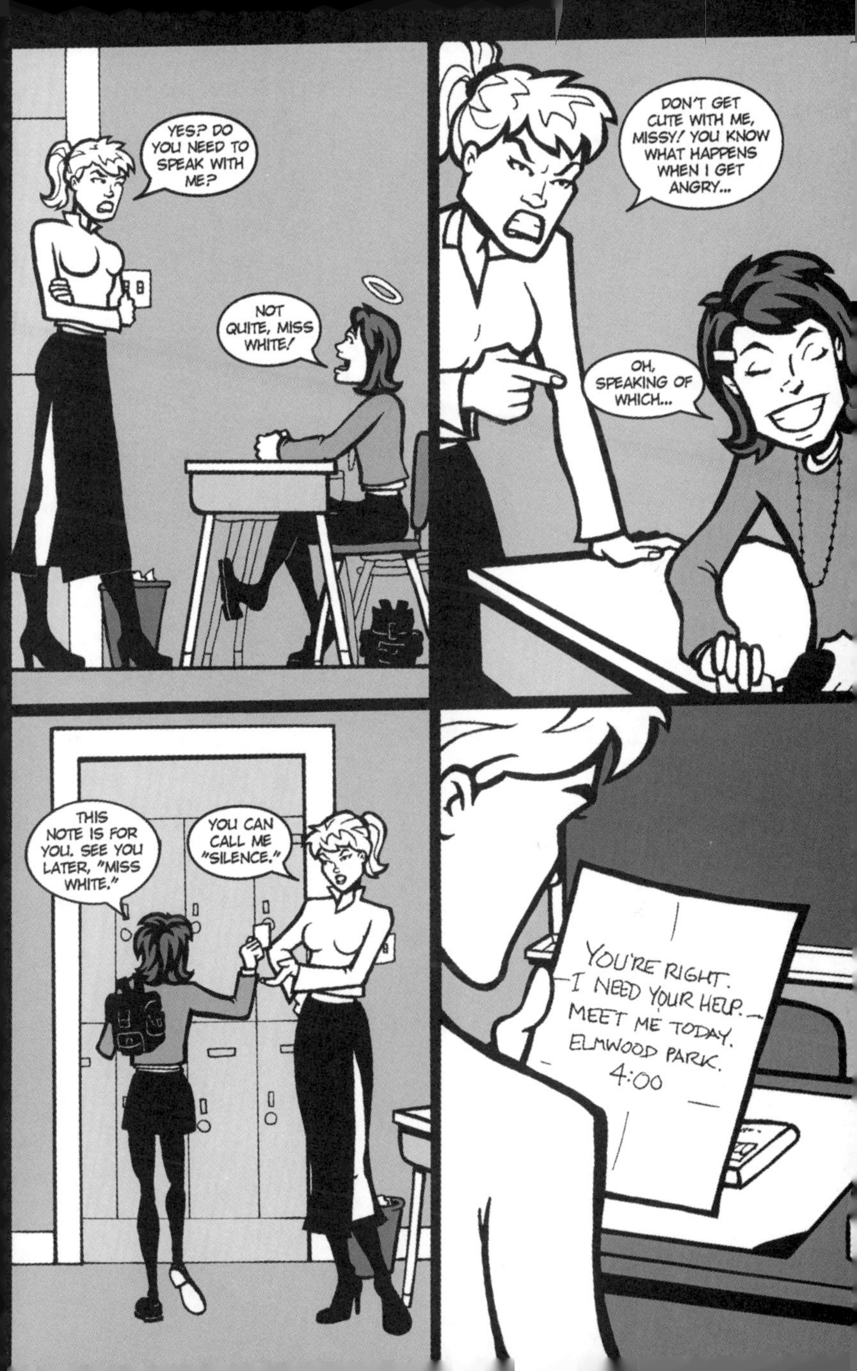
YES? DO YOU NEED TO SPEAK WITH ME?
NOT QUITE, MISS WHITE!
DON'T GET CUTE WITH ME, MISSY! YOU KNOW WHAT HAPPENS WHEN I GET ANGRY...
OH, SPEAKING OF WHICH...
THIS NOTE IS FOR YOU. SEE YOU LATER, "MISS WHITE."
YOU CAN CALL ME "SILENCE."
YOU'RE RIGHT. I NEED YOUR HELP. MEET ME TODAY. ELMWOOD PARK. 4:00

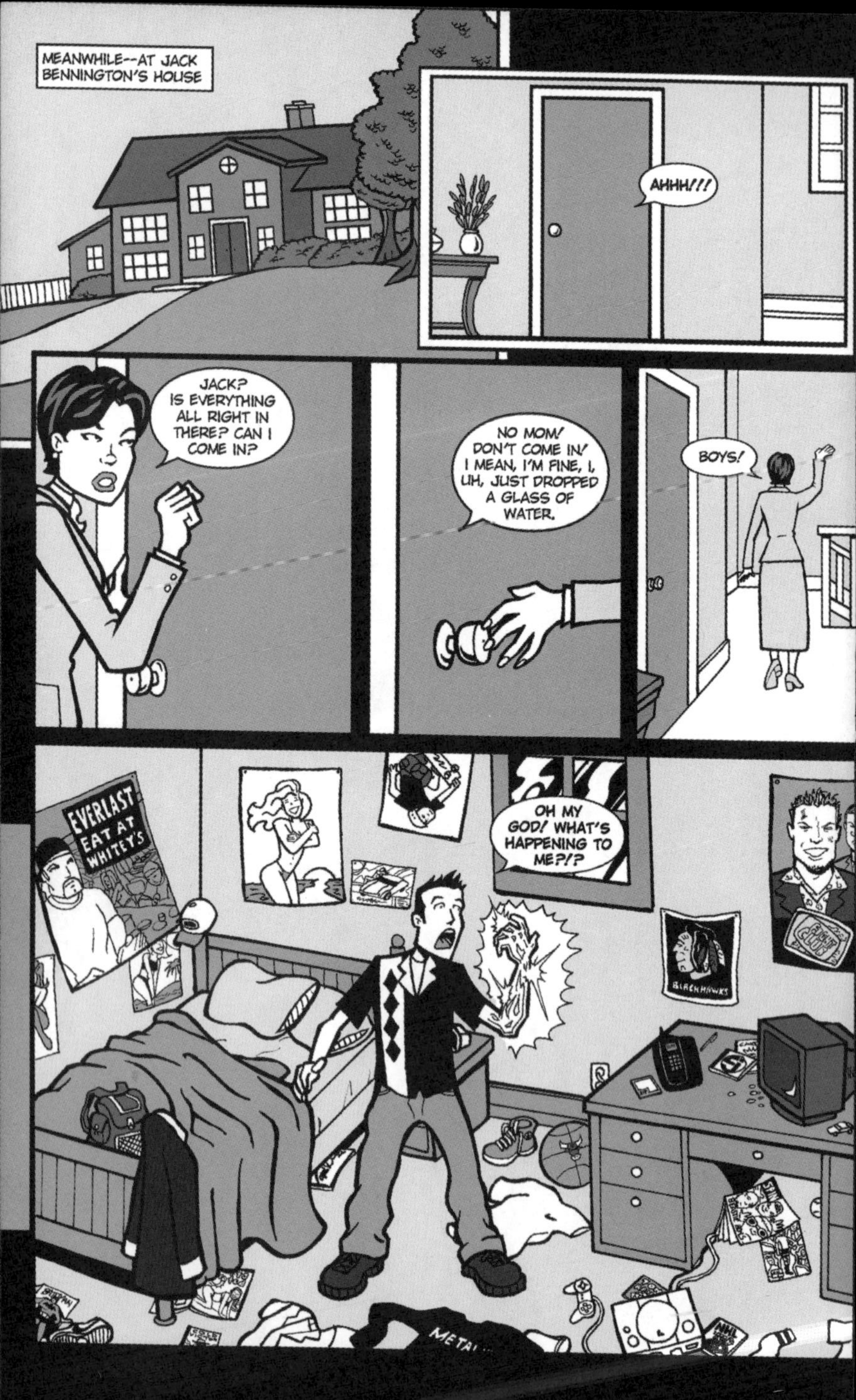
MEANWHILE--AT JACK BENNINGTON'S HOUSE
AHHH!!!
JACK? IS EVERYTHING ALL RIGHT IN THERE? CAN I COME IN?
NO MOM! DON'T COME IN! I MEAN, I'M FINE, I, UH, JUST DROPPED A GLASS OF WATER.
BOYS!
EVERLAST EAT AT WHITEY'S
OH MY GOD! WHAT'S HAPPENING TO ME?!?
BLACKHAWKS
NHL

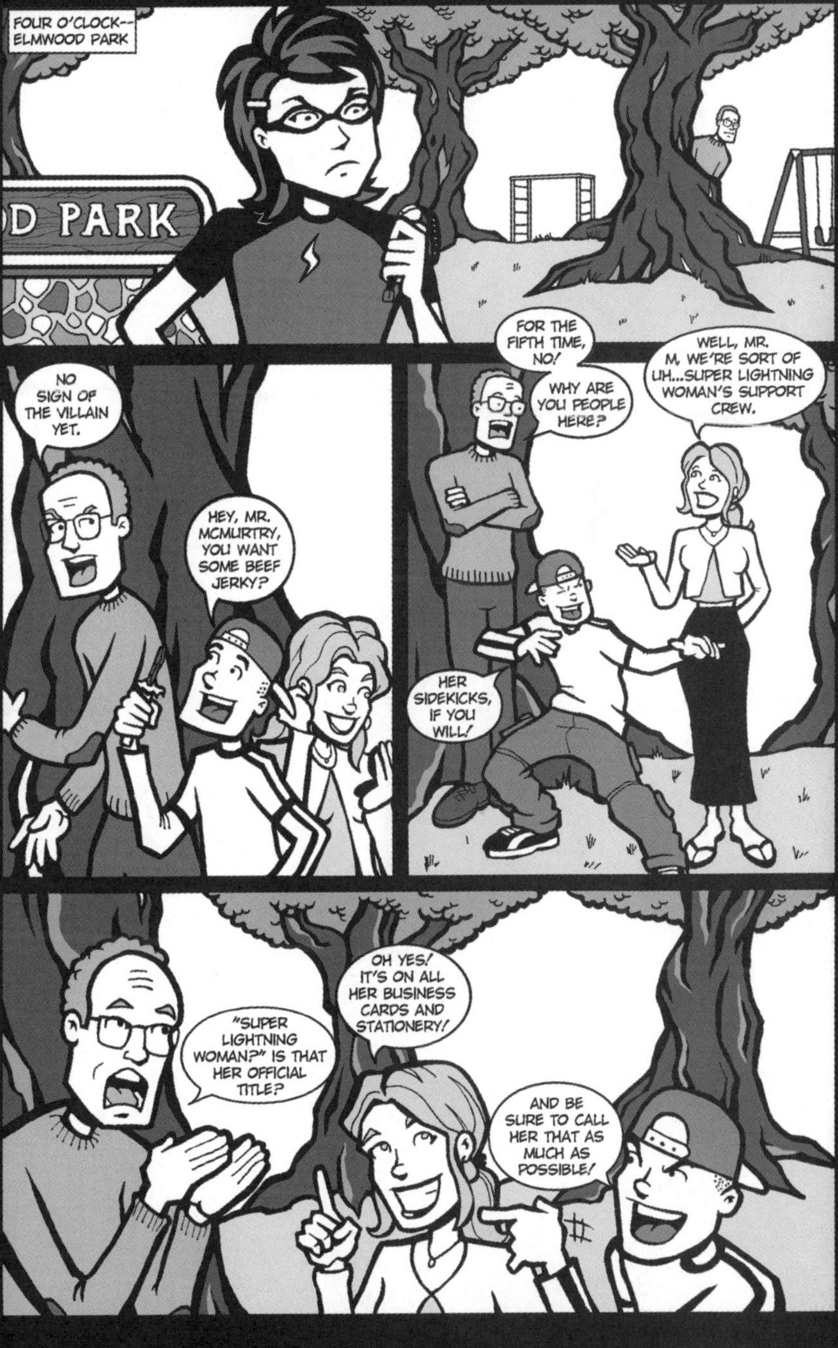
FOUR O'CLOCK--
ELMWOOD PARK
D PARK
NO SIGN OF THE VILLAIN YET.
HEY, MR. MCMURTRY, YOU WANT SOME BEEF JERKY?
FOR THE FIFTH TIME, NO!
WHY ARE YOU PEOPLE HERE?
WELL, MR. M, WE'RE SORT OF UH...SUPER LIGHTNING WOMAN'S SUPPORT CREW.
HER SIDEKICKS, IF YOU WILL!
"SUPER LIGHTNING WOMAN?" IS THAT HER OFFICIAL TITLE?
OH YES! IT'S ON ALL HER BUSINESS CARDS AND STATIONERY!
AND BE SURE TO CALL HER THAT AS MUCH AS POSSIBLE!

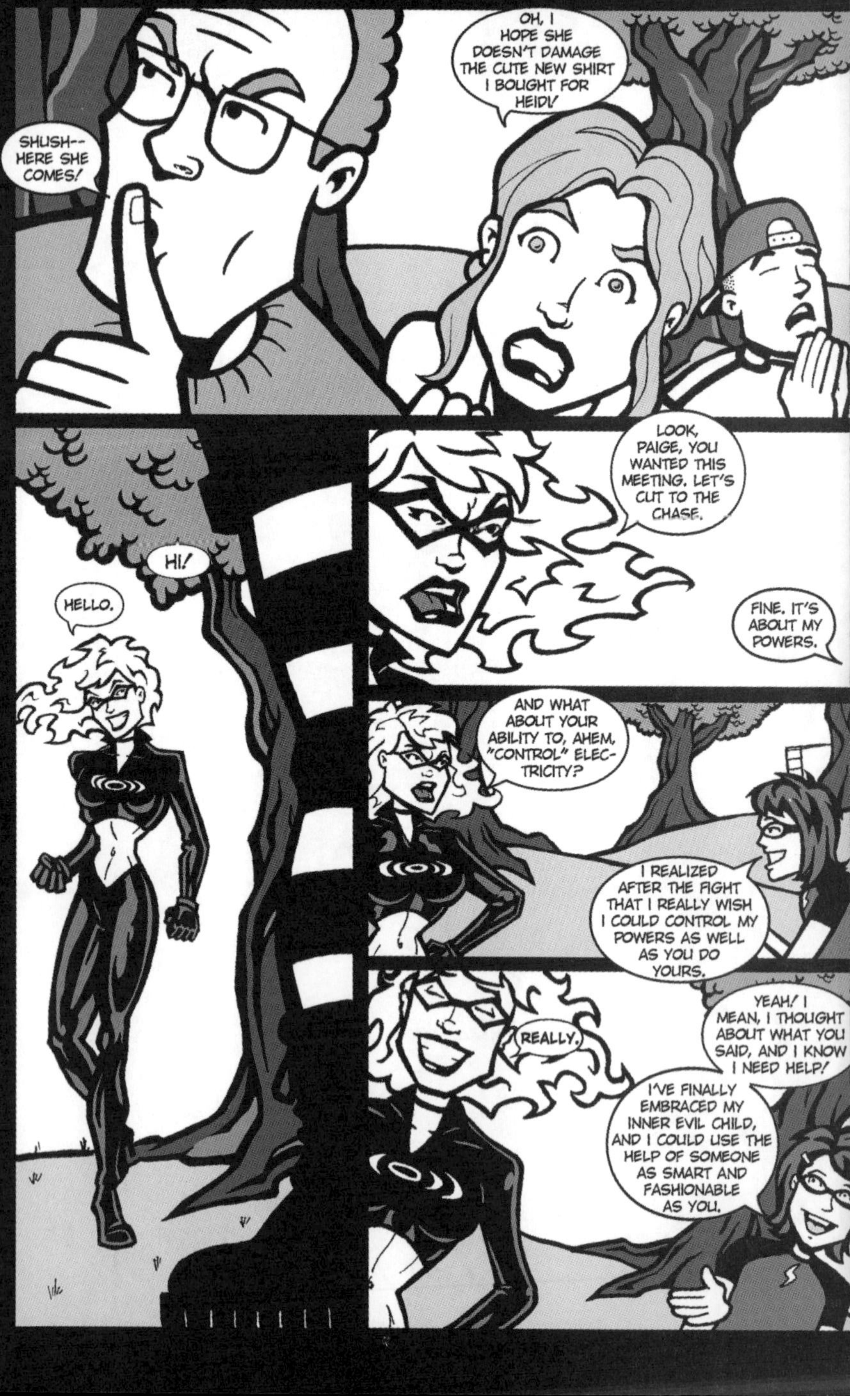
SHUSH--
HERE SHE
COMES!
OH, I
HOPE SHE
DOESN'T DAMAGE
THE CUTE NEW SHIRT
I BOUGHT FOR
HEIDI!
HELLO.
HI!
LOOK,
PAIGE, YOU
WANTED THIS
MEETING. LET'S
CUT TO THE
CHASE.
FINE. IT'S
ABOUT MY
POWERS.
AND WHAT
ABOUT YOUR
ABILITY TO, AHEM,
"CONTROL" ELEC-
TRICITY?
I REALIZED
AFTER THE FIGHT
THAT I REALLY WISH
I COULD CONTROL MY
POWERS AS WELL
AS YOU DO
YOURS.
REALLY.
YEAH! I
MEAN, I THOUGHT
ABOUT WHAT YOU
SAID, AND I KNOW
I NEED HELP!
I'VE FINALLY
EMBRACED MY
INNER EVIL CHILD,
AND I COULD USE THE
HELP OF SOMEONE
AS SMART AND
FASHIONABLE
AS YOU.

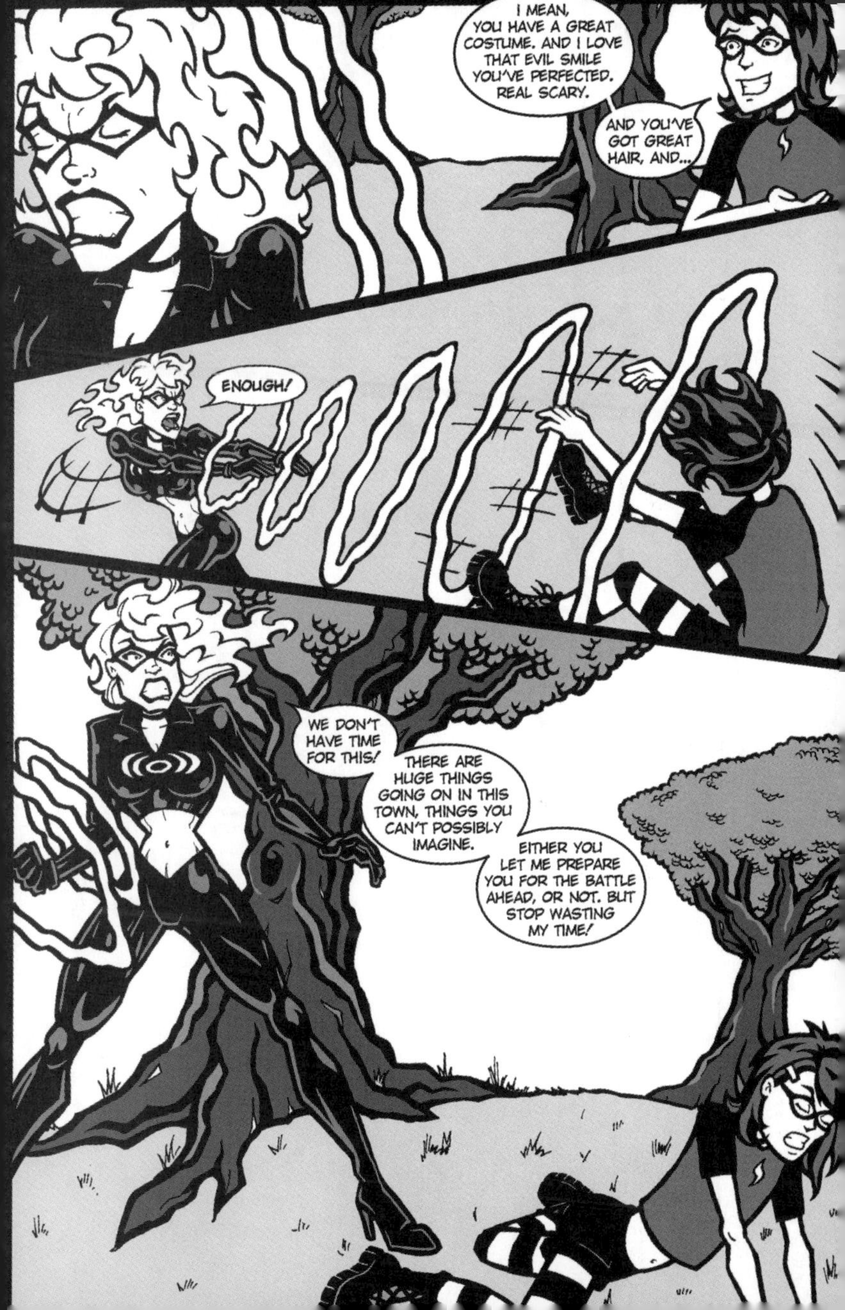
I MEAN, YOU HAVE A GREAT COSTUME. AND I LOVE THAT EVIL SMILE YOU'VE PERFECTED. REAL SCARY.
AND YOU'VE GOT GREAT HAIR, AND...
ENOUGH!
WE DON'T HAVE TIME FOR THIS!
THERE ARE HUGE THINGS GOING ON IN THIS TOWN, THINGS YOU CAN'T POSSIBLY IMAGINE.
EITHER YOU LET ME PREPARE YOU FOR THE BATTLE AHEAD, OR NOT. BUT STOP WASTING MY TIME!

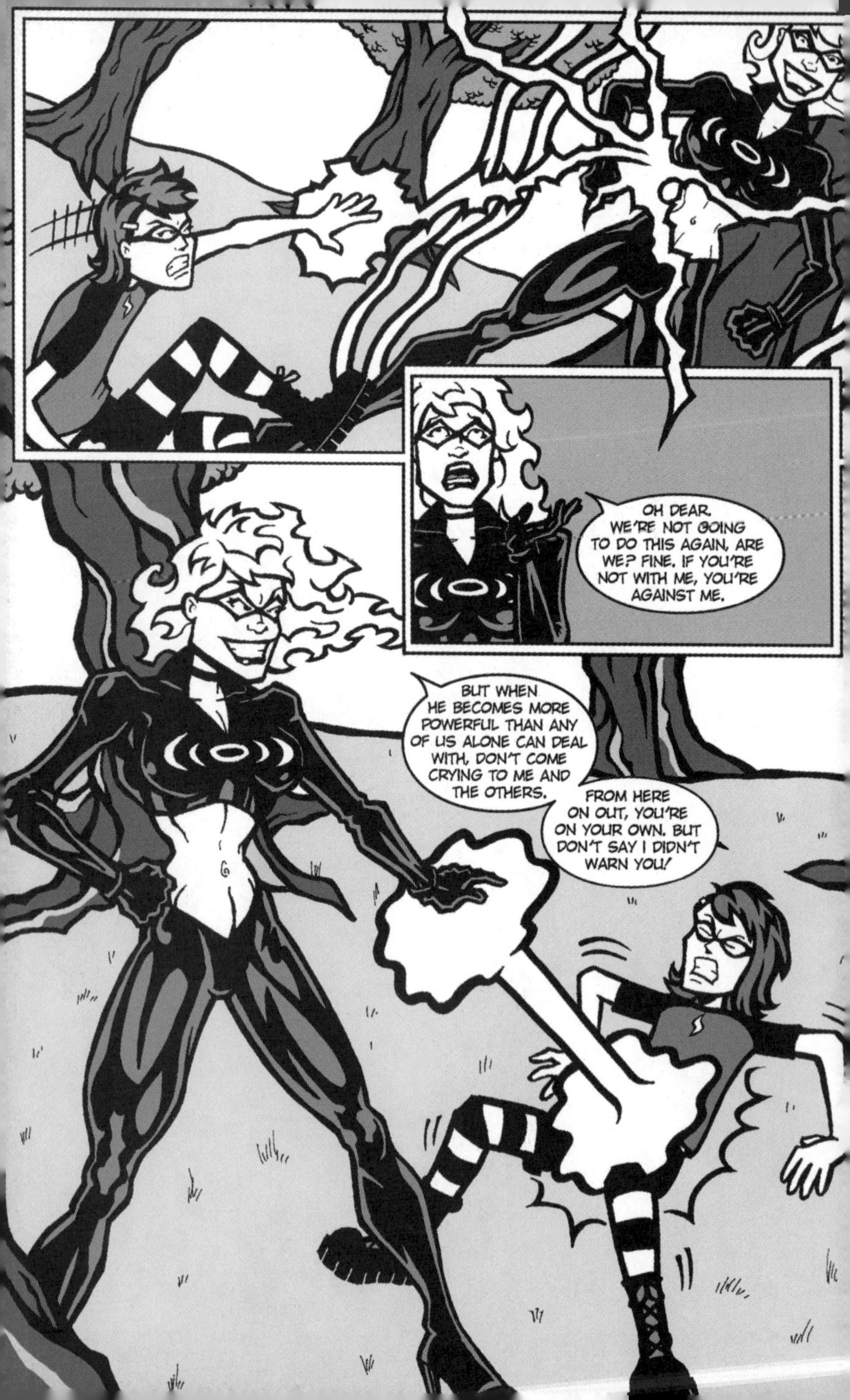
OH DEAR. WE'RE NOT GOING TO DO THIS AGAIN, ARE WE? FINE. IF YOU'RE NOT WITH ME, YOU'RE AGAINST ME.
BUT WHEN HE BECOMES MORE POWERFUL THAN ANY OF US ALONE CAN DEAL WITH, DON'T COME CRYING TO ME AND THE OTHERS.
FROM HERE ON OUT, YOU'RE ON YOUR OWN. BUT DON'T SAY I DIDN'T WARN YOU!

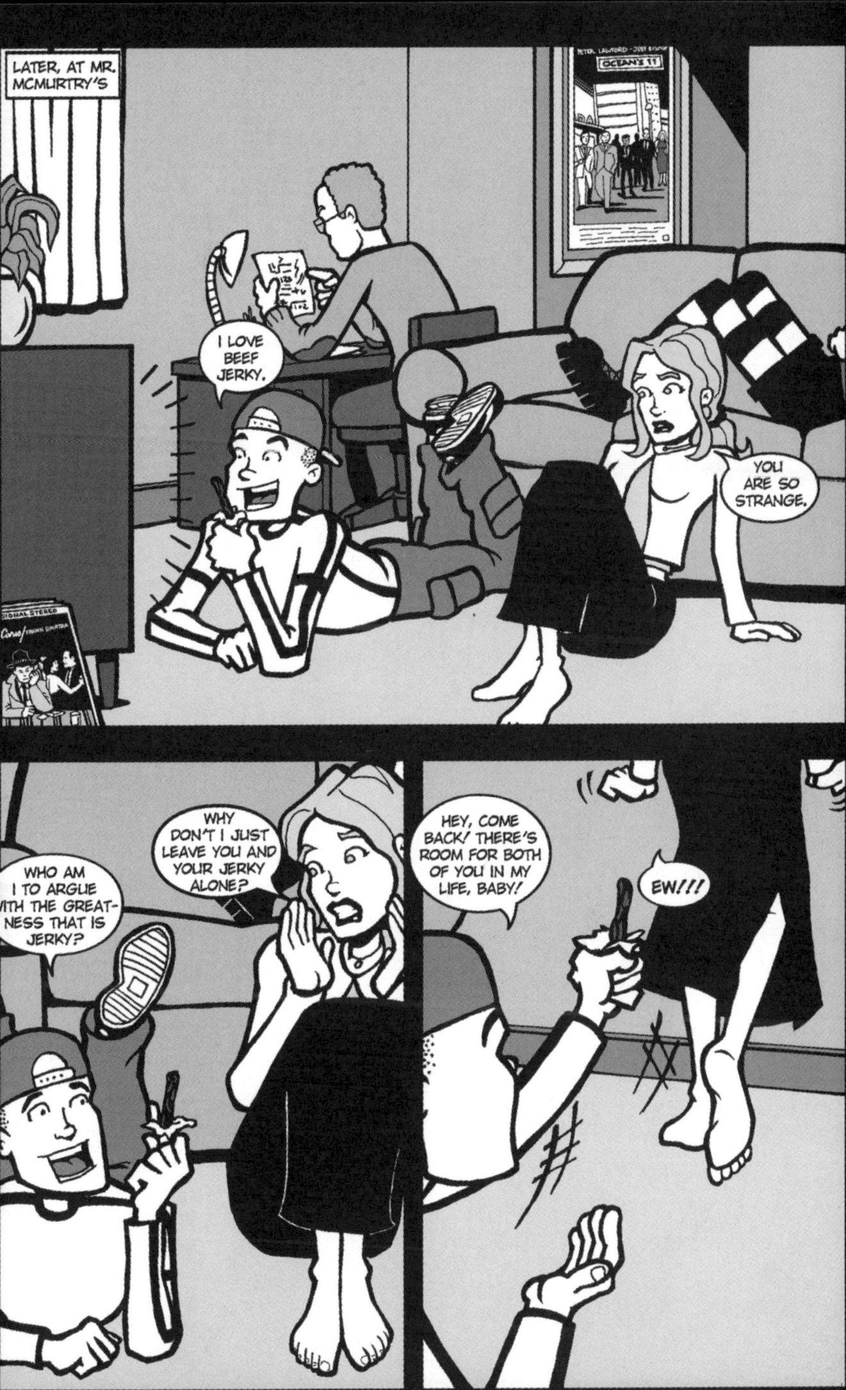
LATER, AT MR. MCMURTRY'S
I LOVE BEEF JERKY.
YOU ARE SO STRANGE.
WHO AM I TO ARGUE WITH THE GREATNESS THAT IS JERKY?
WHY DON'T I JUST LEAVE YOU AND YOUR JERKY ALONE?
HEY, COME BACK! THERE'S ROOM FOR BOTH OF YOU IN MY LIFE, BABY!
EW!!!

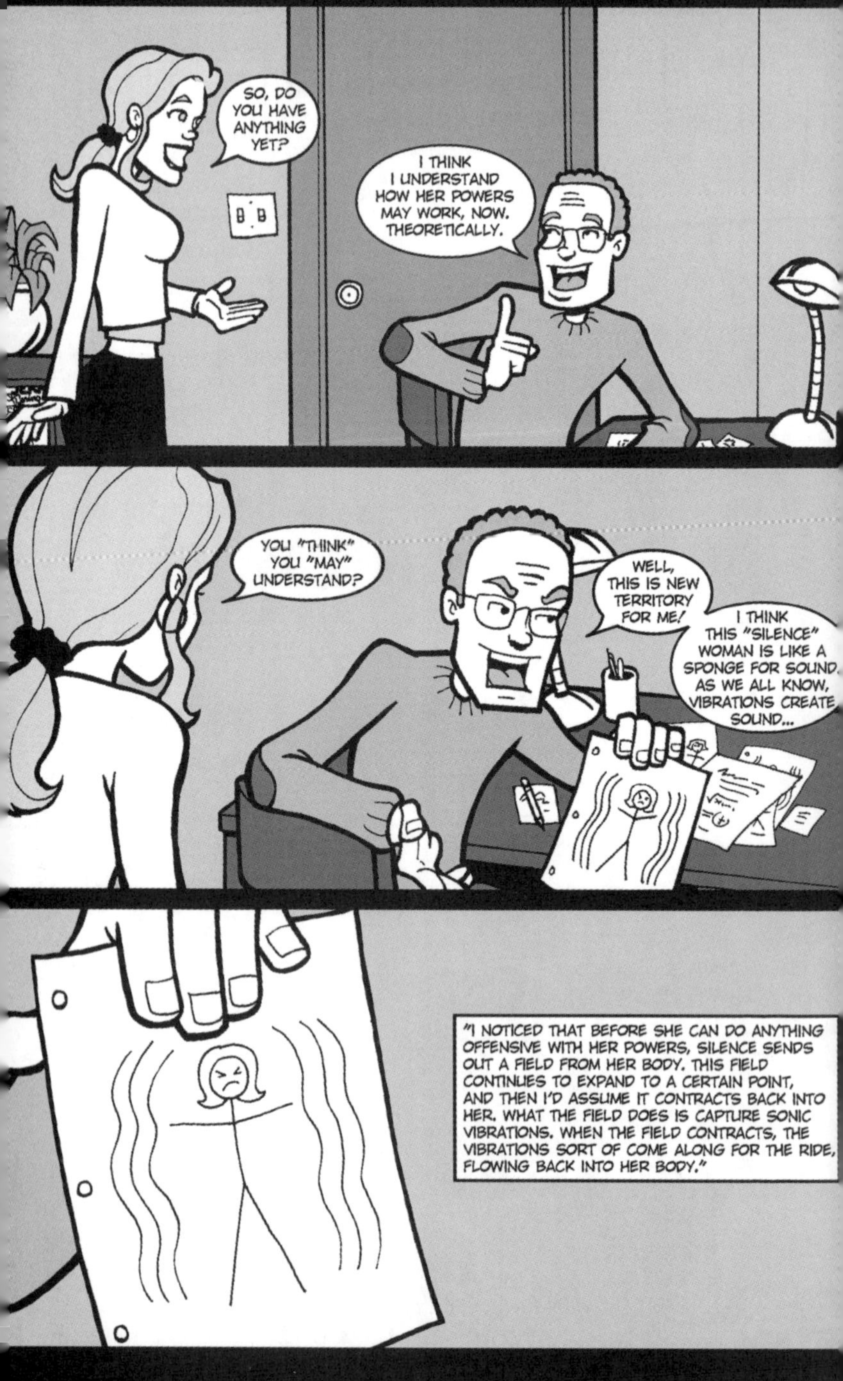
SO, DO YOU HAVE ANYTHING YET?
I THINK I UNDERSTAND HOW HER POWERS MAY WORK, NOW. THEORETICALLY.
YOU "THINK" YOU "MAY" UNDERSTAND?
WELL, THIS IS NEW TERRITORY FOR ME!
I THINK THIS "SILENCE" WOMAN IS LIKE A SPONGE FOR SOUND. AS WE ALL KNOW, VIBRATIONS CREATE SOUND...
"I NOTICED THAT BEFORE SHE CAN DO ANYTHING OFFENSIVE WITH HER POWERS, SILENCE SENDS OUT A FIELD FROM HER BODY. THIS FIELD CONTINUES TO EXPAND TO A CERTAIN POINT, AND THEN I'D ASSUME IT CONTRACTS BACK INTO HER. WHAT THE FIELD DOES IS CAPTURE SONIC VIBRATIONS. WHEN THE FIELD CONTRACTS, THE VIBRATIONS SORT OF COME ALONG FOR THE RIDE, FLOWING BACK INTO HER BODY."

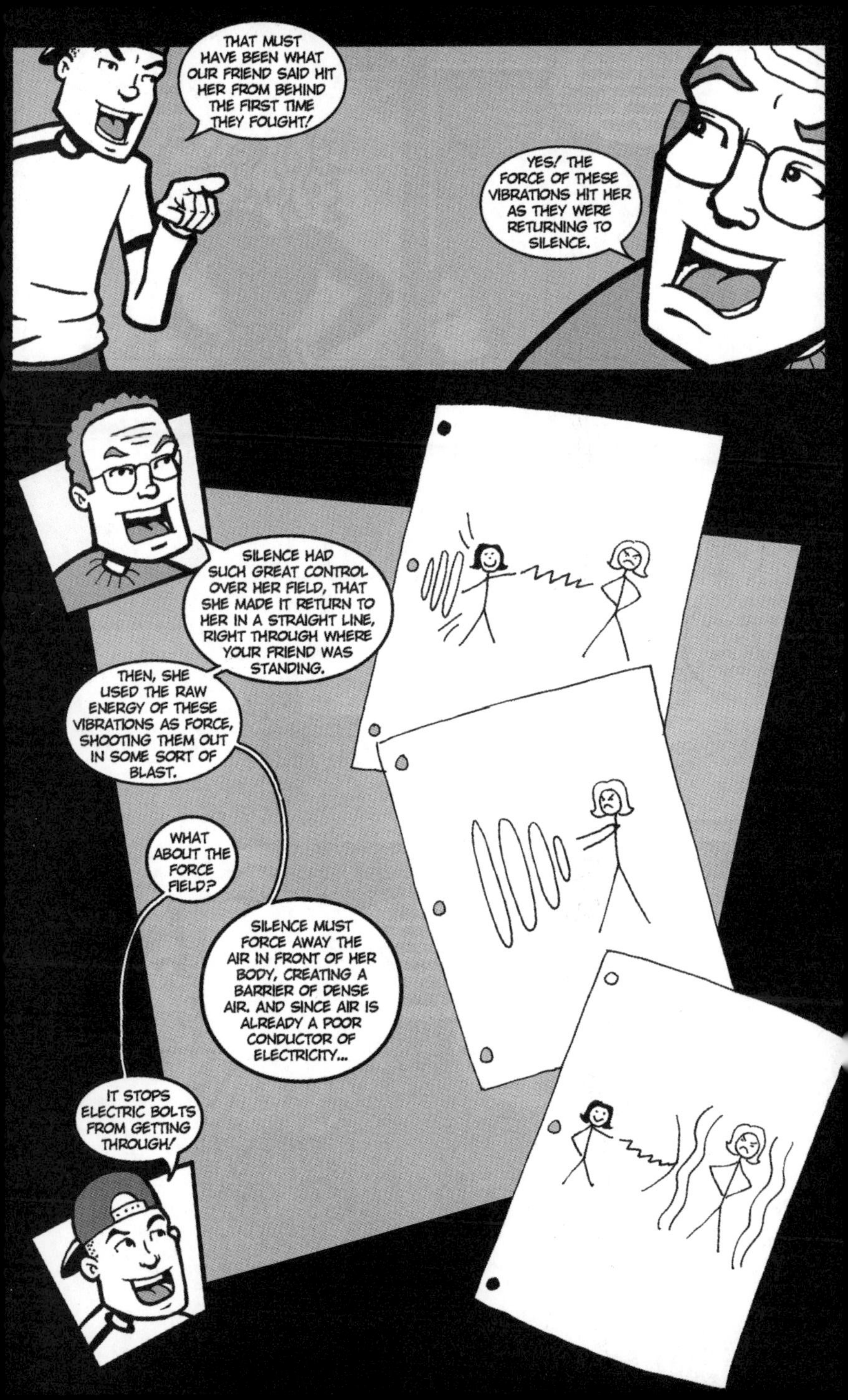
THAT MUST HAVE BEEN WHAT OUR FRIEND SAID HIT HER FROM BEHIND THE FIRST TIME THEY FOUGHT!
YES! THE FORCE OF THESE VIBRATIONS HIT HER AS THEY WERE RETURNING TO SILENCE.
SILENCE HAD SUCH GREAT CONTROL OVER HER FIELD, THAT SHE MADE IT RETURN TO HER IN A STRAIGHT LINE, RIGHT THROUGH WHERE YOUR FRIEND WAS STANDING.
THEN, SHE USED THE RAW ENERGY OF THESE VIBRATIONS AS FORCE, SHOOTING THEM OUT IN SOME SORT OF BLAST.
WHAT ABOUT THE FORCE FIELD?
SILENCE MUST FORCE AWAY THE AIR IN FRONT OF HER BODY, CREATING A BARRIER OF DENSE AIR. AND SINCE AIR IS ALREADY A POOR CONDUCTOR OF ELECTRICITY...
IT STOPS ELECTRIC BOLTS FROM GETTING THROUGH!

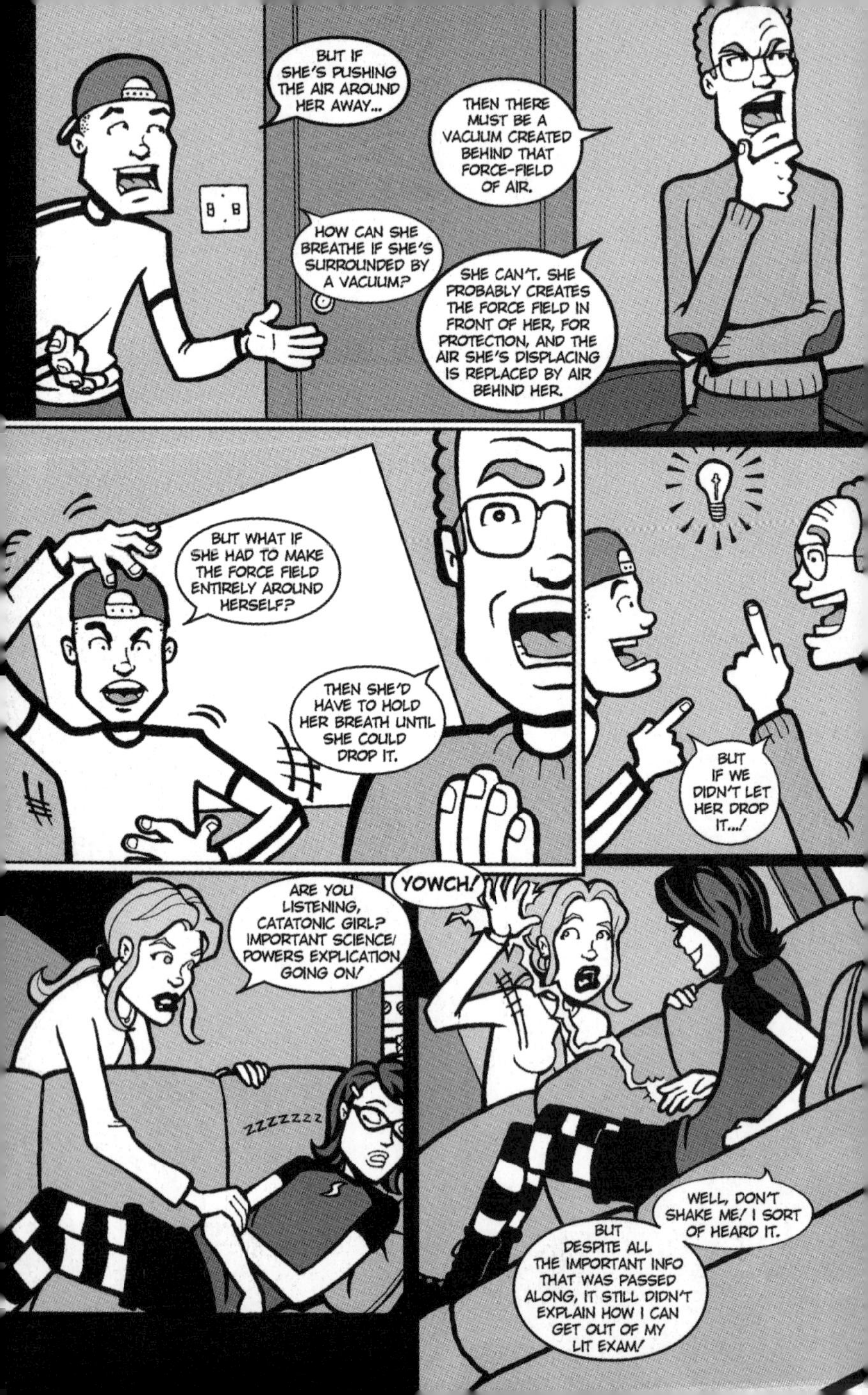
BUT IF SHE'S PUSHING THE AIR AROUND HER AWAY...
THEN THERE MUST BE A VACUUM CREATED BEHIND THAT FORCE-FIELD OF AIR.
HOW CAN SHE BREATHE IF SHE'S SURROUNDED BY A VACUUM?
SHE CAN'T. SHE PROBABLY CREATES THE FORCE FIELD IN FRONT OF HER, FOR PROTECTION, AND THE AIR SHE'S DISPLACING IS REPLACED BY AIR BEHIND HER.
BUT WHAT IF SHE HAD TO MAKE THE FORCE FIELD ENTIRELY AROUND HERSELF?
THEN SHE'D HAVE TO HOLD HER BREATH UNTIL SHE COULD DROP IT.
BUT IF WE DIDN'T LET HER DROP IT...!
ARE YOU LISTENING, CATATONIC GIRL? IMPORTANT SCIENCE/POWERS EXPLICATION GOING ON!
ZZZZZZZ
YOWCH!
WELL, DON'T SHAKE ME! I SORT OF HEARD IT.
BUT DESPITE ALL THE IMPORTANT INFO THAT WAS PASSED ALONG, IT STILL DIDN'T EXPLAIN HOW I CAN GET OUT OF MY LIT EXAM!

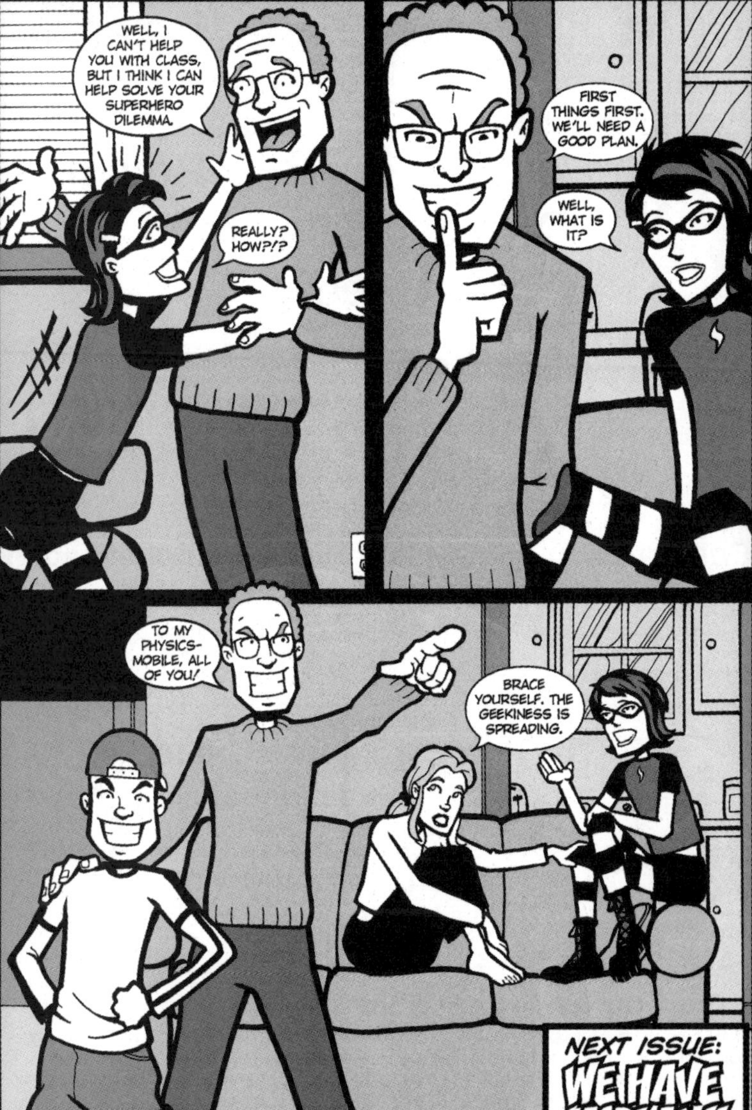
WELL, I CAN'T HELP YOU WITH CLASS, BUT I THINK I CAN HELP SOLVE YOUR SUPERHERO DILEMMA.
REALLY? HOW?!?
FIRST THINGS FIRST. WE'LL NEED A GOOD PLAN.
WELL, WHAT IS IT?
TO MY PHYSICS-MOBILE, ALL OF YOU!
BRACE YOURSELF. THE GEEKINESS IS SPREADING.
NEXT ISSUE:
WE HAVE A PLAN!!

Vol. 68 No. 19

𝕳arrington 𝕻ost-𝕲azette

www.ampcomics.com   "Serving the Town of Harrington since 1946"

Thunderstorms, High 68 Details on Page 2   Final Edition

Ice Skating Sub-Regional Quarterfinals are in 2 short weeks!

Recent Harrington arrival and Harrington High junior Ilsa Daniel, the 16 year old phenom who has drawn some national attention, is one of a few who will be looking to qualify for the regional finals with a victory. The victor will then advance to the Sub-Regional Semis in Chicago, then the Sub-Regional Finals in Indianapolis, then will be entered into a group who may have a chance to possibly qualify for the Olympic qualifier qualifier! So let's go and cheer on these bright stars of tomorrow!

Construction on new laboratory complex begins

Mr. John Reeves, head of the Harrington Mental Health Institute, is pleased to announce that work has begun on a new, 5 million dollar laboratory complex at the Institute! Though exact details on the new wing are sketchy, and the reasoning behind building a laboratory onto a Mental Health Institute seems questionable, we here at Harrington Happenings wish Mr. Reeves all the luck in the construction of his new…laboratory.

File photo

The New Harrington High locker rooms are now finished!

Coach Linda Breitsman, Swimming Coach and P.E. Teacher at H.H., said she's excited by the re-design, and "hopes no wannabe superheroes trash it in some testosterone fueled battle. "Well, Coach, we're sure that won't happen!

Amp Comics looks to the future

Amp Comics announces upcoming plans for series "Shades of Blue." James S. Harris of Amp Comics outlined the company's plans for the next few issues of their comic today. "Issue 5 contains the 3rd and final part of the 'Silence' storyline. Heidi and her arch-nemesis have a knock-down drag out tussle, and the newly re-designed locker rooms at Harrington High will never be the same!"

Last night's Powerball Super-Lotto results
19 11 68 4 23 1

Sports............................3a
Around the World...........2b
Classifieds.....................7j
Today.............................5c
Tomorrrow......................6d

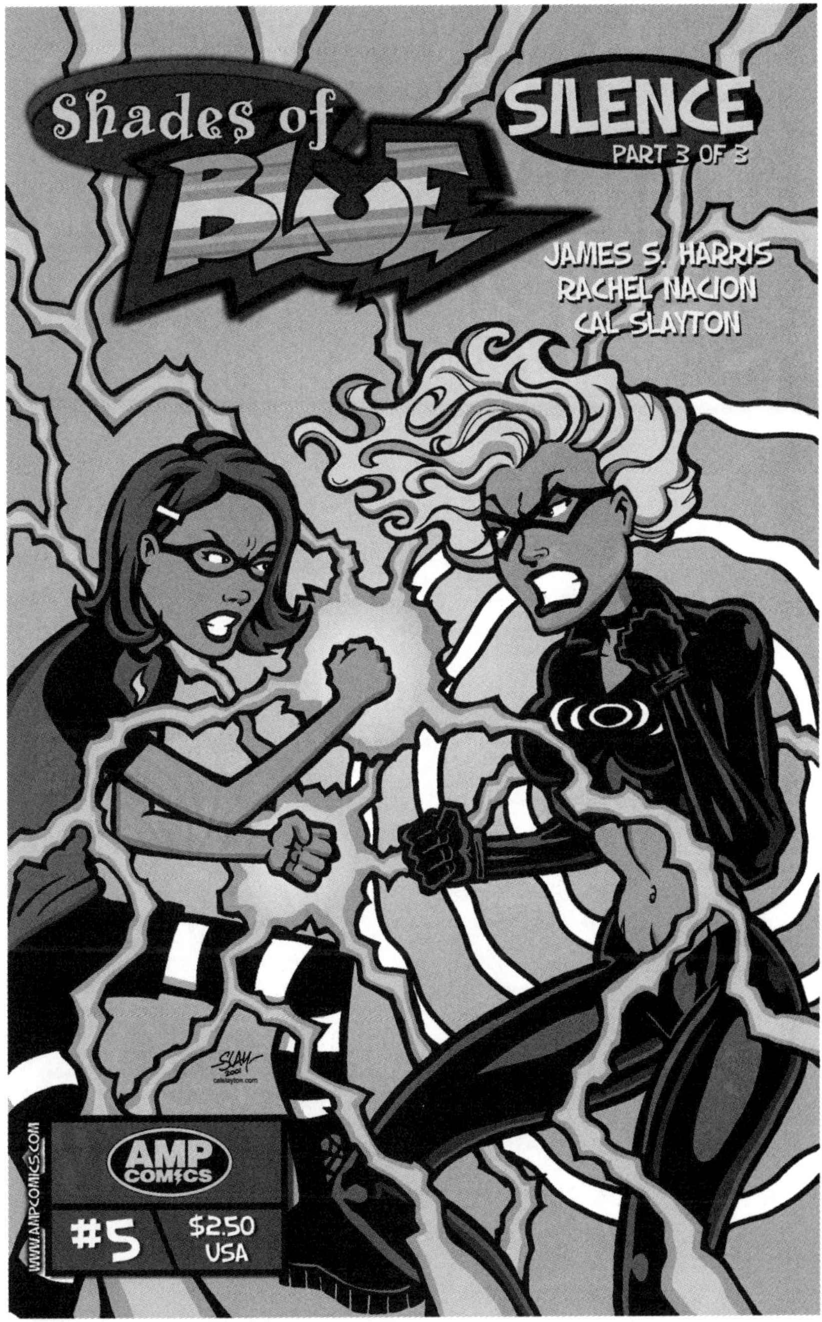
Shades of
BLUE
SILENCE
PART 3 OF 3
JAMES S. HARRIS
RACHEL NACION
CAL SLAYTON
AMP COMICS
#5
$2.50 USA
WWW.AMPCOMICS.COM

And now, to catch you, the reader, up to speed, we're proud to present Miss K.T. O'Hara, best friend of our hero, Heidi Paige.

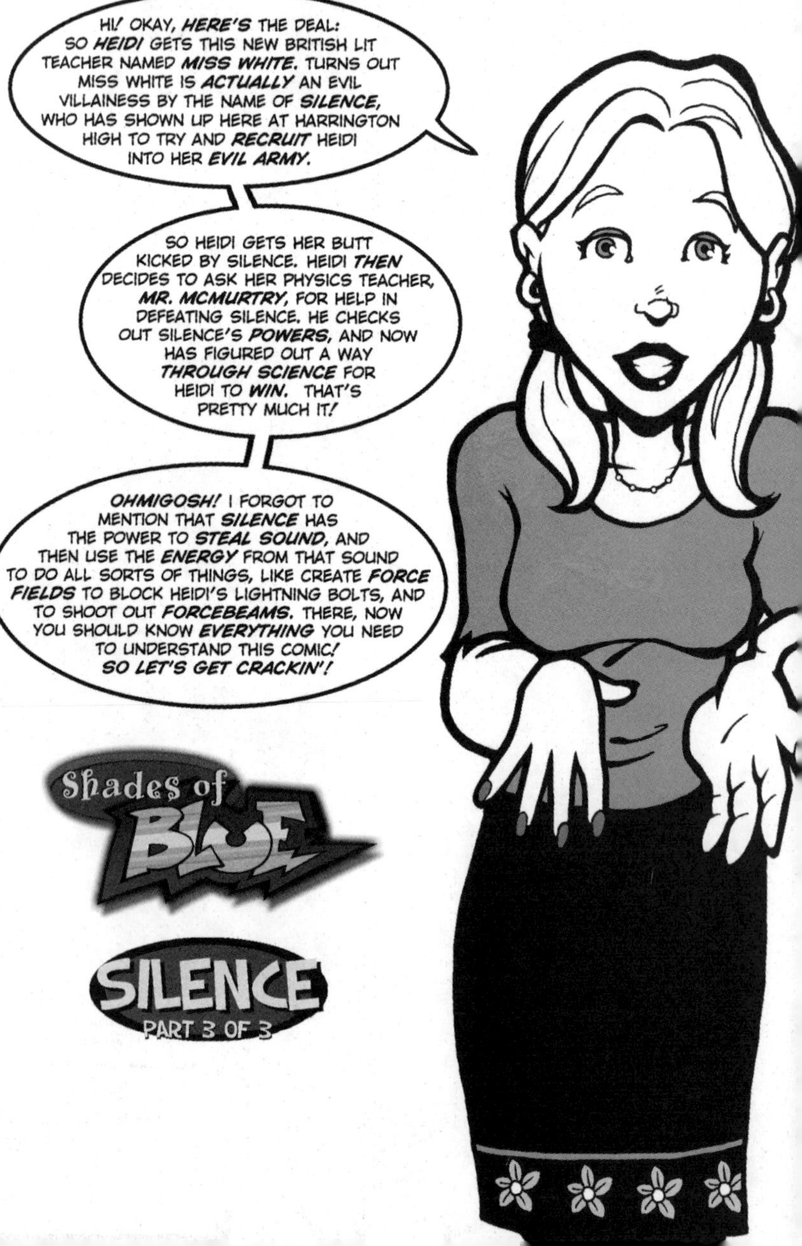
HI! OKAY, HERE'S THE DEAL: SO HEIDI GETS THIS NEW BRITISH LIT TEACHER NAMED MISS WHITE. TURNS OUT MISS WHITE IS ACTUALLY AN EVIL VILLAINESS BY THE NAME OF SILENCE, WHO HAS SHOWN UP HERE AT HARRINGTON HIGH TO TRY AND RECRUIT HEIDI INTO HER EVIL ARMY.
SO HEIDI GETS HER BUTT KICKED BY SILENCE. HEIDI THEN DECIDES TO ASK HER PHYSICS TEACHER, MR. MCMURTRY, FOR HELP IN DEFEATING SILENCE. HE CHECKS OUT SILENCE'S POWERS, AND NOW HAS FIGURED OUT A WAY THROUGH SCIENCE FOR HEIDI TO WIN. THAT'S PRETTY MUCH IT!
OHMIGOSH! I FORGOT TO MENTION THAT SILENCE HAS THE POWER TO STEAL SOUND, AND THEN USE THE ENERGY FROM THAT SOUND TO DO ALL SORTS OF THINGS, LIKE CREATE FORCE FIELDS TO BLOCK HEIDI'S LIGHTNING BOLTS, AND TO SHOOT OUT FORCEBEAMS. THERE, NOW YOU SHOULD KNOW EVERYTHING YOU NEED TO UNDERSTAND THIS COMIC! SO LET'S GET CRACKIN'!
Shades of BLUE
SILENCE
PART 3 OF 3

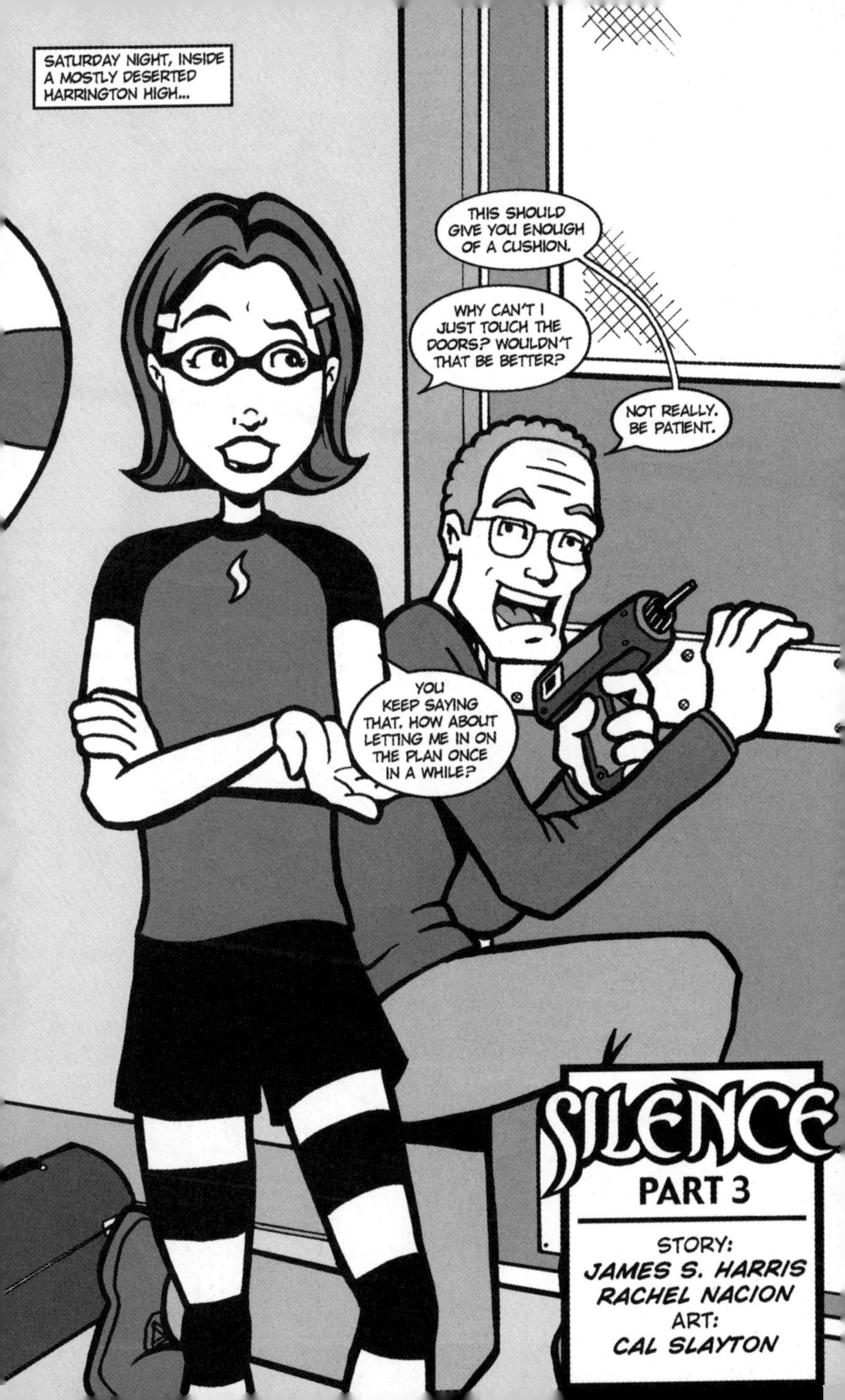
SATURDAY NIGHT, INSIDE A MOSTLY DESERTED HARRINGTON HIGH...
THIS SHOULD GIVE YOU ENOUGH OF A CUSHION.
WHY CAN'T I JUST TOUCH THE DOORS? WOULDN'T THAT BE BETTER?
NOT REALLY. BE PATIENT.
YOU KEEP SAYING THAT. HOW ABOUT LETTING ME IN ON THE PLAN ONCE IN A WHILE?
SILENCE
PART 3
STORY:
JAMES S. HARRIS
RACHEL NACION
ART:
CAL SLAYTON

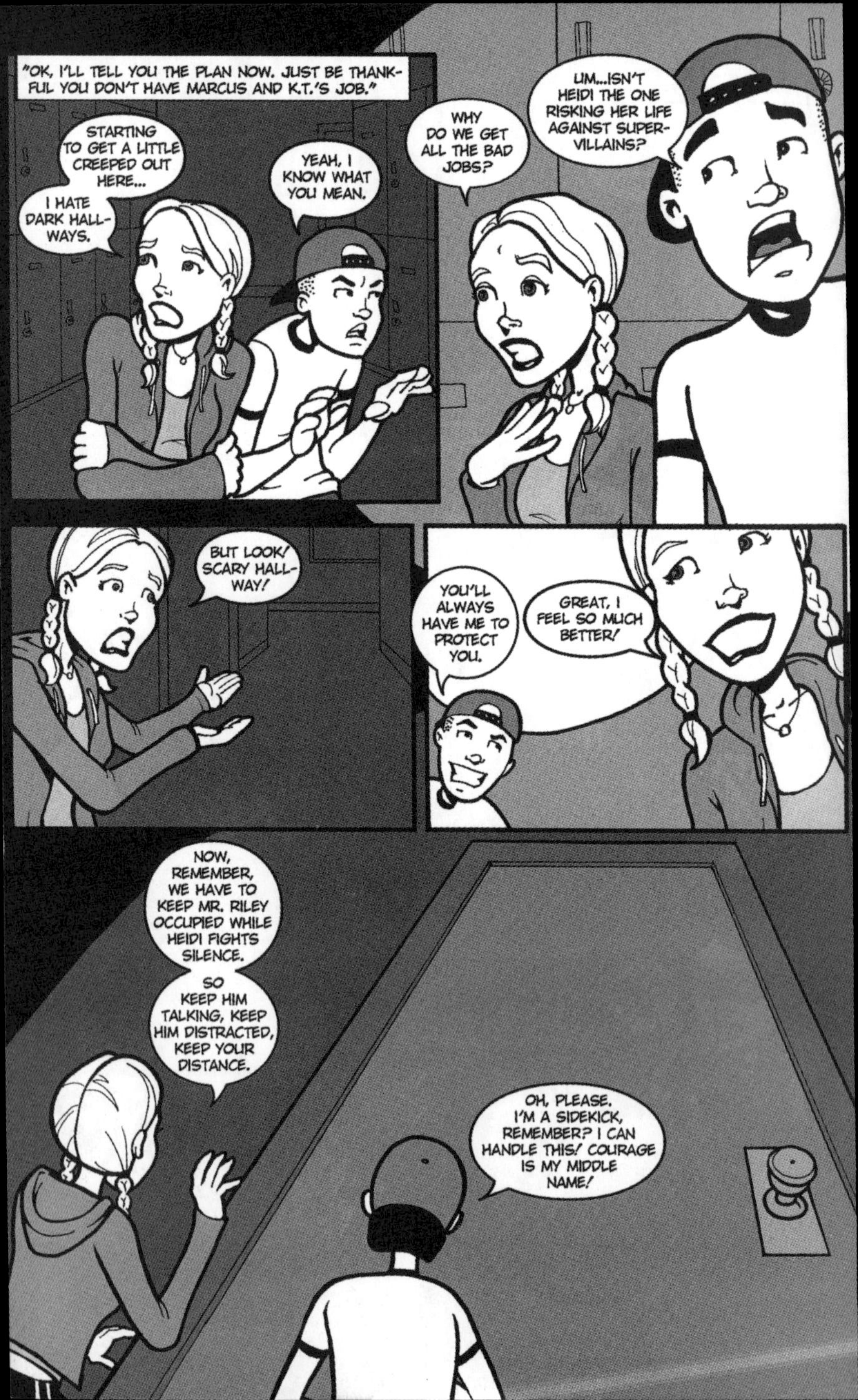
"OK, I'LL TELL YOU THE PLAN NOW. JUST BE THANKFUL YOU DON'T HAVE MARCUS AND K.T.'S JOB."
STARTING TO GET A LITTLE CREEPED OUT HERE...
I HATE DARK HALLWAYS.
YEAH, I KNOW WHAT YOU MEAN.
WHY DO WE GET ALL THE BAD JOBS?
UM...ISN'T HEIDI THE ONE RISKING HER LIFE AGAINST SUPER-VILLAINS?
BUT LOOK! SCARY HALLWAY!
YOU'LL ALWAYS HAVE ME TO PROTECT YOU.
GREAT, I FEEL SO MUCH BETTER!
NOW, REMEMBER, WE HAVE TO KEEP MR. RILEY OCCUPIED WHILE HEIDI FIGHTS SILENCE.
SO KEEP HIM TALKING, KEEP HIM DISTRACTED, KEEP YOUR DISTANCE.
OH, PLEASE. I'M A SIDEKICK, REMEMBER? I CAN HANDLE THIS! COURAGE IS MY MIDDLE NAME!

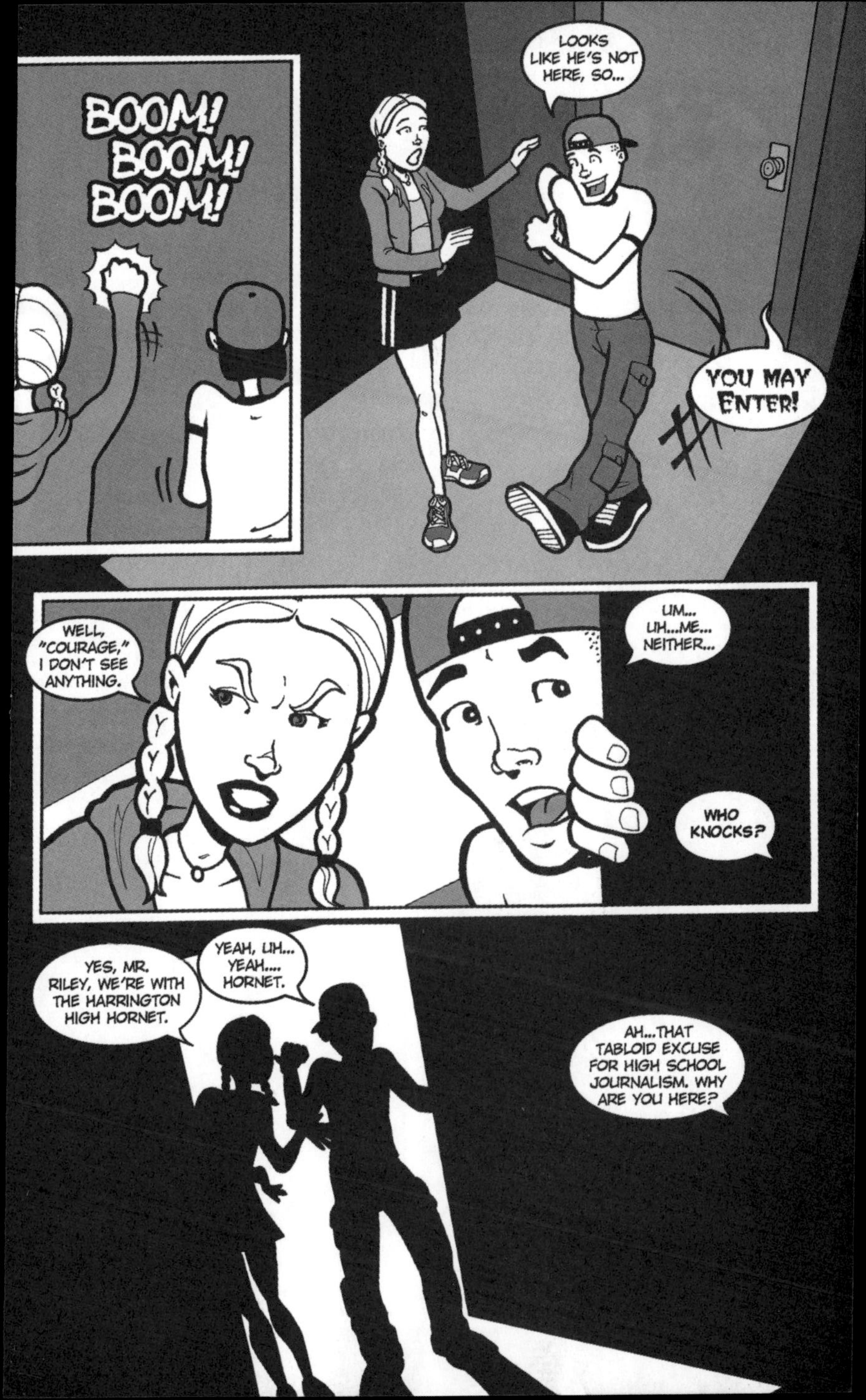
BOOM! BOOM! BOOM!
LOOKS LIKE HE'S NOT HERE, SO...
YOU MAY ENTER!
WELL, "COURAGE," I DON'T SEE ANYTHING.
UM... UH...ME... NEITHER...
WHO KNOCKS?
YES, MR. RILEY, WE'RE WITH THE HARRINGTON HIGH HORNET.
YEAH, UH... YEAH.... HORNET.
AH...THAT TABLOID EXCUSE FOR HIGH SCHOOL JOURNALISM. WHY ARE YOU HERE?

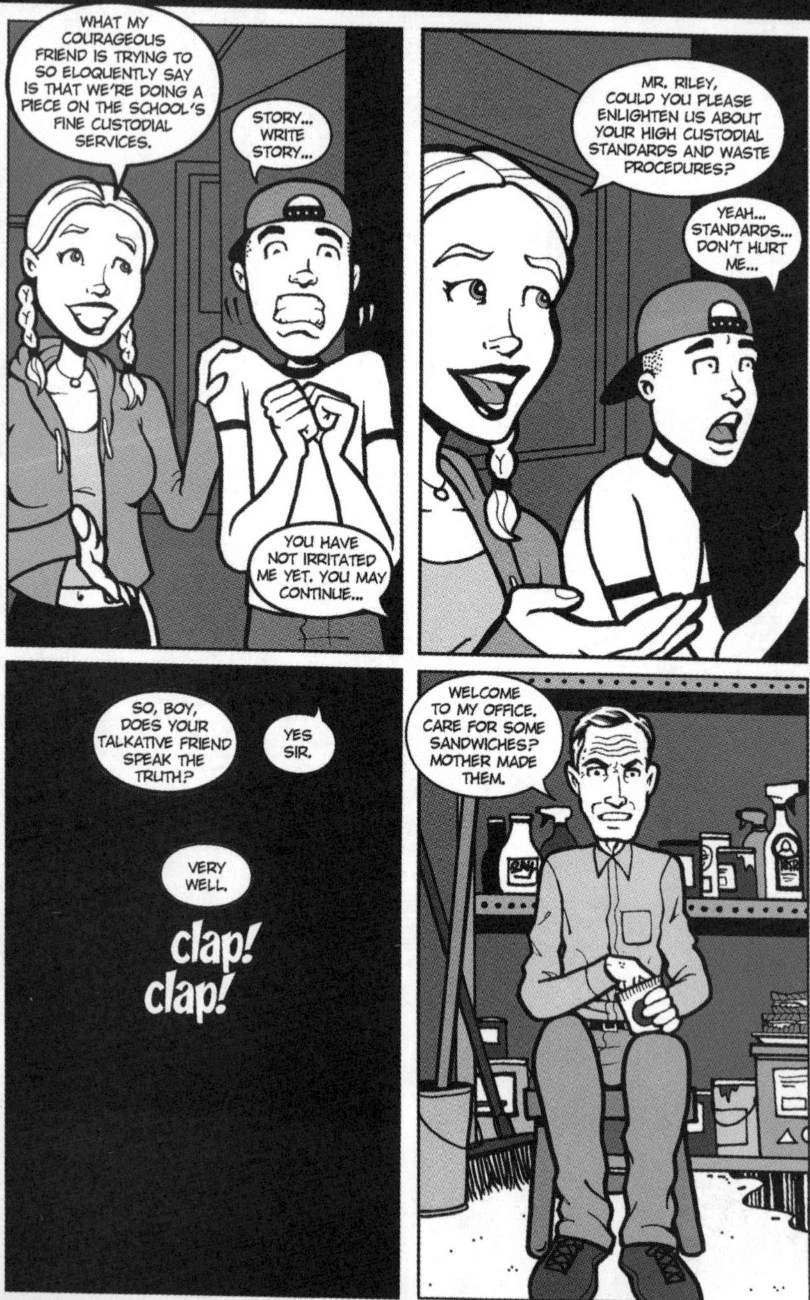
WHAT MY COURAGEOUS FRIEND IS TRYING TO SO ELOQUENTLY SAY IS THAT WE'RE DOING A PIECE ON THE SCHOOL'S FINE CUSTODIAL SERVICES.
STORY... WRITE STORY...
YOU HAVE NOT IRRITATED ME YET. YOU MAY CONTINUE...
MR. RILEY, COULD YOU PLEASE ENLIGHTEN US ABOUT YOUR HIGH CUSTODIAL STANDARDS AND WASTE PROCEDURES?
YEAH... STANDARDS... DON'T HURT ME...
SO, BOY, DOES YOUR TALKATIVE FRIEND SPEAK THE TRUTH?
YES SIR.
VERY WELL.
clap! clap!
WELCOME TO MY OFFICE. CARE FOR SOME SANDWICHES? MOTHER MADE THEM.

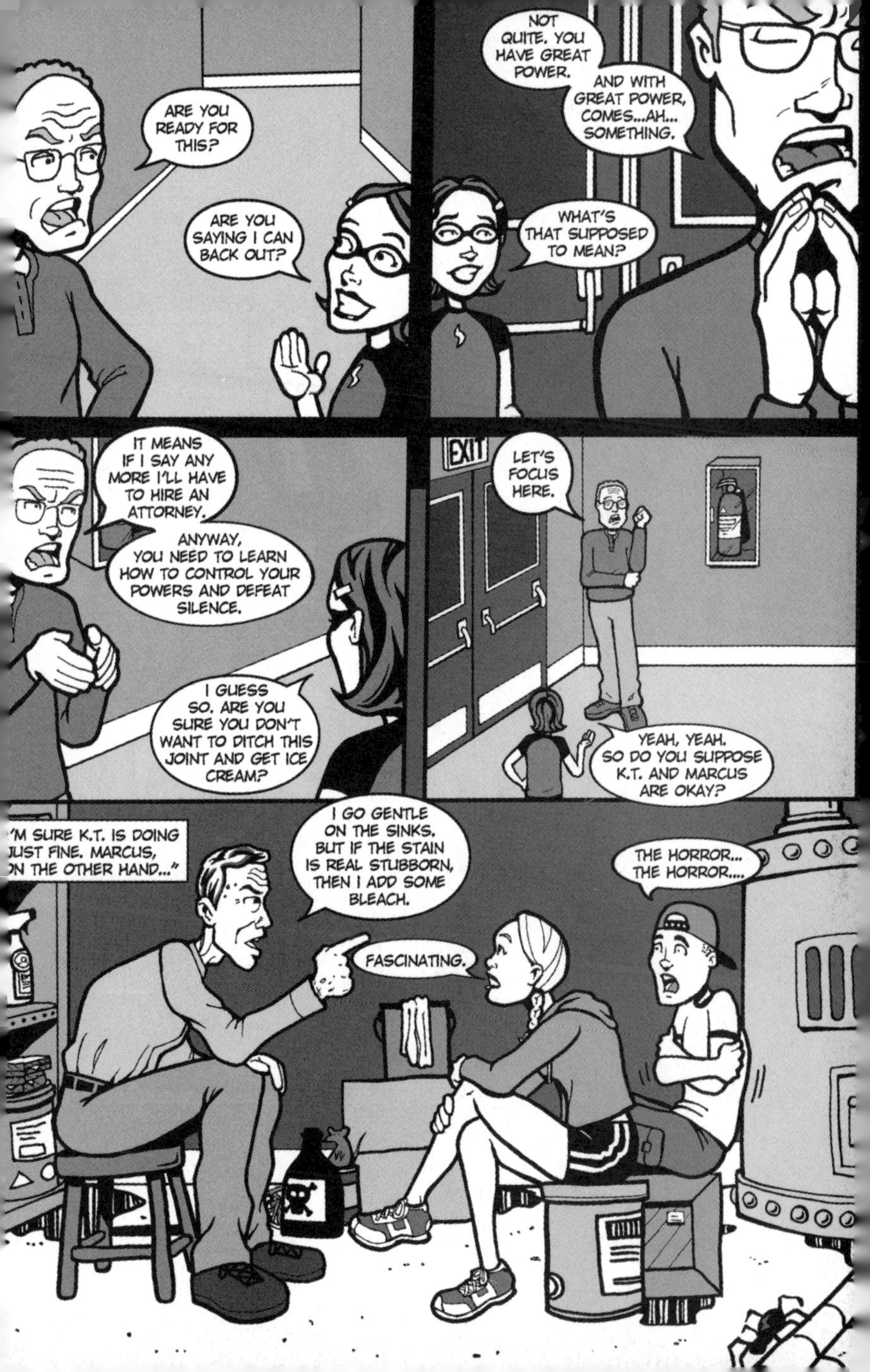
ARE YOU READY FOR THIS?
ARE YOU SAYING I CAN BACK OUT?
NOT QUITE. YOU HAVE GREAT POWER.
AND WITH GREAT POWER, COMES...AH... SOMETHING.
WHAT'S THAT SUPPOSED TO MEAN?
IT MEANS IF I SAY ANY MORE I'LL HAVE TO HIRE AN ATTORNEY.
ANYWAY, YOU NEED TO LEARN HOW TO CONTROL YOUR POWERS AND DEFEAT SILENCE.
I GUESS SO. ARE YOU SURE YOU DON'T WANT TO DITCH THIS JOINT AND GET ICE CREAM?
EXIT
LET'S FOCUS HERE.
YEAH, YEAH. SO DO YOU SUPPOSE K.T. AND MARCUS ARE OKAY?
'M SURE K.T. IS DOING JUST FINE. MARCUS, ON THE OTHER HAND..."
I GO GENTLE ON THE SINKS. BUT IF THE STAIN IS REAL STUBBORN, THEN I ADD SOME BLEACH.
FASCINATING.
THE HORROR... THE HORROR....

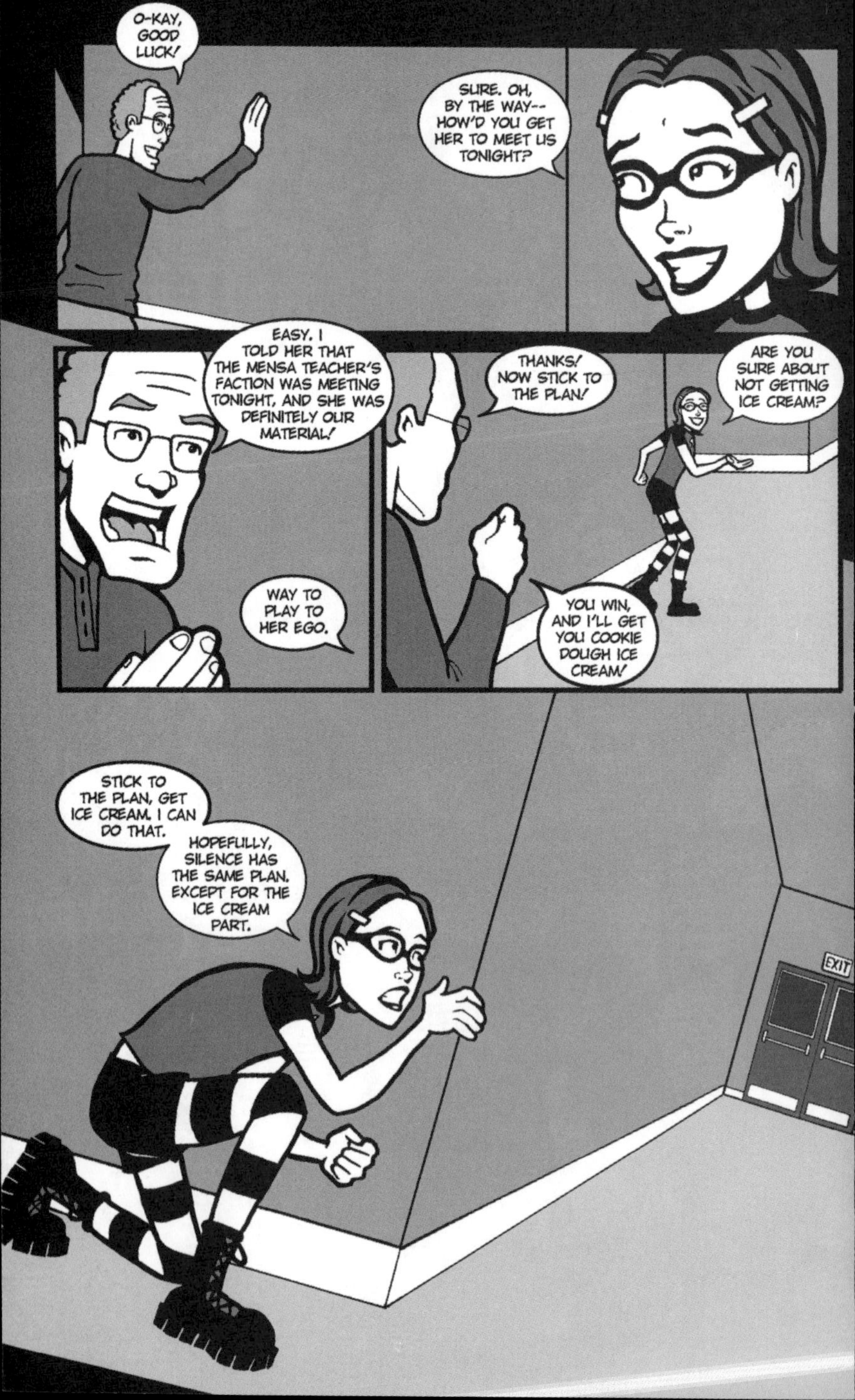
O-KAY, GOOD LUCK!
SURE. OH, BY THE WAY-- HOW'D YOU GET HER TO MEET US TONIGHT?
EASY. I TOLD HER THAT THE MENSA TEACHER'S FACTION WAS MEETING TONIGHT, AND SHE WAS DEFINITELY OUR MATERIAL!
WAY TO PLAY TO HER EGO.
THANKS! NOW STICK TO THE PLAN!
YOU WIN, AND I'LL GET YOU COOKIE DOUGH ICE CREAM!
ARE YOU SURE ABOUT NOT GETTING ICE CREAM?
STICK TO THE PLAN, GET ICE CREAM. I CAN DO THAT.
HOPEFULLY, SILENCE HAS THE SAME PLAN. EXCEPT FOR THE ICE CREAM PART.
EXIT

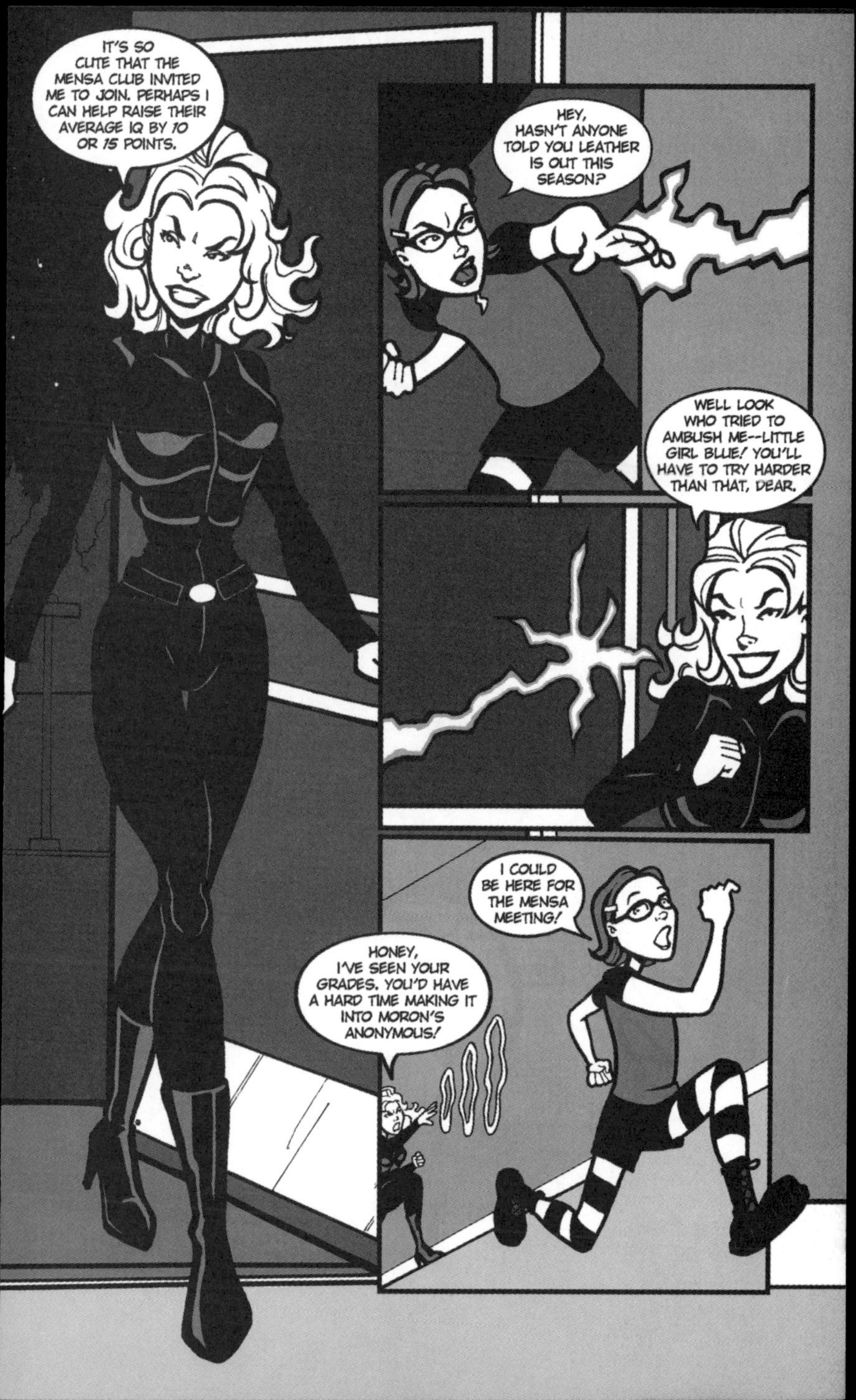

IT'S SO CUTE THAT THE MENSA CLUB INVITED ME TO JOIN. PERHAPS I CAN HELP RAISE THEIR AVERAGE IQ BY 10 OR 15 POINTS.
HEY, HASN'T ANYONE TOLD YOU LEATHER IS OUT THIS SEASON?
WELL LOOK WHO TRIED TO AMBUSH ME--LITTLE GIRL BLUE! YOU'LL HAVE TO TRY HARDER THAN THAT, DEAR.
I COULD BE HERE FOR THE MENSA MEETING!
HONEY, I'VE SEEN YOUR GRADES. YOU'D HAVE A HARD TIME MAKING IT INTO MORON'S ANONYMOUS!

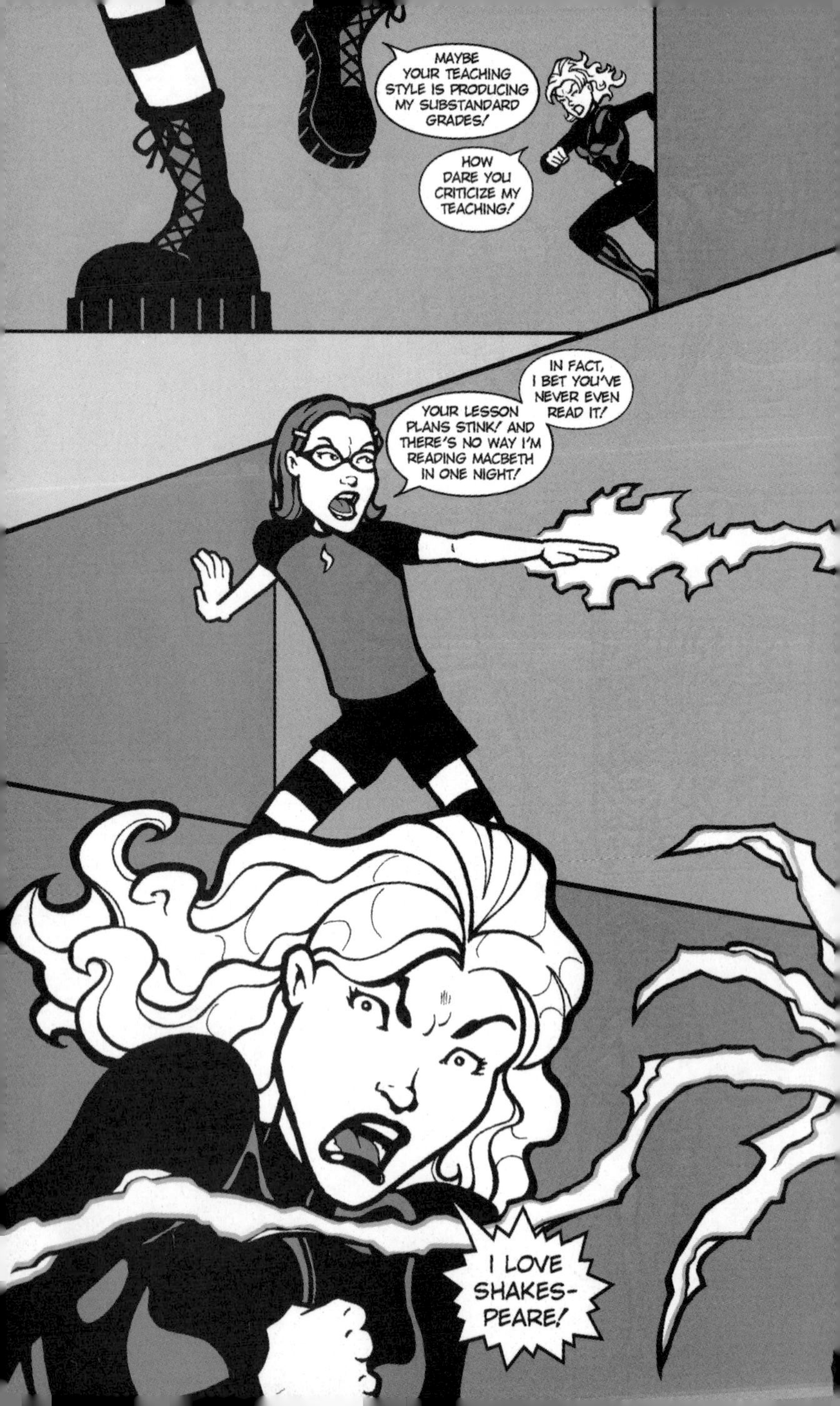
MAYBE YOUR TEACHING STYLE IS PRODUCING MY SUBSTANDARD GRADES!
HOW DARE YOU CRITICIZE MY TEACHING!
YOUR LESSON PLANS STINK! AND THERE'S NO WAY I'M READING MACBETH IN ONE NIGHT!
IN FACT, I BET YOU'VE NEVER EVEN READ IT!
I LOVE SHAKES-PEARE!

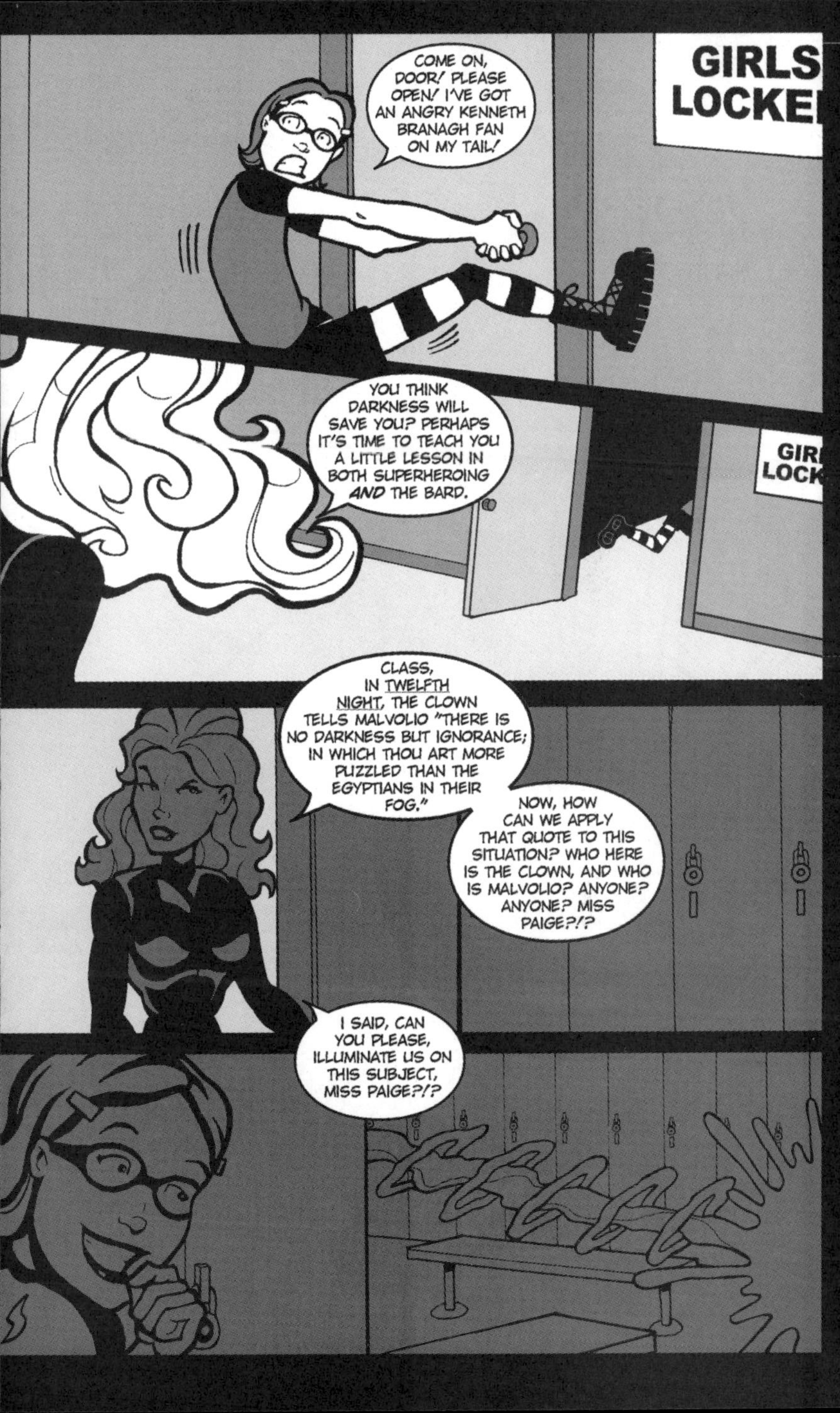

COME ON, DOOR! PLEASE OPEN! I'VE GOT AN ANGRY KENNETH BRANAGH FAN ON MY TAIL!
GIRLS LOCKE
YOU THINK DARKNESS WILL SAVE YOU? PERHAPS IT'S TIME TO TEACH YOU A LITTLE LESSON IN BOTH SUPERHEROING *AND* THE BARD.
CLASS, IN TWELFTH NIGHT, THE CLOWN TELLS MALVOLIO "THERE IS NO DARKNESS BUT IGNORANCE; IN WHICH THOU ART MORE PUZZLED THAN THE EGYPTIANS IN THEIR FOG."
NOW, HOW CAN WE APPLY THAT QUOTE TO THIS SITUATION? WHO HERE IS THE CLOWN, AND WHO IS MALVOLIO? ANYONE? ANYONE? MISS PAIGE?!?
I SAID, CAN YOU PLEASE, ILLUMINATE US ON THIS SUBJECT, MISS PAIGE?!?

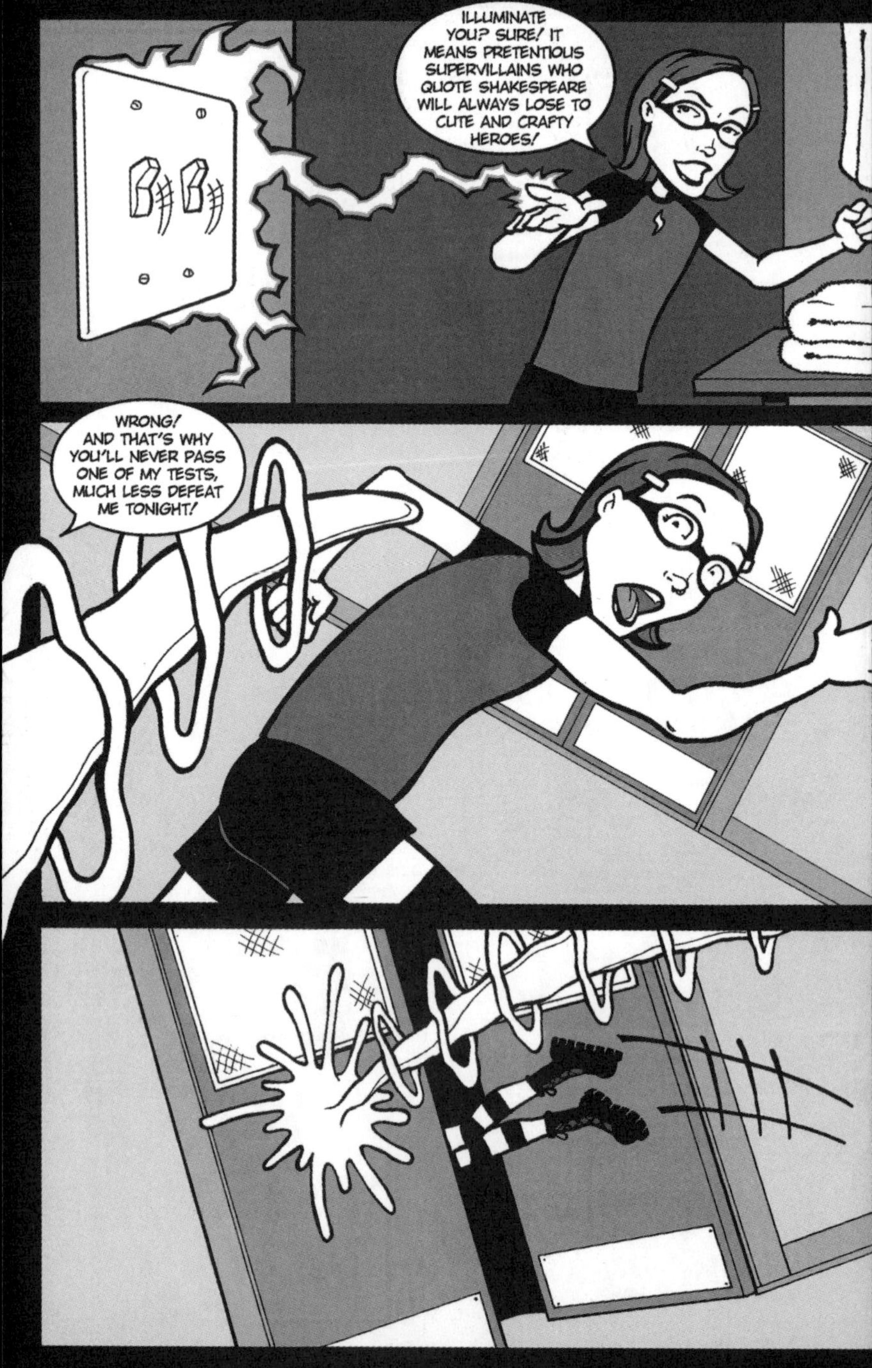
ILLUMINATE YOU? SURE! IT MEANS PRETENTIOUS SUPERVILLAINS WHO QUOTE SHAKESPEARE WILL ALWAYS LOSE TO CUTE AND CRAFTY HEROES!
WRONG! AND THAT'S WHY YOU'LL NEVER PASS ONE OF MY TESTS, MUCH LESS DEFEAT ME TONIGHT!

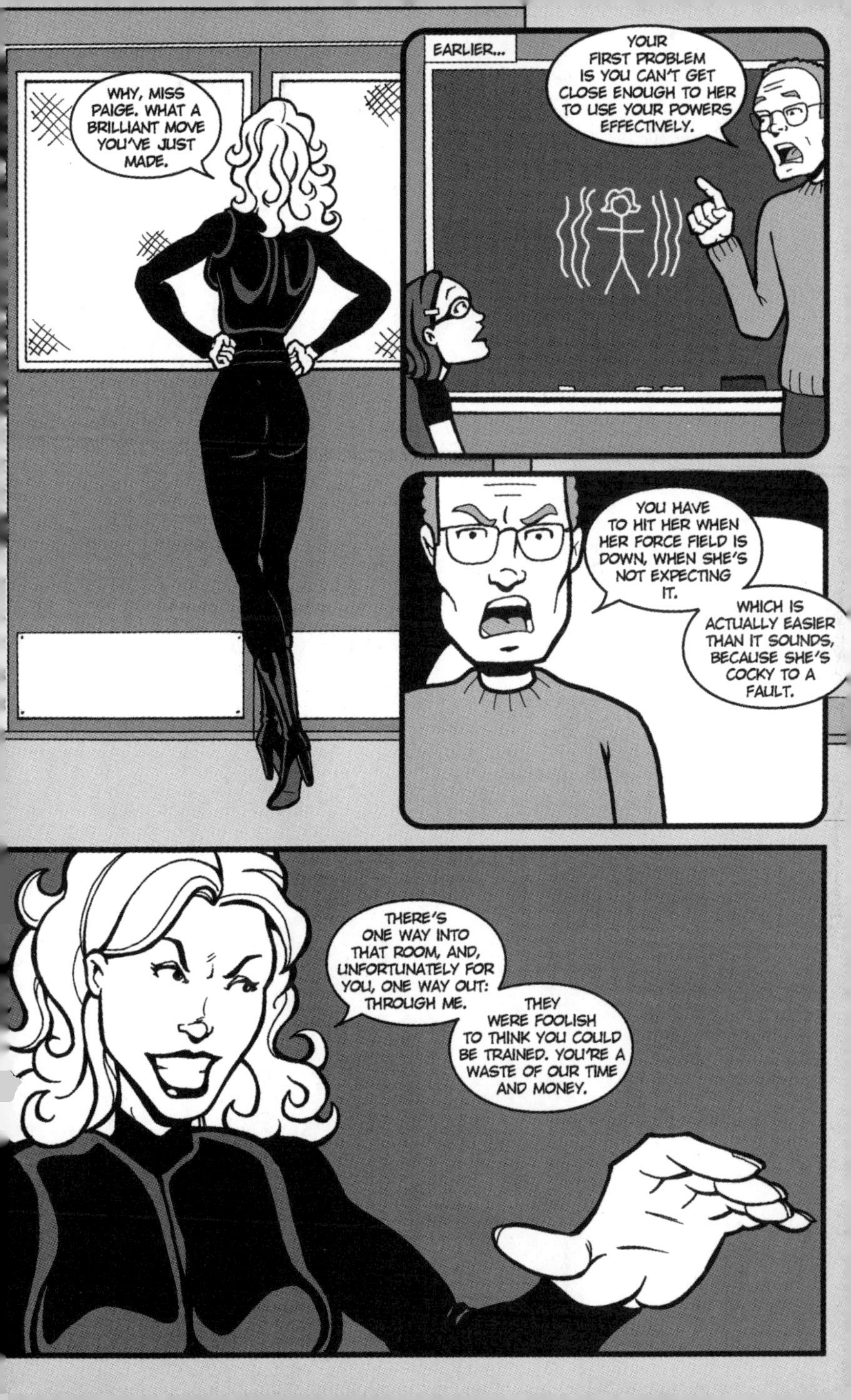
WHY, MISS PAIGE. WHAT A BRILLIANT MOVE YOU'VE JUST MADE.
EARLIER...
YOUR FIRST PROBLEM IS YOU CAN'T GET CLOSE ENOUGH TO HER TO USE YOUR POWERS EFFECTIVELY.
YOU HAVE TO HIT HER WHEN HER FORCE FIELD IS DOWN, WHEN SHE'S NOT EXPECTING IT.
WHICH IS ACTUALLY EASIER THAN IT SOUNDS, BECAUSE SHE'S COCKY TO A FAULT.
THERE'S ONE WAY INTO THAT ROOM, AND, UNFORTUNATELY FOR YOU, ONE WAY OUT: THROUGH ME.
THEY WERE FOOLISH TO THINK YOU COULD BE TRAINED. YOU'RE A WASTE OF OUR TIME AND MONEY.

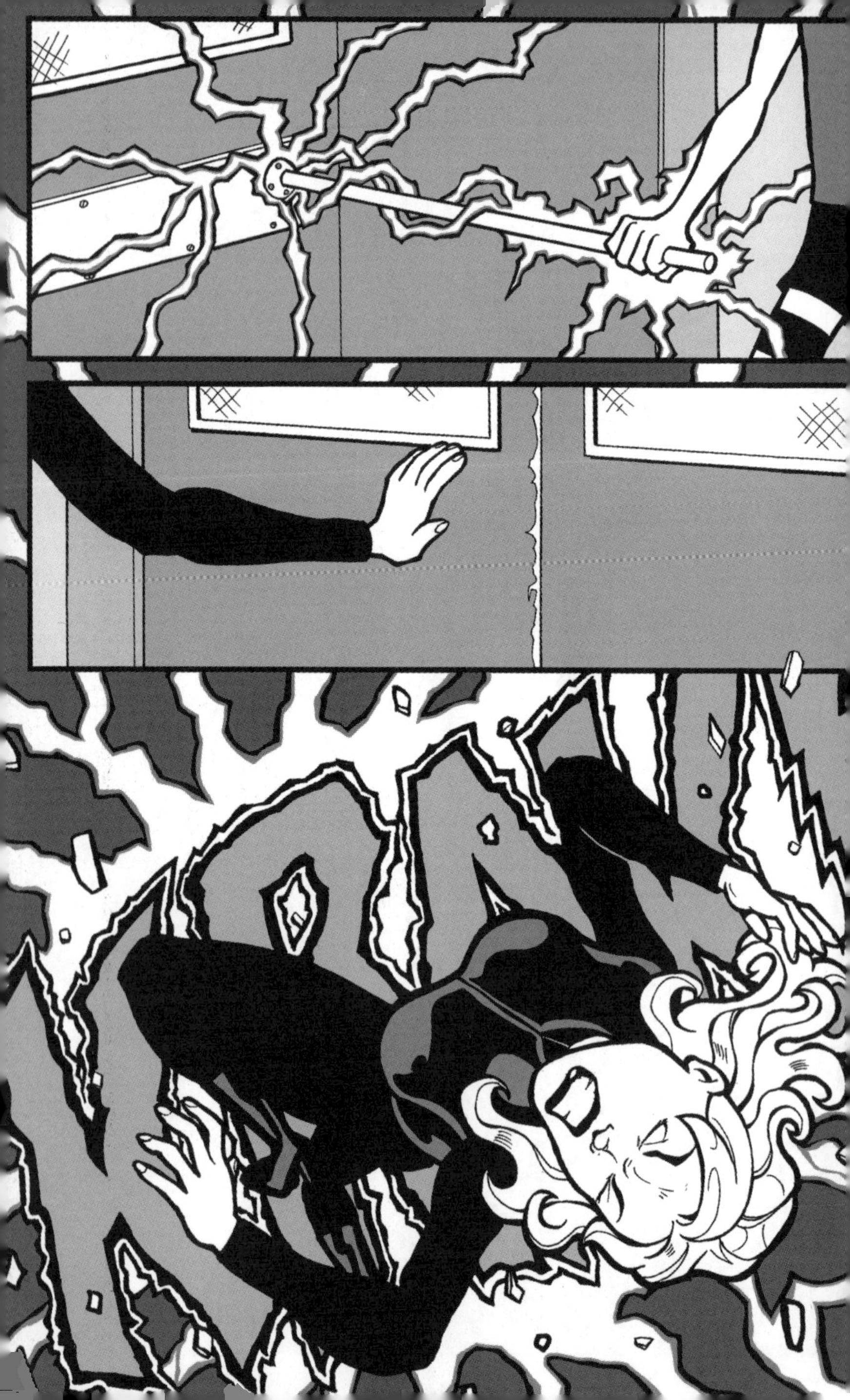

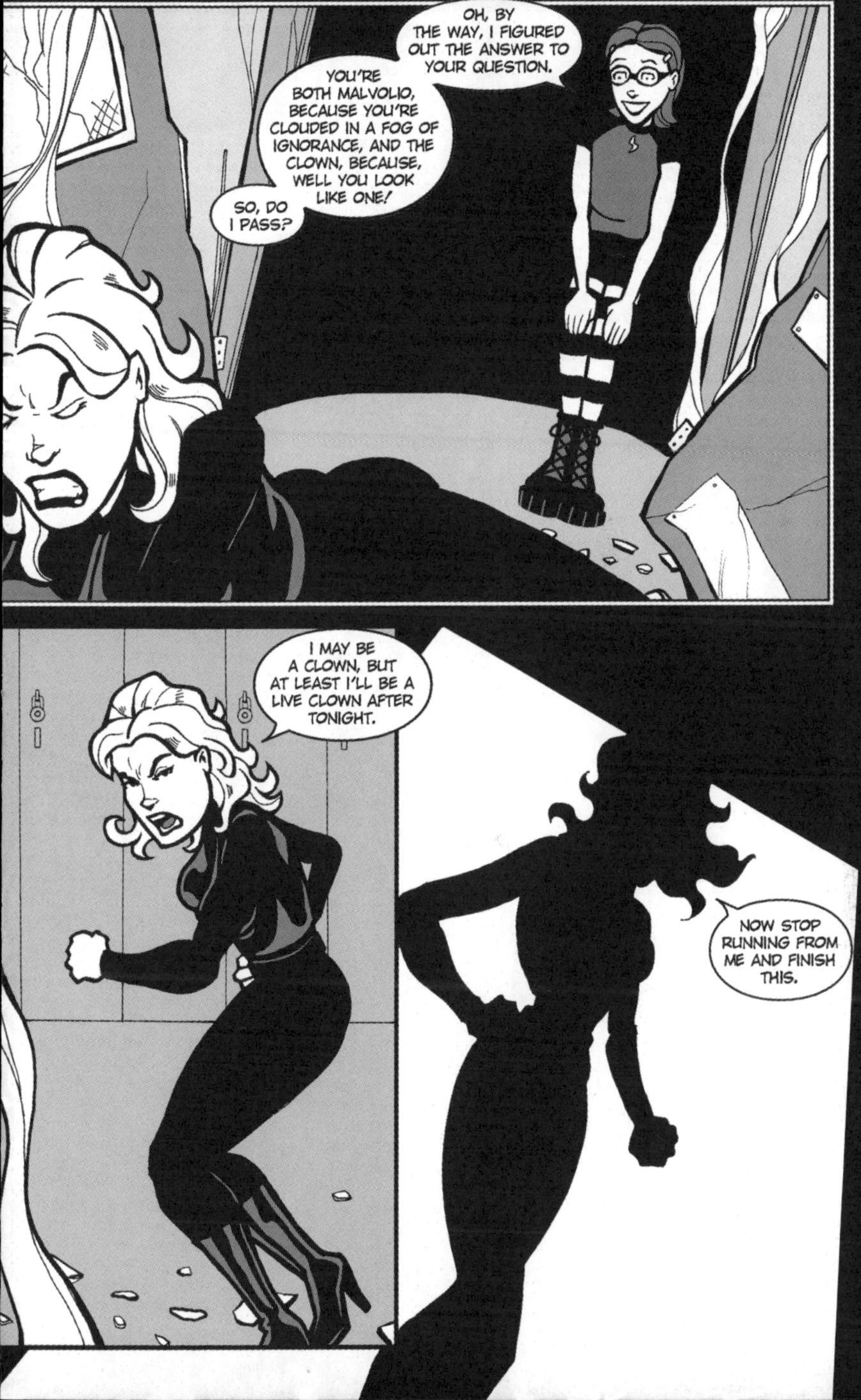
OH, BY THE WAY, I FIGURED OUT THE ANSWER TO YOUR QUESTION.
YOU'RE BOTH MALVOLIO, BECAUSE YOU'RE CLOUDED IN A FOG OF IGNORANCE, AND THE CLOWN, BECAUSE, WELL YOU LOOK LIKE ONE!
SO, DO I PASS?
I MAY BE A CLOWN, BUT AT LEAST I'LL BE A LIVE CLOWN AFTER TONIGHT.
NOW STOP RUNNING FROM ME AND FINISH THIS.

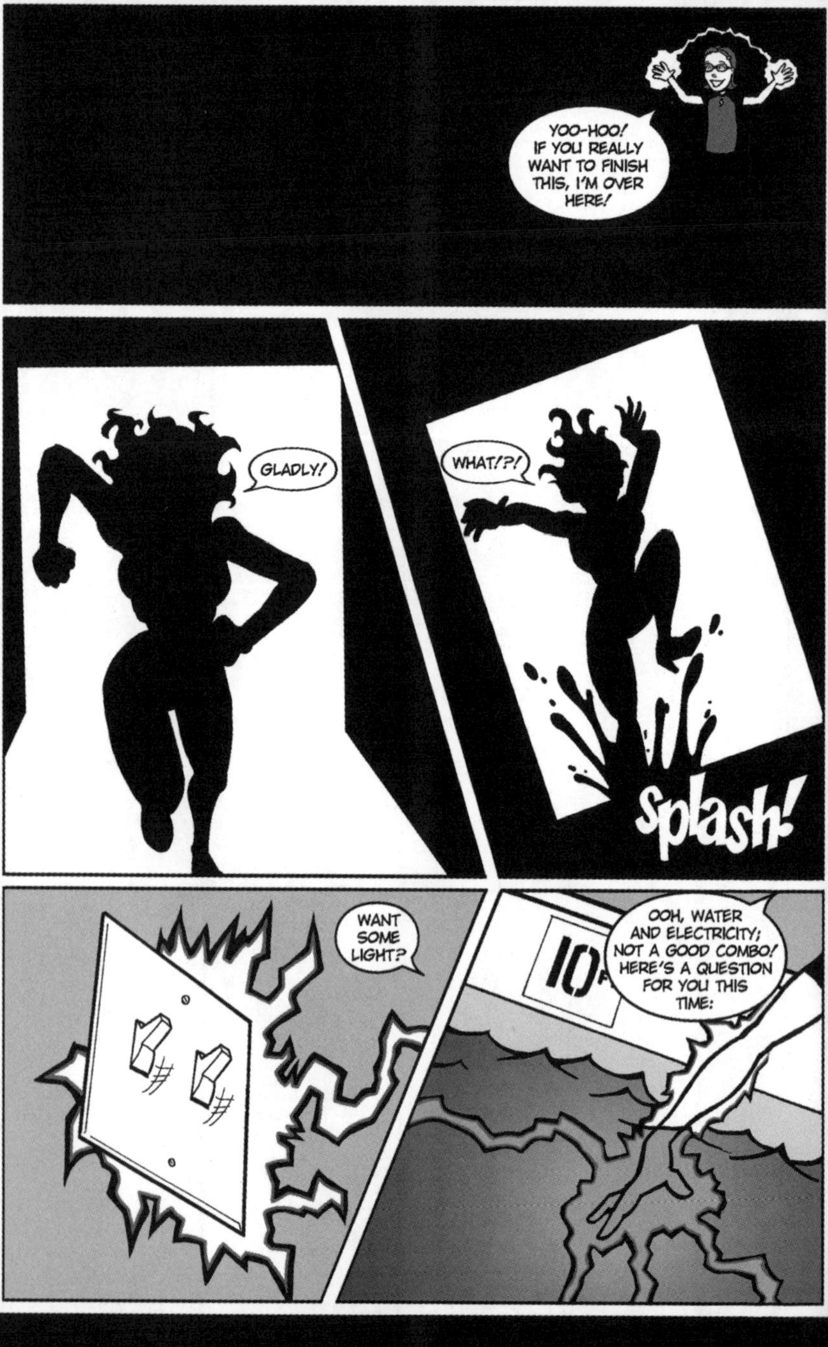
YOO-HOO! IF YOU REALLY WANT TO FINISH THIS, I'M OVER HERE!
GLADLY!
WHAT!?!
Splash!
WANT SOME LIGHT?
10
OOH, WATER AND ELECTRICITY; NOT A GOOD COMBO! HERE'S A QUESTION FOR YOU THIS TIME:

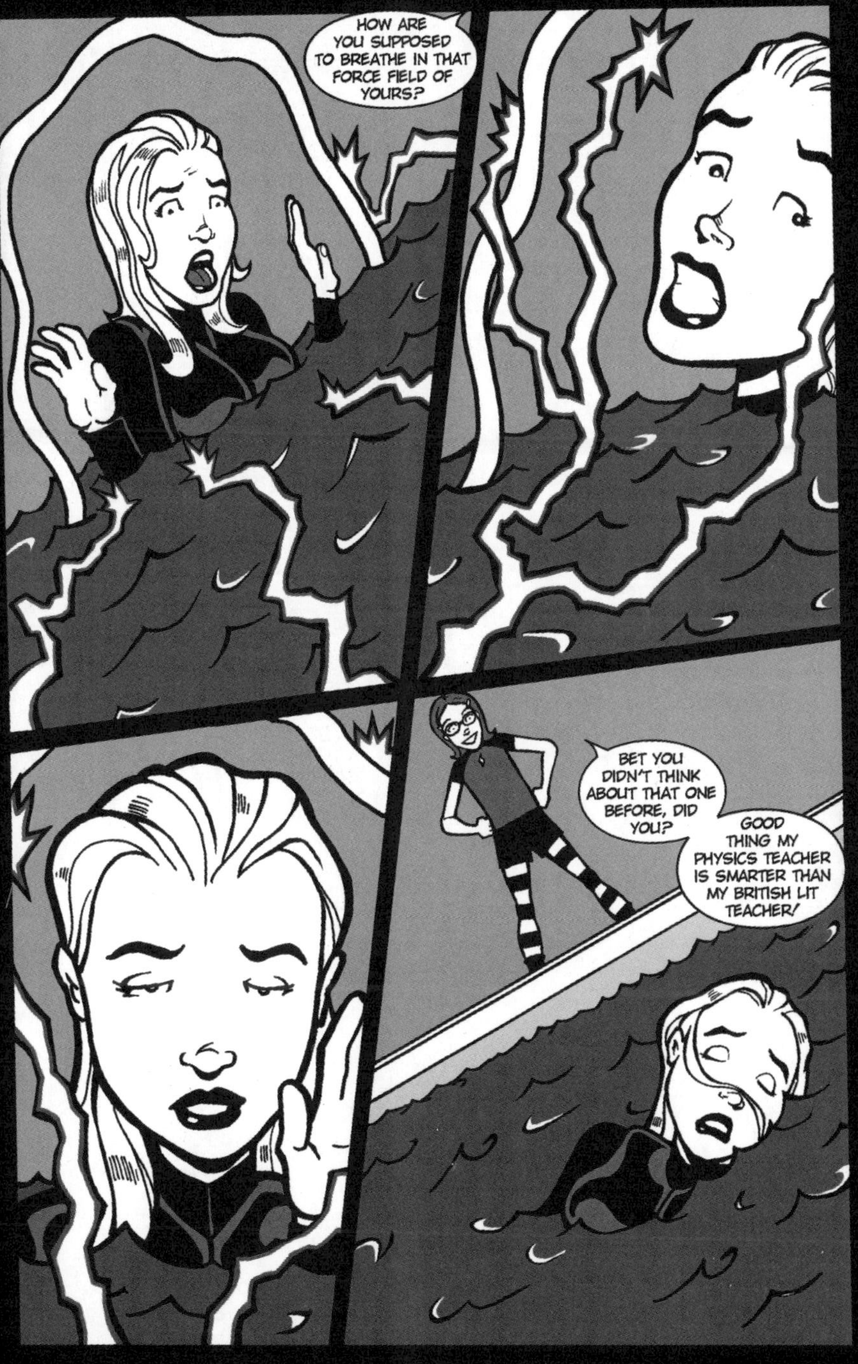
HOW ARE YOU SUPPOSED TO BREATHE IN THAT FORCE FIELD OF YOURS?
BET YOU DIDN'T THINK ABOUT THAT ONE BEFORE, DID YOU?
GOOD THING MY PHYSICS TEACHER IS SMARTER THAN MY BRITISH LIT TEACHER!

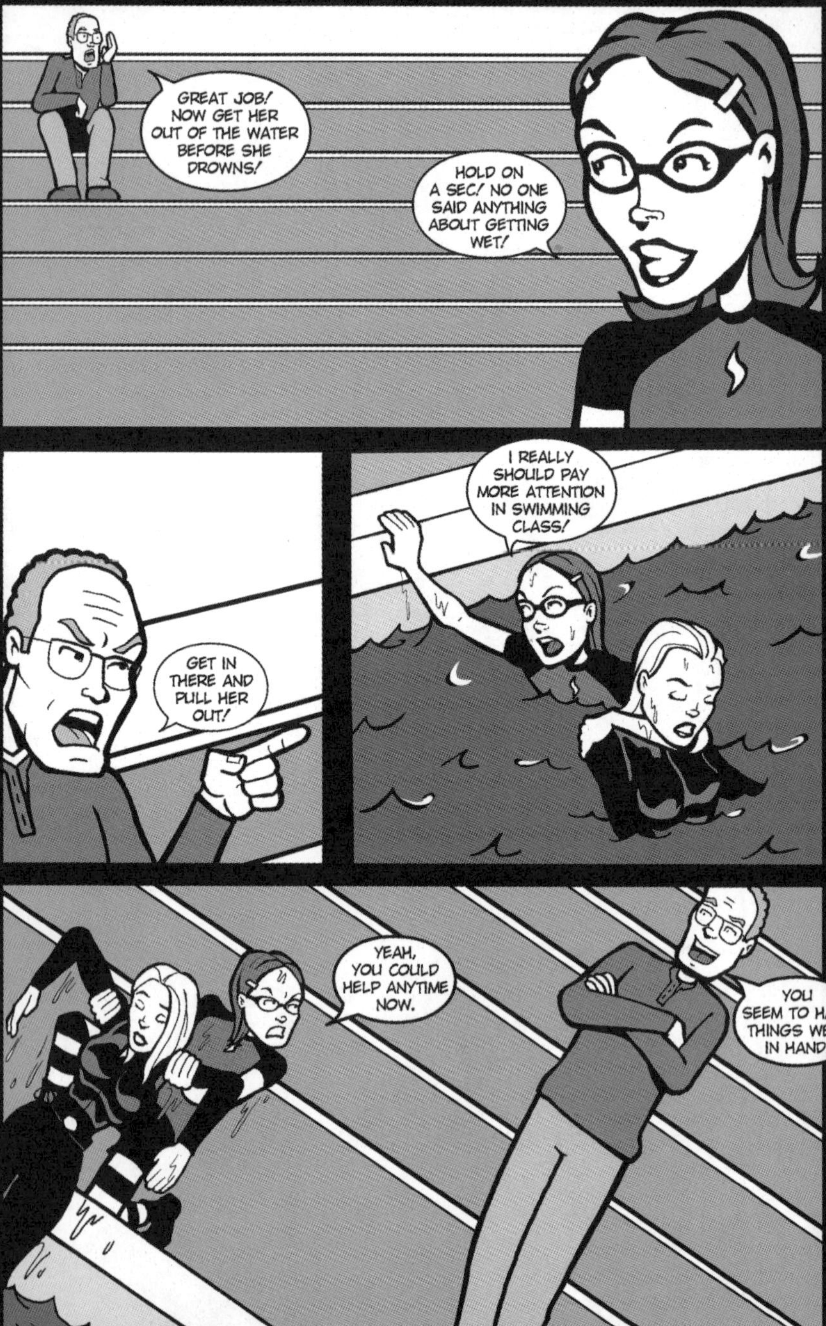
GREAT JOB! NOW GET HER OUT OF THE WATER BEFORE SHE DROWNS!
HOLD ON A SEC! NO ONE SAID ANYTHING ABOUT GETTING WET!
GET IN THERE AND PULL HER OUT!
I REALLY SHOULD PAY MORE ATTENTION IN SWIMMING CLASS!
YEAH, YOU COULD HELP ANYTIME NOW.
YOU SEEM TO HAV THINGS WEL IN HAND.

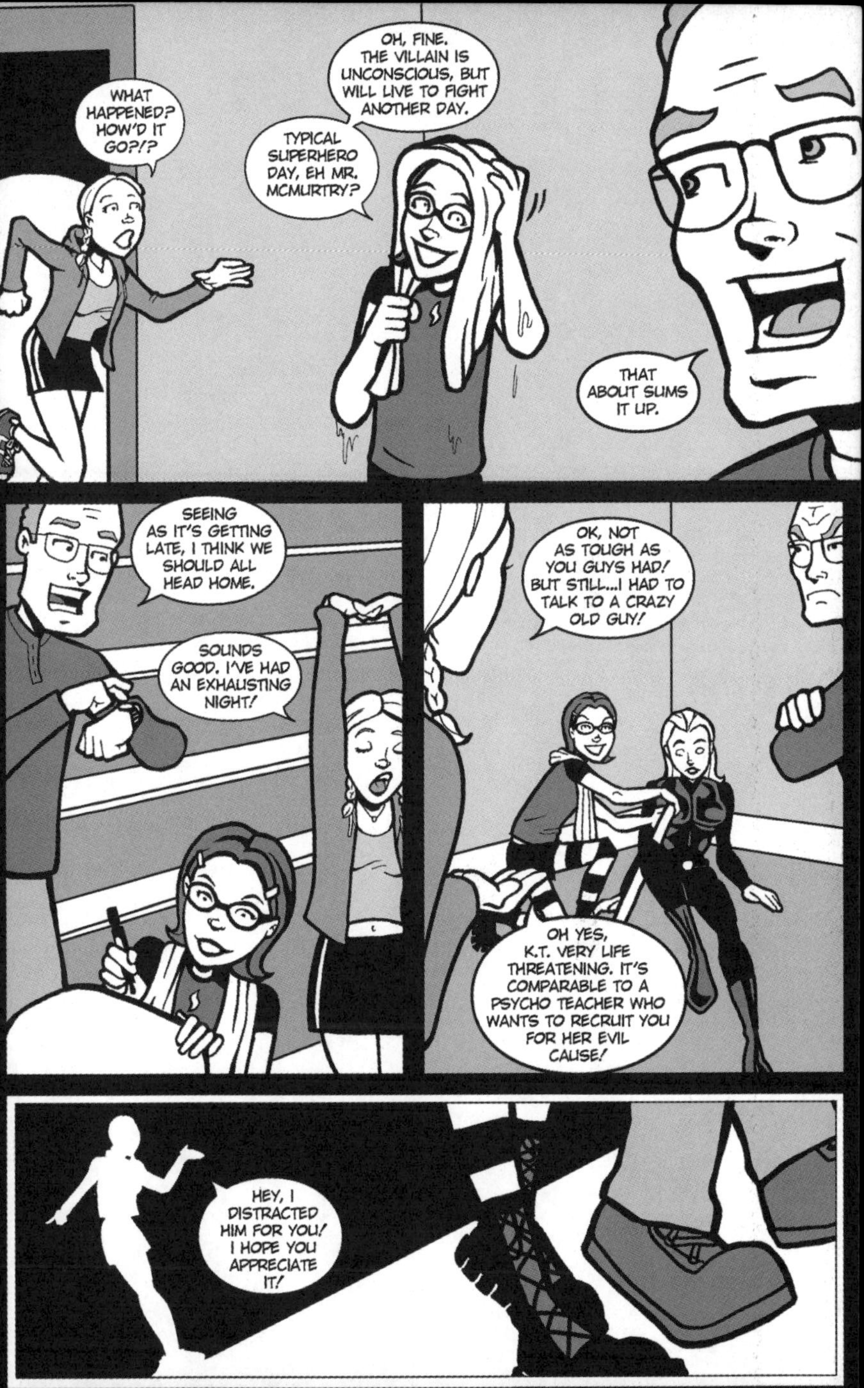
WHAT HAPPENED? HOW'D IT GO?!?
OH, FINE. THE VILLAIN IS UNCONSCIOUS, BUT WILL LIVE TO FIGHT ANOTHER DAY.
TYPICAL SUPERHERO DAY, EH MR. MCMURTRY?
THAT ABOUT SUMS IT UP.
SEEING AS IT'S GETTING LATE, I THINK WE SHOULD ALL HEAD HOME.
SOUNDS GOOD. I'VE HAD AN EXHAUSTING NIGHT!
OK, NOT AS TOUGH AS YOU GUYS HAD! BUT STILL...I HAD TO TALK TO A CRAZY OLD GUY!
OH YES, K.T. VERY LIFE THREATENING. IT'S COMPARABLE TO A PSYCHO TEACHER WHO WANTS TO RECRUIT YOU FOR HER EVIL CAUSE!
HEY, I DISTRACTED HIM FOR YOU! I HOPE YOU APPRECIATE IT!

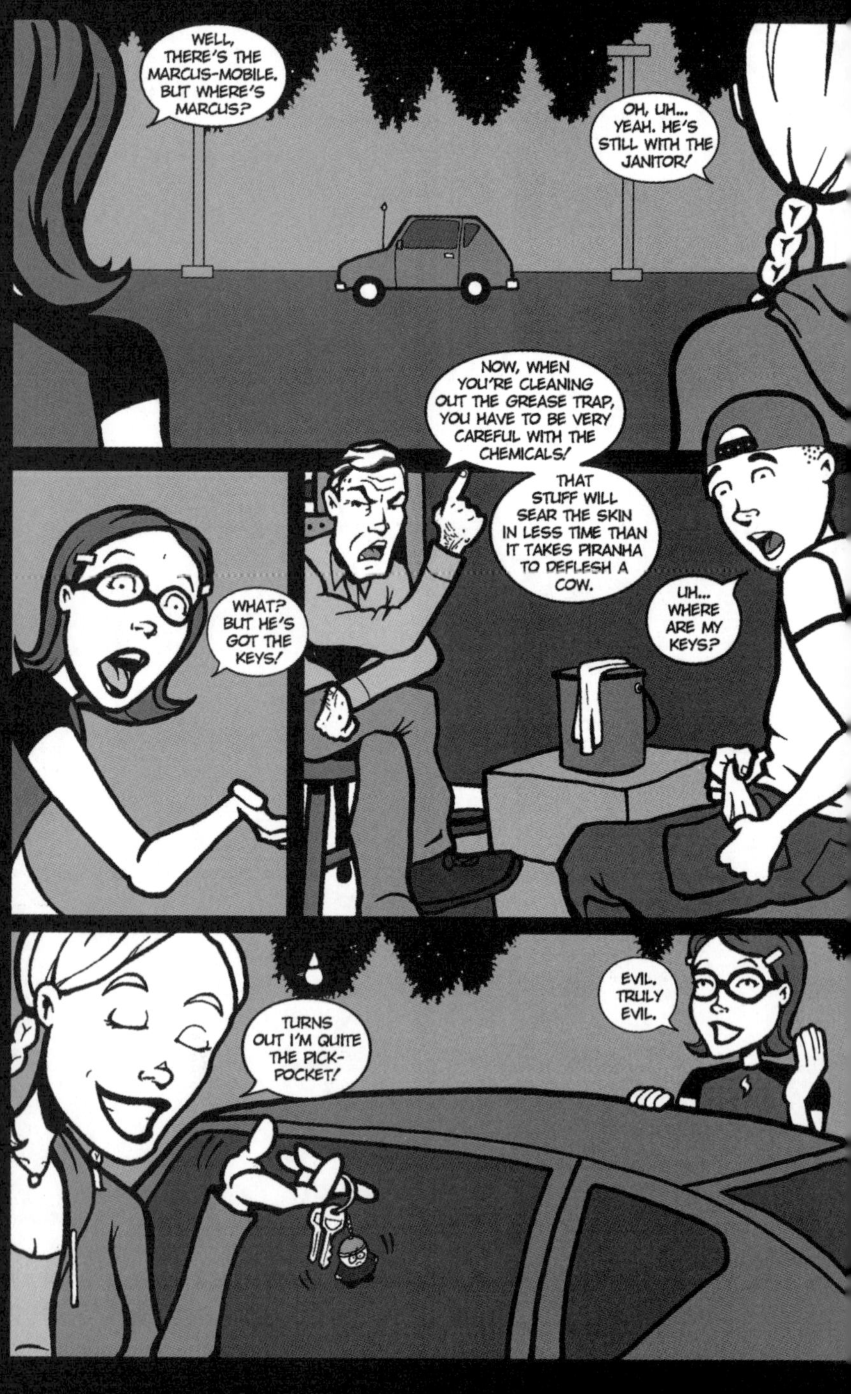
WELL, THERE'S THE MARCUS-MOBILE. BUT WHERE'S MARCUS?
OH, UH... YEAH. HE'S STILL WITH THE JANITOR!
WHAT? BUT HE'S GOT THE KEYS!
NOW, WHEN YOU'RE CLEANING OUT THE GREASE TRAP, YOU HAVE TO BE VERY CAREFUL WITH THE CHEMICALS!
THAT STUFF WILL SEAR THE SKIN IN LESS TIME THAN IT TAKES PIRANHA TO DEFLESH A COW.
UH... WHERE ARE MY KEYS?
TURNS OUT I'M QUITE THE PICK-POCKET!
EVIL. TRULY EVIL.

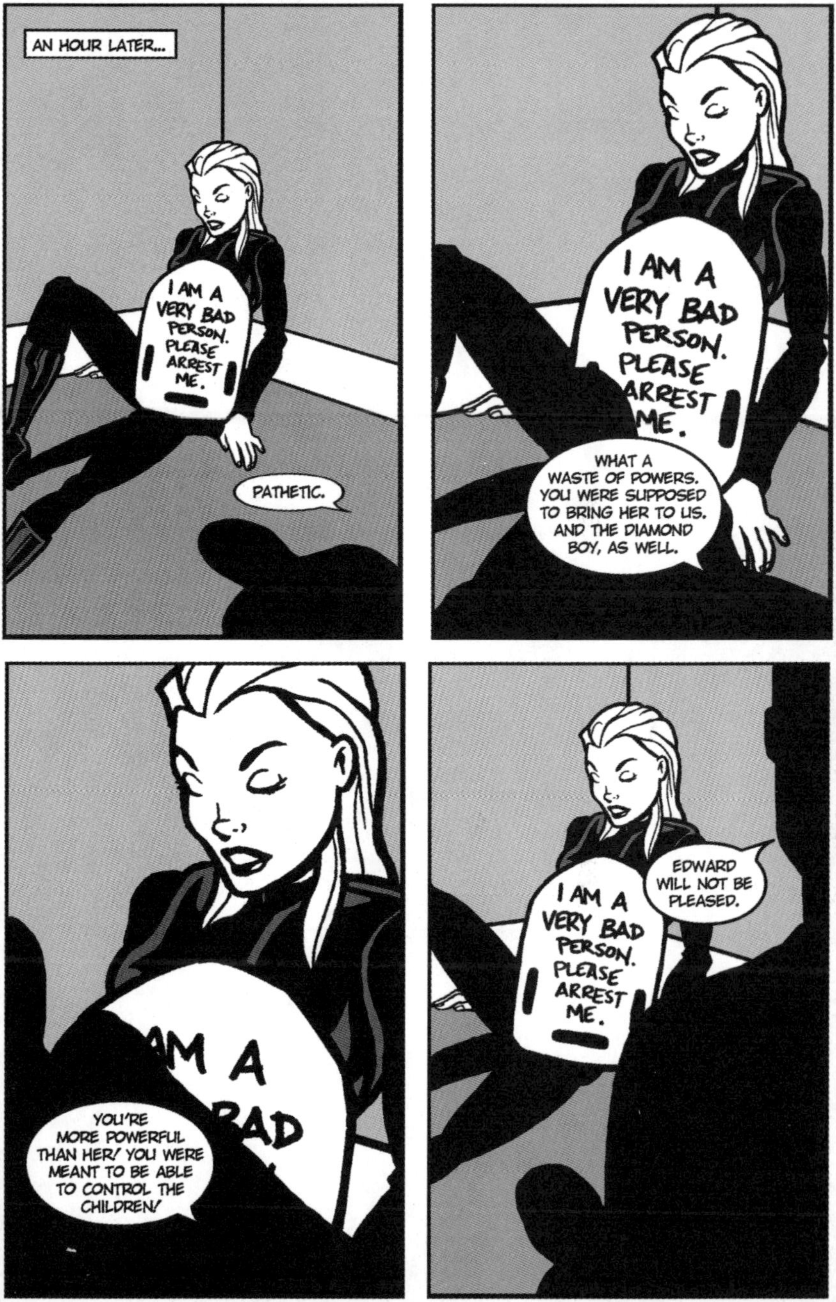
AN HOUR LATER...
I AM A VERY BAD PERSON. PLEASE ARREST ME.
PATHETIC.
I AM A VERY BAD PERSON. PLEASE ARREST ME.
WHAT A WASTE OF POWERS. YOU WERE SUPPOSED TO BRING HER TO US. AND THE DIAMOND BOY, AS WELL.
YOU'RE MORE POWERFUL THAN HER! YOU WERE MEANT TO BE ABLE TO CONTROL THE CHILDREN!
I AM A VERY BAD PERSON. PLEASE ARREST ME.
EDWARD WILL NOT BE PLEASED.

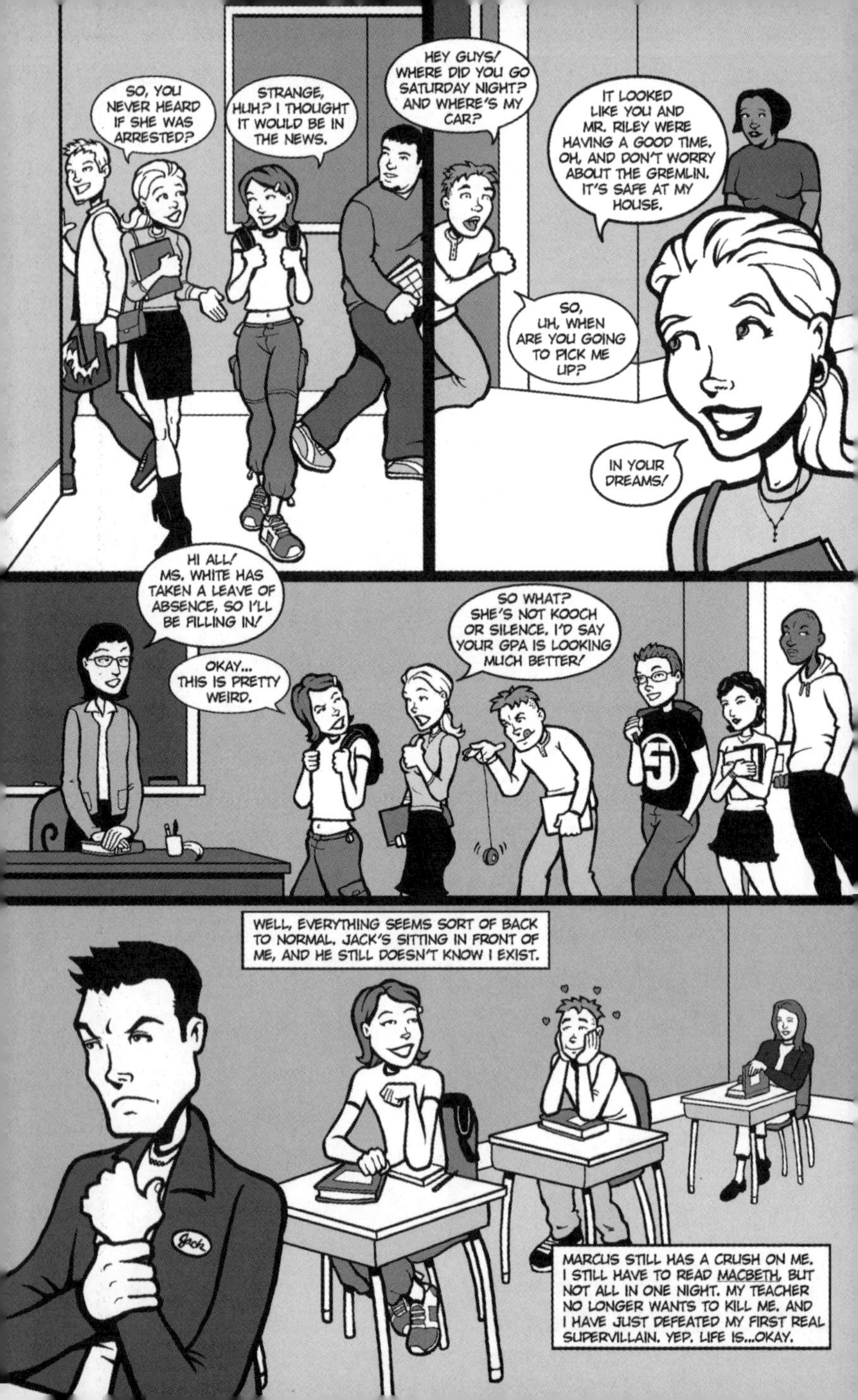

SO, YOU NEVER HEARD IF SHE WAS ARRESTED?
STRANGE, HUH? I THOUGHT IT WOULD BE IN THE NEWS.
HEY GUYS! WHERE DID YOU GO SATURDAY NIGHT? AND WHERE'S MY CAR?
IT LOOKED LIKE YOU AND MR. RILEY WERE HAVING A GOOD TIME. OH, AND DON'T WORRY ABOUT THE GREMLIN. IT'S SAFE AT MY HOUSE.
SO, UH, WHEN ARE YOU GOING TO PICK ME UP?
IN YOUR DREAMS!
HI ALL! MS. WHITE HAS TAKEN A LEAVE OF ABSENCE, SO I'LL BE FILLING IN!
OKAY... THIS IS PRETTY WEIRD.
SO WHAT? SHE'S NOT KOOCH OR SILENCE. I'D SAY YOUR GPA IS LOOKING MUCH BETTER!
WELL, EVERYTHING SEEMS SORT OF BACK TO NORMAL. JACK'S SITTING IN FRONT OF ME, AND HE STILL DOESN'T KNOW I EXIST.
Jack
MARCUS STILL HAS A CRUSH ON ME. I STILL HAVE TO READ MACBETH, BUT NOT ALL IN ONE NIGHT. MY TEACHER NO LONGER WANTS TO KILL ME. AND I HAVE JUST DEFEATED MY FIRST REAL SUPERVILLAIN. YEP. LIFE IS...OKAY.

Epilogue

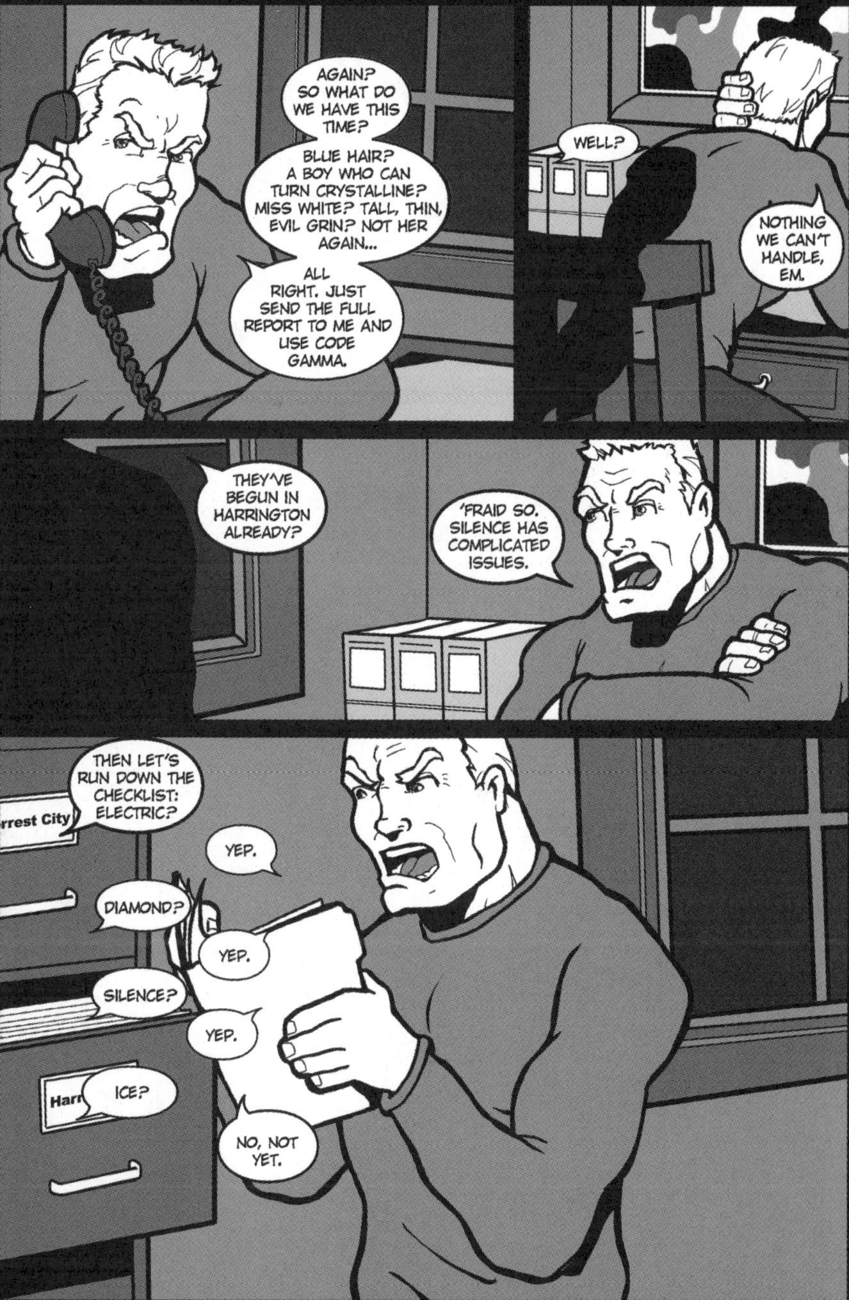

AGAIN? SO WHAT DO WE HAVE THIS TIME?
BLUE HAIR? A BOY WHO CAN TURN CRYSTALLINE? MISS WHITE? TALL, THIN, EVIL GRIN? NOT HER AGAIN...
ALL RIGHT. JUST SEND THE FULL REPORT TO ME AND USE CODE GAMMA.
WELL?
NOTHING WE CAN'T HANDLE, EM.
THEY'VE BEGUN IN HARRINGTON ALREADY?
'FRAID SO. SILENCE HAS COMPLICATED ISSUES.
THEN LET'S RUN DOWN THE CHECKLIST: ELECTRIC?
rrest City
YEP.
DIAMOND?
YEP.
SILENCE?
YEP.
Harr
ICE?
NO, NOT YET.

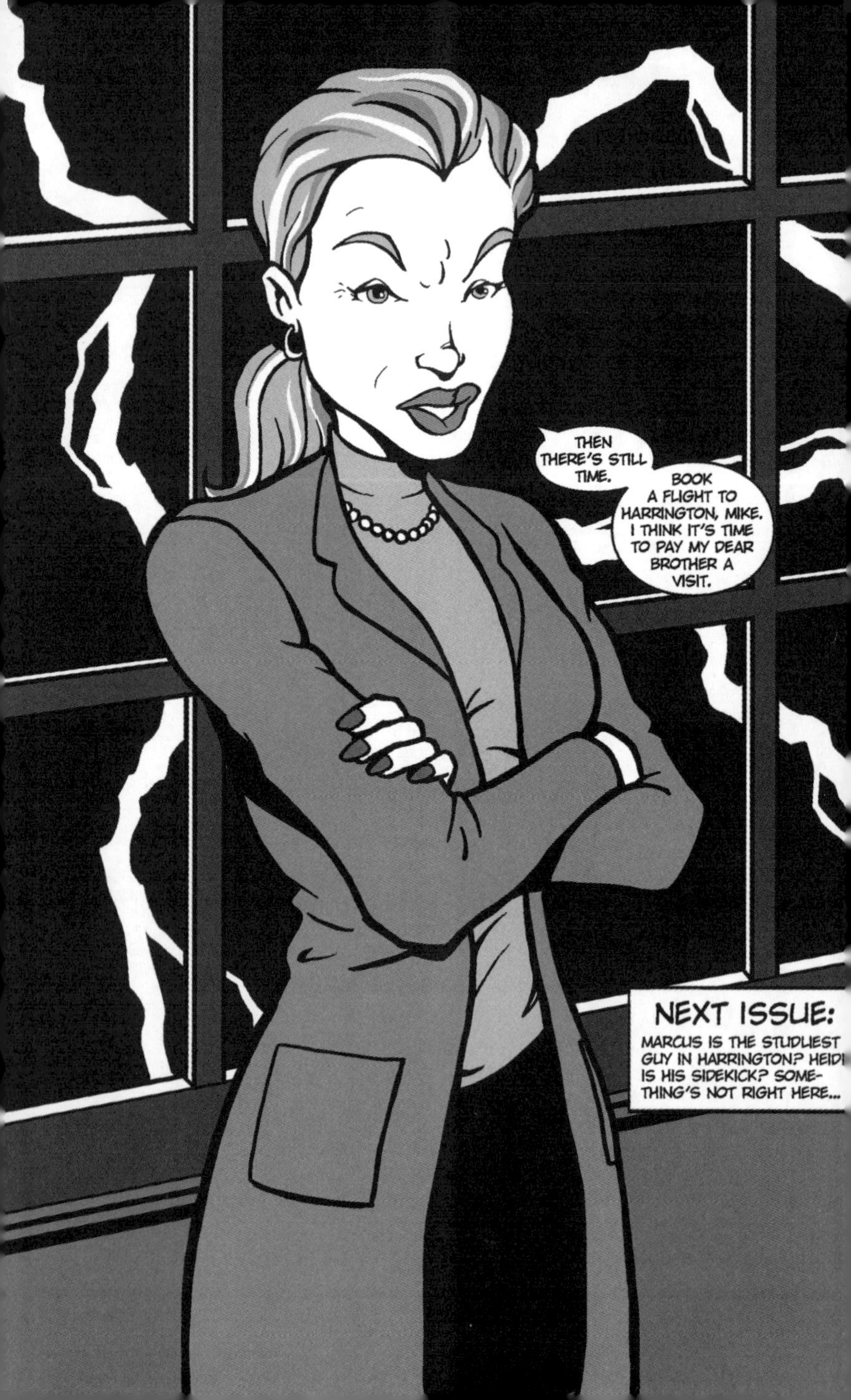
THEN THERE'S STILL TIME.
BOOK A FLIGHT TO HARRINGTON, MIKE. I THINK IT'S TIME TO PAY MY DEAR BROTHER A VISIT.
NEXT ISSUE:
MARCUS IS THE STUDLIEST GUY IN HARRINGTON? HEIDI IS HIS SIDEKICK? SOME-THING'S NOT RIGHT HERE...

EPILOGUE: "Return to the Mall"

Originally published in Digital Webbing
Presents #7, February, 2003

Writer:
James S. Harris

Art:
Cal Slayton

Lettering:
Ed Dukeshire

Editor:
Michelle Harris

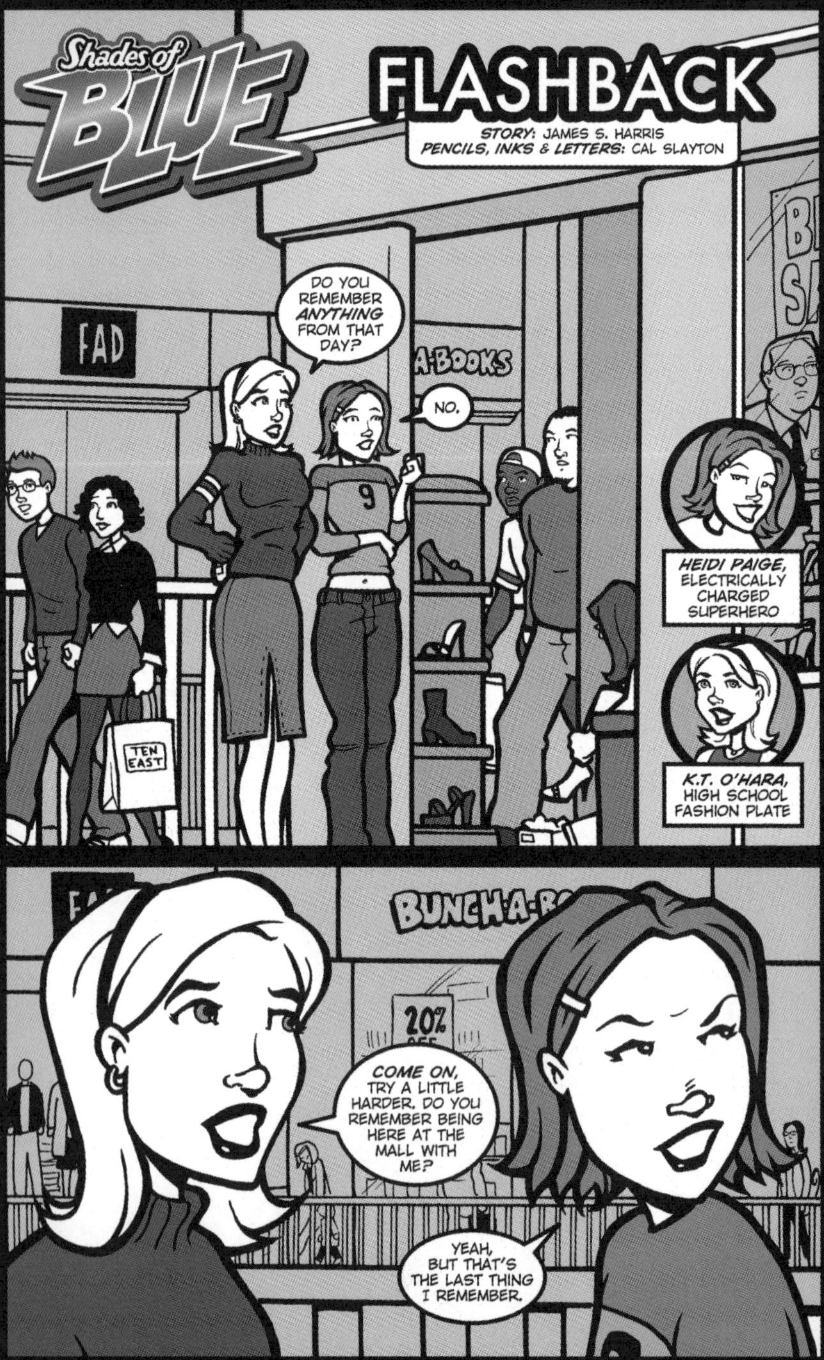
Shades of BLUE
FLASHBACK
STORY: JAMES S. HARRIS
PENCILS, INKS & LETTERS: CAL SLAYTON
FAD
DO YOU REMEMBER ANYTHING FROM THAT DAY?
NO.
HEIDI PAIGE, ELECTRICALLY CHARGED SUPERHERO
K.T. O'HARA, HIGH SCHOOL FASHION PLATE
TEN EAST
20%
COME ON, TRY A LITTLE HARDER. DO YOU REMEMBER BEING HERE AT THE MALL WITH ME?
YEAH, BUT THAT'S THE LAST THING I REMEMBER.

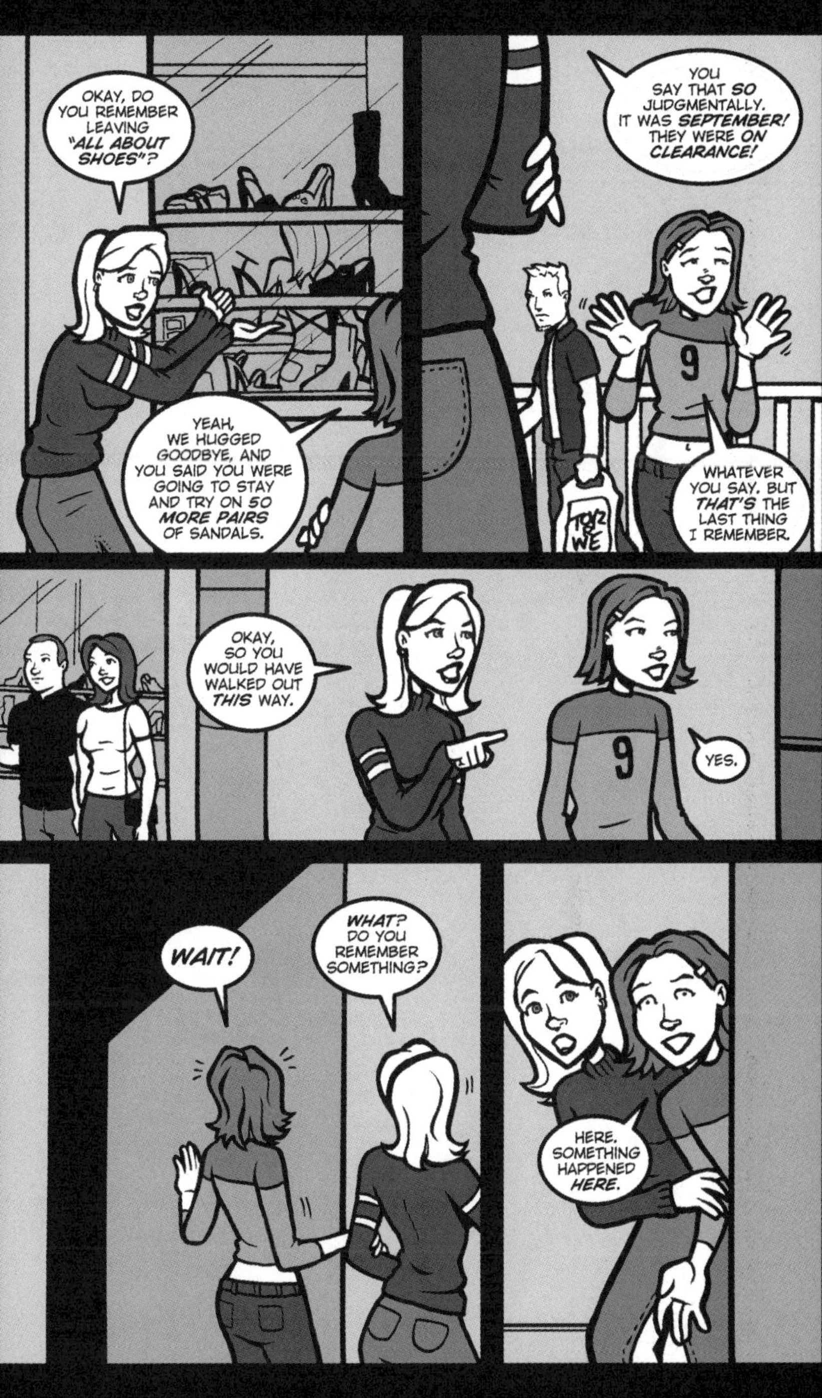
OKAY, DO YOU REMEMBER LEAVING "ALL ABOUT SHOES"?
YEAH, WE HUGGED GOODBYE, AND YOU SAID YOU WERE GOING TO STAY AND TRY ON 50 MORE PAIRS OF SANDALS.
YOU SAY THAT SO JUDGMENTALLY. IT WAS SEPTEMBER! THEY WERE ON CLEARANCE!
WHATEVER YOU SAY. BUT THAT'S THE LAST THING I REMEMBER.
OKAY, SO YOU WOULD HAVE WALKED OUT THIS WAY.
YES.
WAIT!
WHAT? DO YOU REMEMBER SOMETHING?
HERE. SOMETHING HAPPENED HERE.

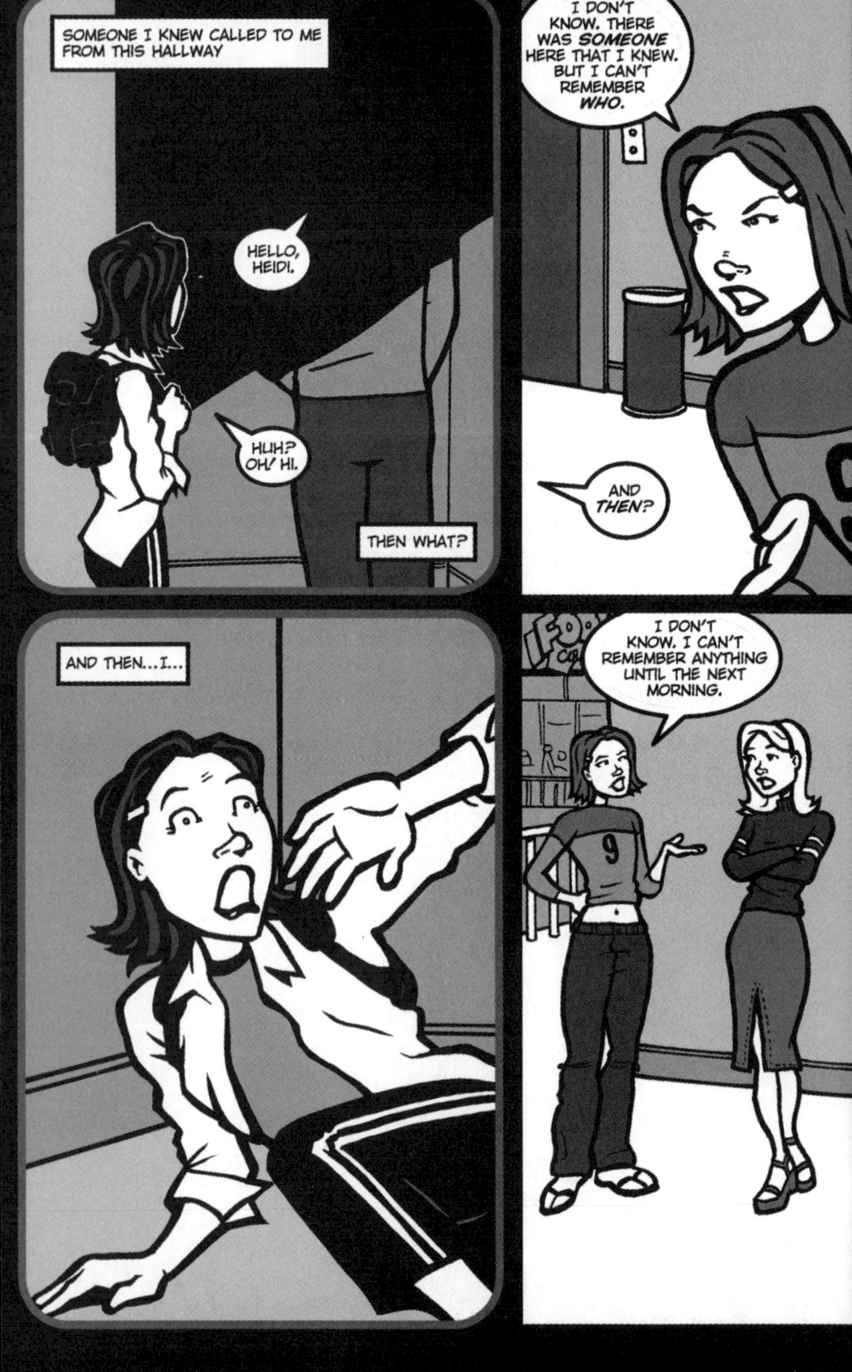
SOMEONE I KNEW CALLED TO ME FROM THIS HALLWAY
HELLO, HEIDI.
HUH? OH! HI.
THEN WHAT?
I DON'T KNOW. THERE WAS SOMEONE HERE THAT I KNEW. BUT I CAN'T REMEMBER WHO.
AND THEN?
AND THEN...I...
I DON'T KNOW. I CAN'T REMEMBER ANYTHING UNTIL THE NEXT MORNING.

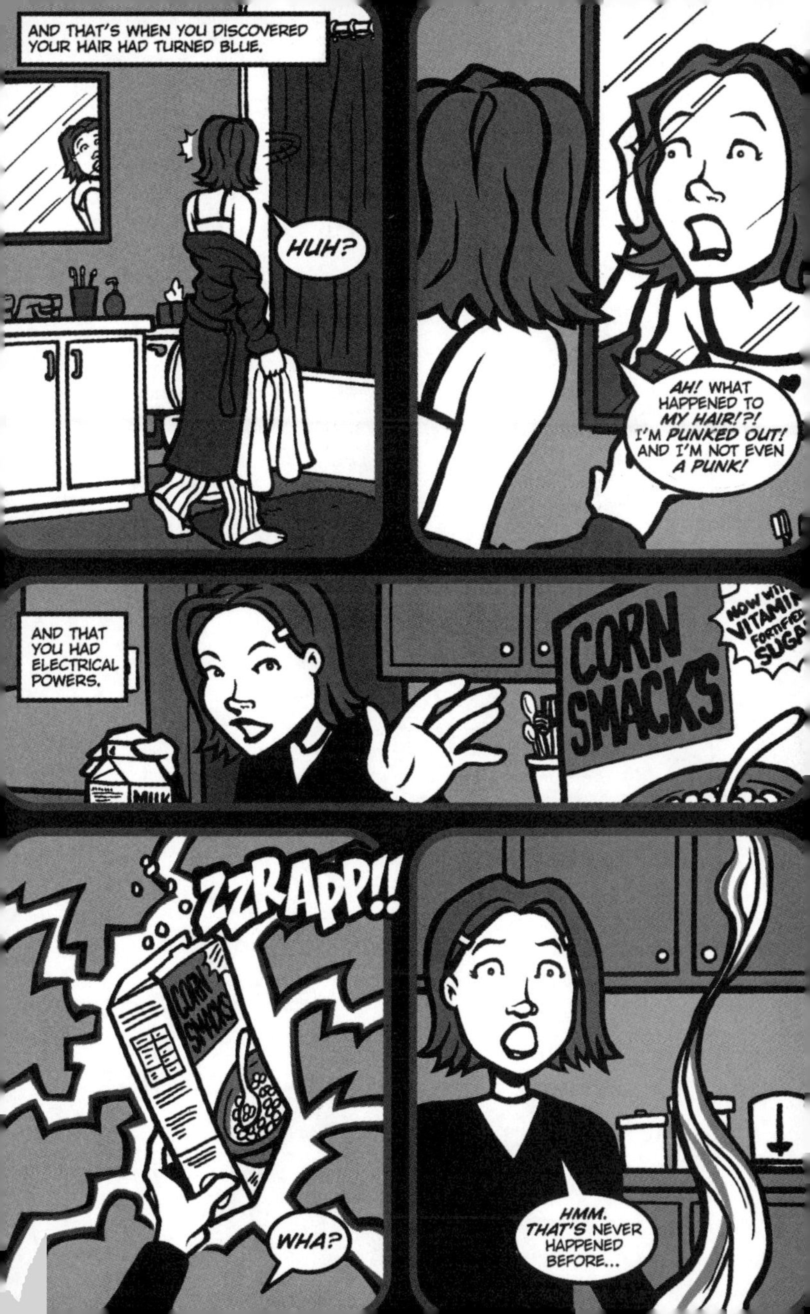
AND THAT'S WHEN YOU DISCOVERED YOUR HAIR HAD TURNED BLUE.
HUH?
AH! WHAT HAPPENED TO MY HAIR!?! I'M PUNKED OUT! AND I'M NOT EVEN A PUNK!
AND THAT YOU HAD ELECTRICAL POWERS.
CORN SMACKS
MILK
ZZRAPP!!
CORN SMACKS
WHA?
HMM. THAT'S NEVER HAPPENED BEFORE...

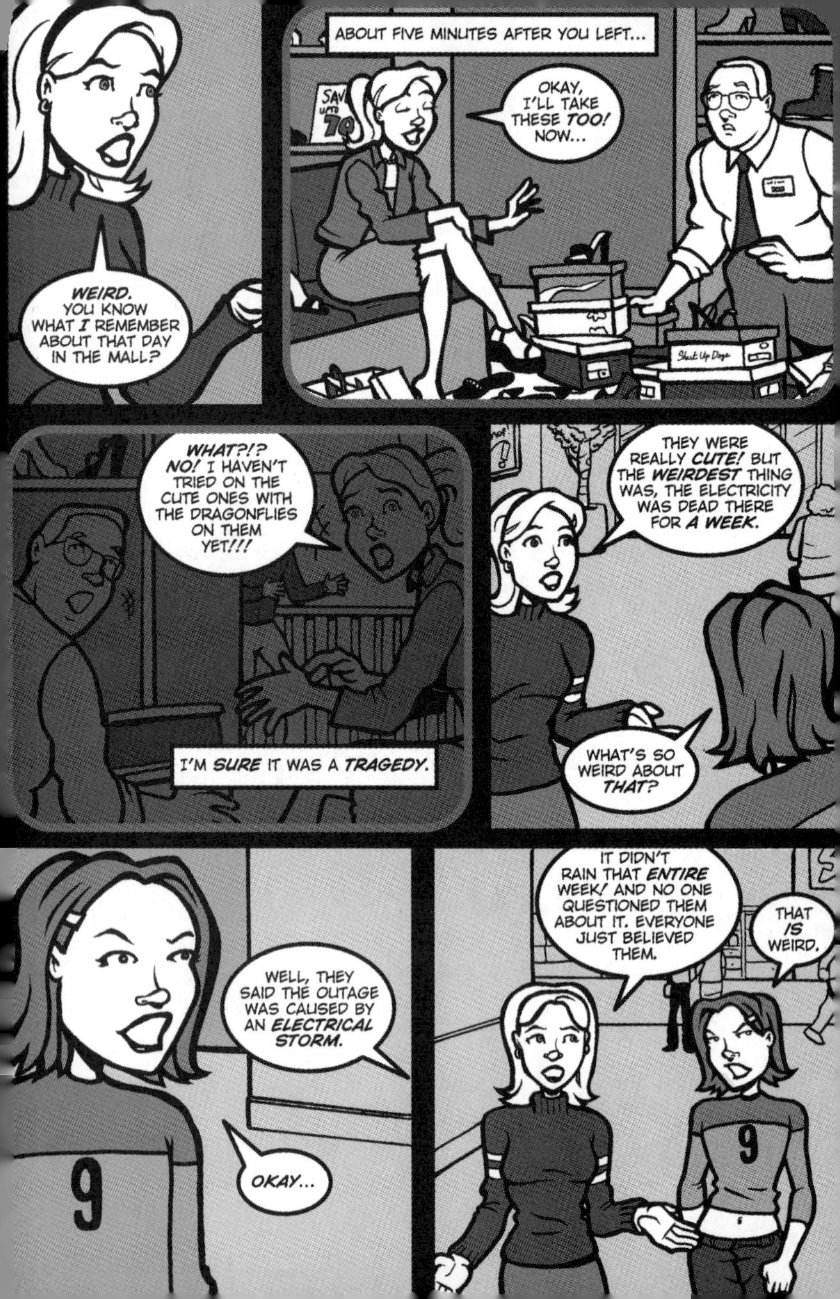
WEIRD. YOU KNOW WHAT I REMEMBER ABOUT THAT DAY IN THE MALL?
ABOUT FIVE MINUTES AFTER YOU LEFT...
OKAY, I'LL TAKE THESE TOO! NOW...
WHAT?!? NO! I HAVEN'T TRIED ON THE CUTE ONES WITH THE DRAGONFLIES ON THEM YET!!!
I'M SURE IT WAS A TRAGEDY.
THEY WERE REALLY CUTE! BUT THE WEIRDEST THING WAS, THE ELECTRICITY WAS DEAD THERE FOR A WEEK.
WHAT'S SO WEIRD ABOUT THAT?
WELL, THEY SAID THE OUTAGE WAS CAUSED BY AN ELECTRICAL STORM.
OKAY...
IT DIDN'T RAIN THAT ENTIRE WEEK! AND NO ONE QUESTIONED THEM ABOUT IT. EVERYONE JUST BELIEVED THEM.
THAT IS WEIRD.

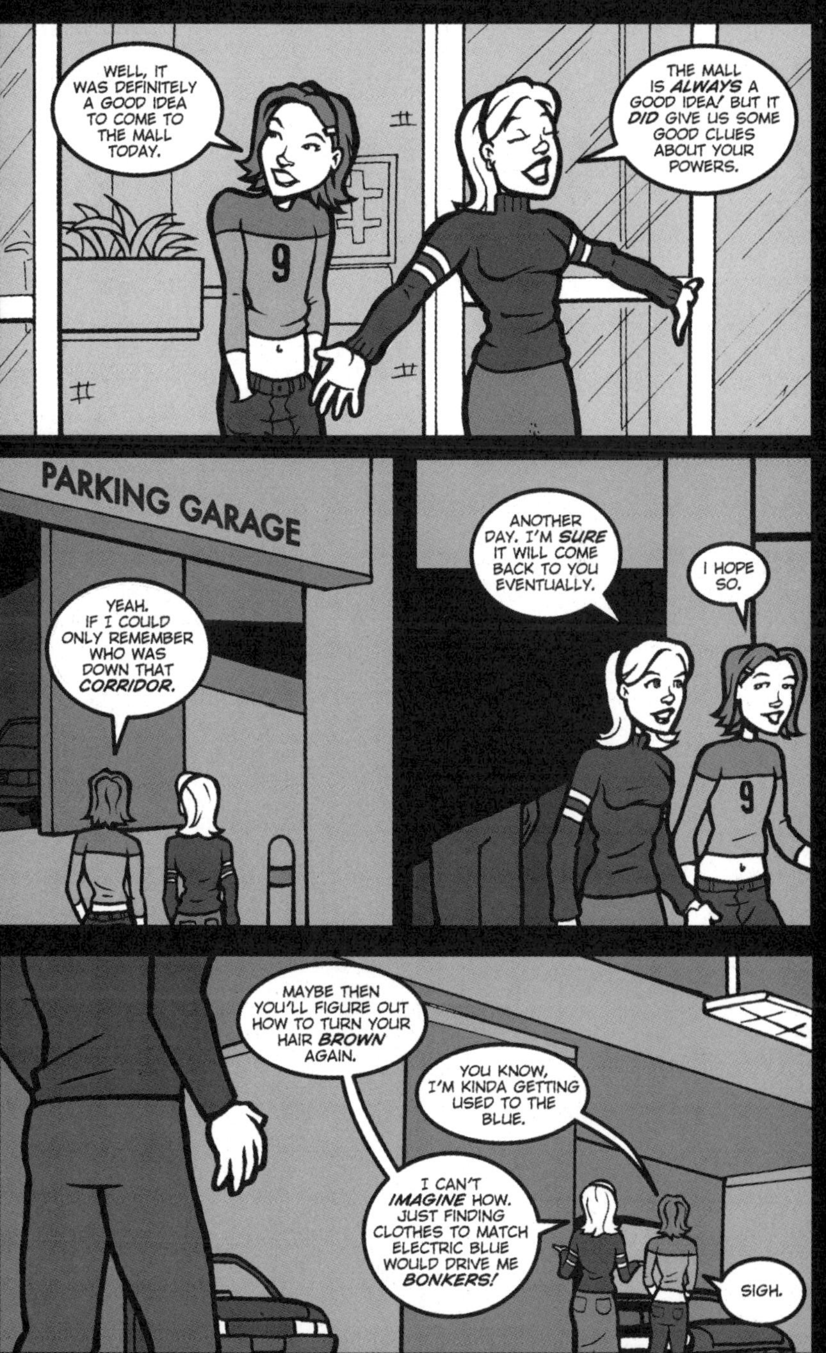
WELL, IT WAS DEFINITELY A GOOD IDEA TO COME TO THE MALL TODAY.
THE MALL IS *ALWAYS* A GOOD IDEA! BUT IT *DID* GIVE US SOME GOOD CLUES ABOUT YOUR POWERS.
PARKING GARAGE
YEAH. IF I COULD ONLY REMEMBER WHO WAS DOWN THAT *CORRIDOR.*
ANOTHER DAY. I'M *SURE* IT WILL COME BACK TO YOU EVENTUALLY.
I HOPE SO.
MAYBE THEN YOU'LL FIGURE OUT HOW TO TURN YOUR HAIR *BROWN* AGAIN.
YOU KNOW, I'M KINDA GETTING USED TO THE BLUE.
I CAN'T *IMAGINE* HOW. JUST FINDING CLOTHES TO MATCH ELECTRIC BLUE WOULD DRIVE ME *BONKERS!*
SIGH.

2001 Convention Tour Promotional Mini-Comic

Question: How can I still have 100 of these left when I only printed up like a thousand and I've given them out everywhere for the last three years? Oh well, it's a funny little piece starring none other than Cal, Rachel and I (I'm not happy with my portrayal, by the way. Cal made me look a little on the chunky side!).

Writer:
James S. Harris

Art:
Cal Slayton

Lettering:
Cal Slayton

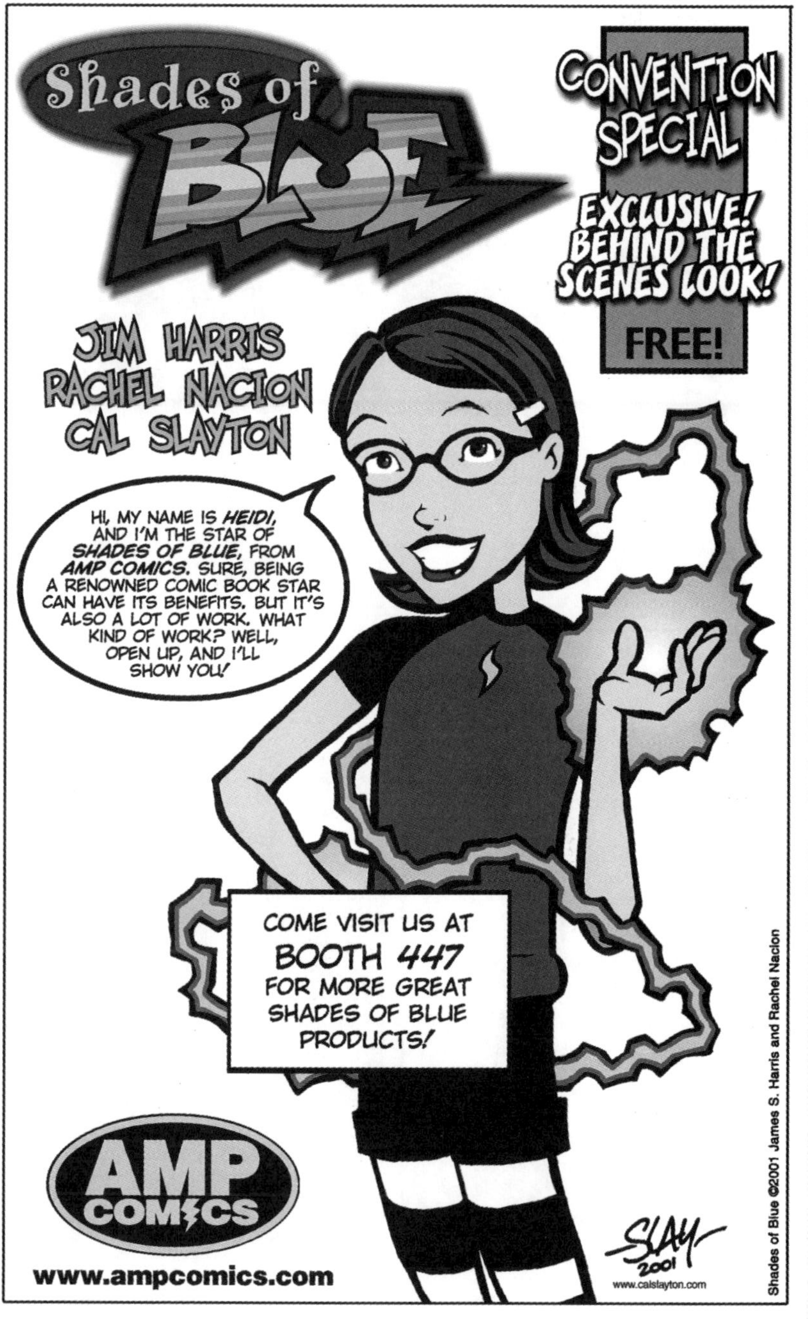
Shades of BLUE
CONVENTION SPECIAL
EXCLUSIVE! BEHIND THE SCENES LOOK!
FREE!
JIM HARRIS
RACHEL NACION
CAL SLAYTON
HI, MY NAME IS HEIDI, AND I'M THE STAR OF SHADES OF BLUE, FROM AMP COMICS. SURE, BEING A RENOWNED COMIC BOOK STAR CAN HAVE ITS BENEFITS. BUT IT'S ALSO A LOT OF WORK. WHAT KIND OF WORK? WELL, OPEN UP, AND I'LL SHOW YOU!
COME VISIT US AT BOOTH 447 FOR MORE GREAT SHADES OF BLUE PRODUCTS!
AMP COMICS
www.ampcomics.com
SLAY 2001
www.calslayton.com
Shades of Blue ©2001 James S. Harris and Rachel Nacion

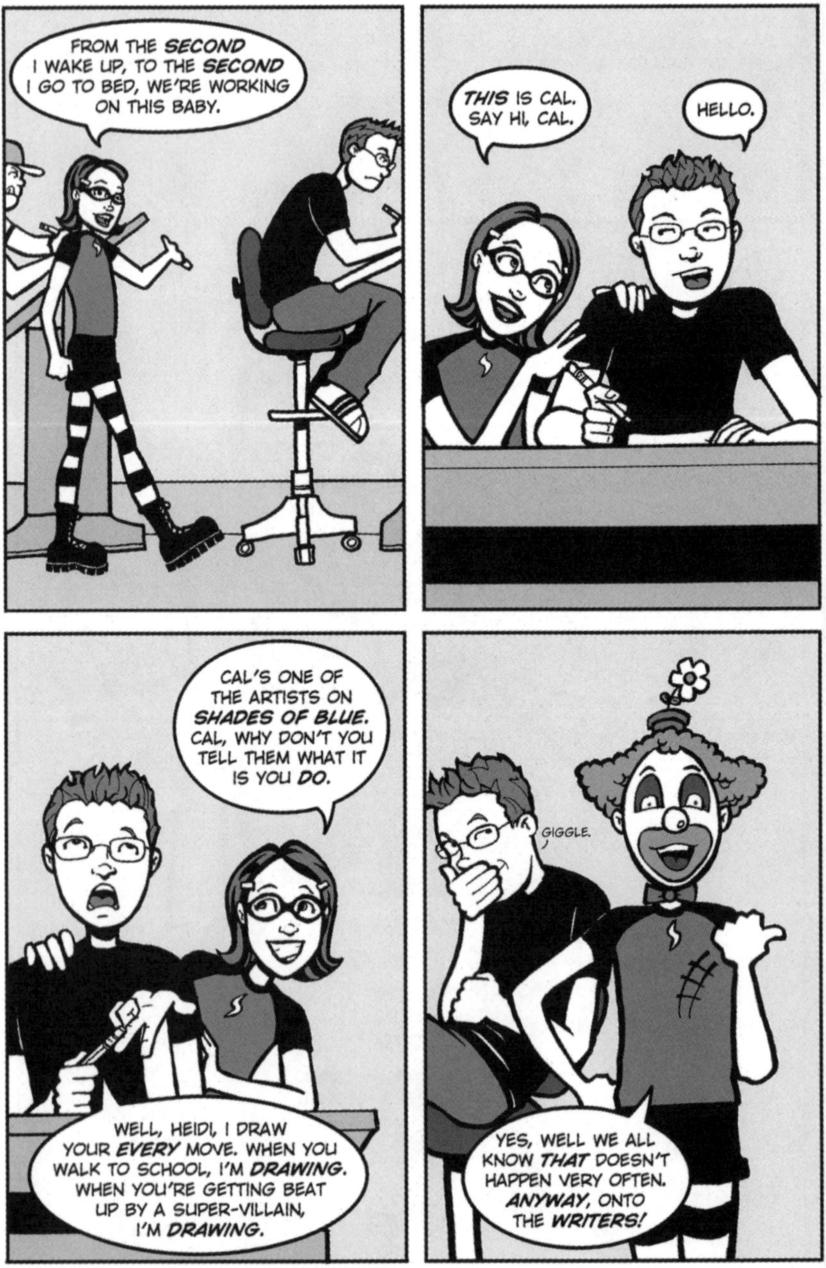
FROM THE *SECOND* I WAKE UP, TO THE *SECOND* I GO TO BED, WE'RE WORKING ON THIS BABY.
THIS IS CAL. SAY HI, CAL.
HELLO.
CAL'S ONE OF THE ARTISTS ON *SHADES OF BLUE.* CAL, WHY DON'T YOU TELL THEM WHAT IT IS YOU *DO.*
WELL, HEIDI, I DRAW YOUR *EVERY* MOVE. WHEN YOU WALK TO SCHOOL, I'M *DRAWING.* WHEN YOU'RE GETTING BEAT UP BY A SUPER-VILLAIN, I'M *DRAWING.*
GIGGLE.
YES, WELL WE ALL KNOW *THAT* DOESN'T HAPPEN VERY OFTEN. *ANYWAY,* ONTO THE *WRITERS!*

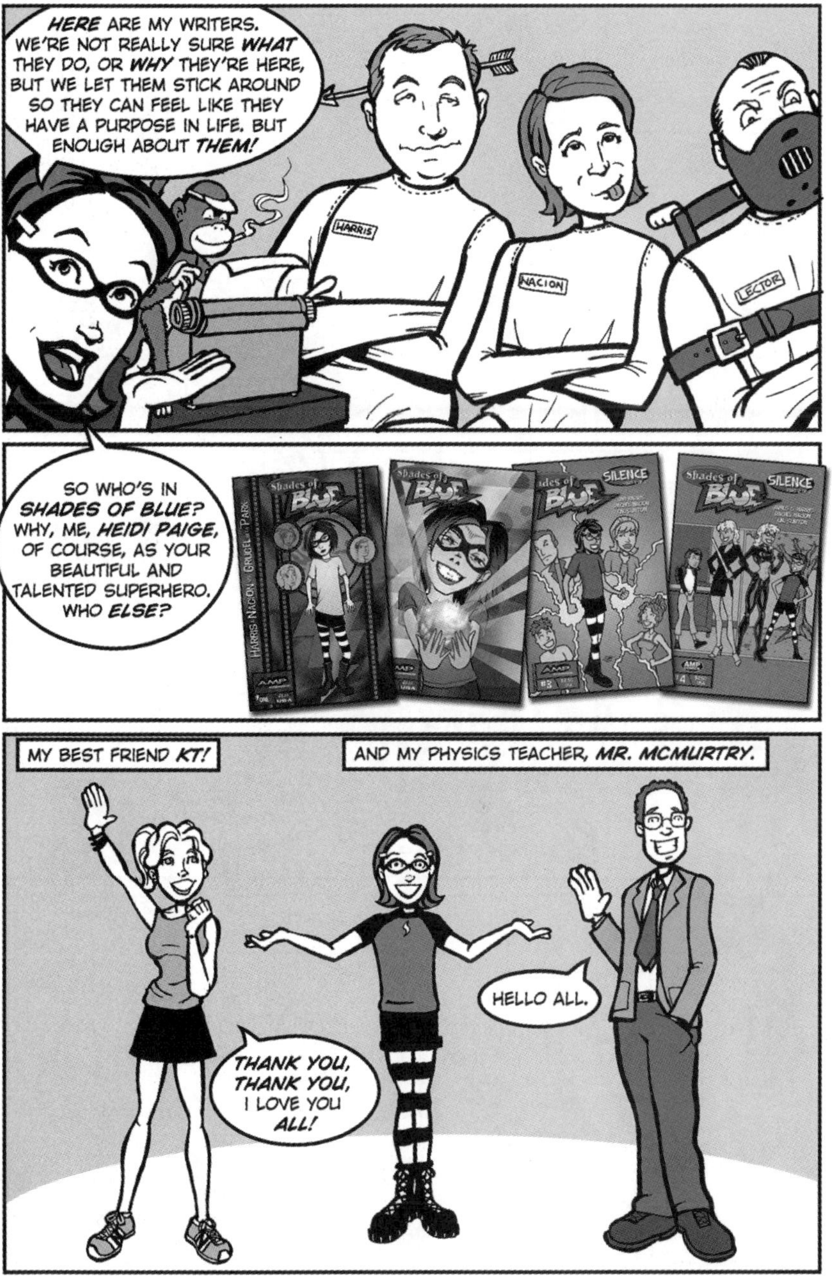
HERE ARE MY WRITERS. WE'RE NOT REALLY SURE WHAT THEY DO, OR WHY THEY'RE HERE, BUT WE LET THEM STICK AROUND SO THEY CAN FEEL LIKE THEY HAVE A PURPOSE IN LIFE. BUT ENOUGH ABOUT THEM!
HARRIS
NACION
LECTOR
SO WHO'S IN SHADES OF BLUE? WHY, ME, HEIDI PAIGE, OF COURSE, AS YOUR BEAUTIFUL AND TALENTED SUPERHERO. WHO ELSE?
Shades of BLUE
SILENCE
MY BEST FRIEND KT!
AND MY PHYSICS TEACHER, MR. MCMURTRY.
HELLO ALL.
THANK YOU, THANK YOU, I LOVE YOU ALL!

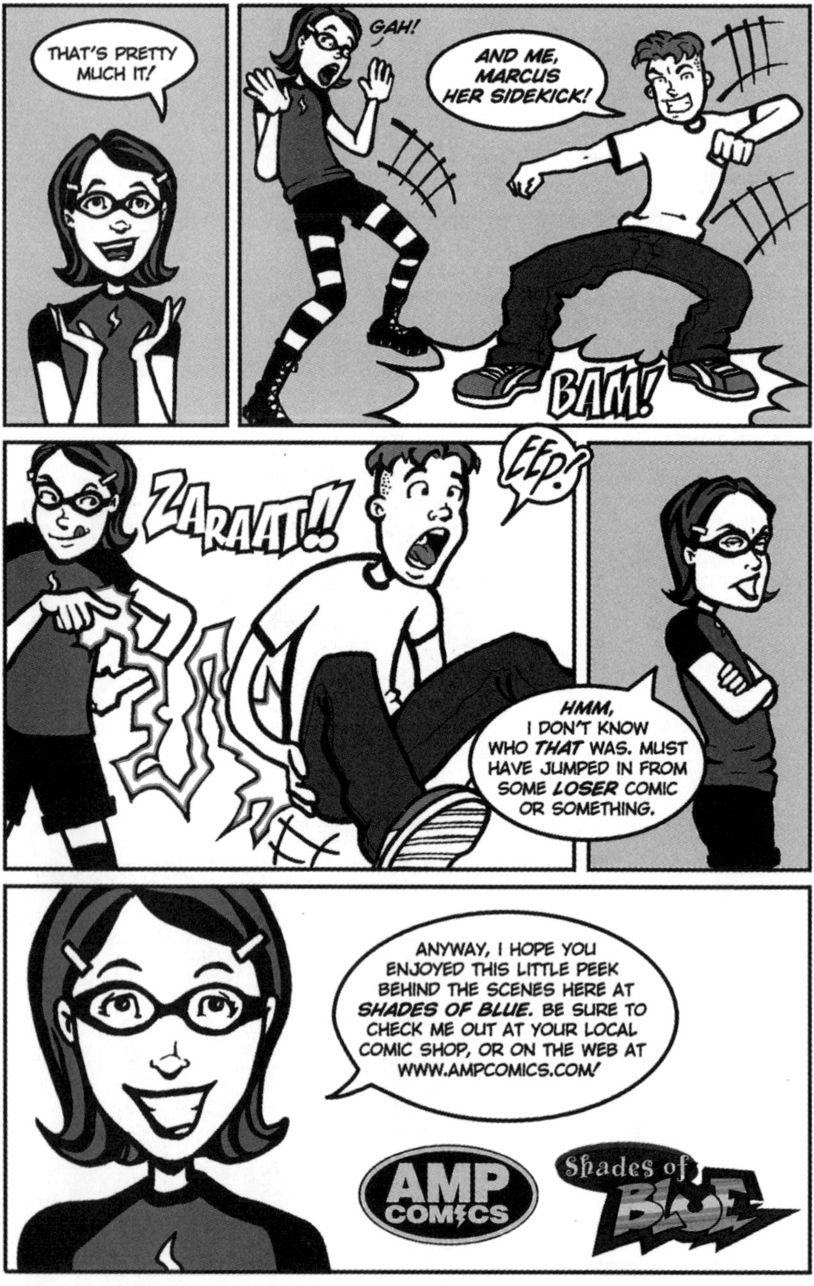
THAT'S PRETTY MUCH IT!
GAH!
AND ME, MARCUS HER SIDEKICK!
BAM!
ZARAAT!!
EEP!
HMM, I DON'T KNOW WHO THAT WAS. MUST HAVE JUMPED IN FROM SOME LOSER COMIC OR SOMETHING.
ANYWAY, I HOPE YOU ENJOYED THIS LITTLE PEEK BEHIND THE SCENES HERE AT SHADES OF BLUE. BE SURE TO CHECK ME OUT AT YOUR LOCAL COMIC SHOP, OR ON THE WEB AT WWW.AMPCOMICS.COM!
AMP COMICS
Shades of BLUE

ARTWORK

We put together some extra goodies for this section. First we have an ad we did that plays off the various awards shows out there. I hate when people ramble on. Hate it more when the producers cut them off.

Next up is the back cover to issue 4, followed by the back cover to issue 5. You can see the evolution of the characters even over the course of one issue with those two drawings. I would have loved to make a poster out of the back cover to issue 5, but the opportunity never presented itself (by opportunity, I mean money!)

And finally Cal has put together some of his production art for your amusement.

Enjoy!

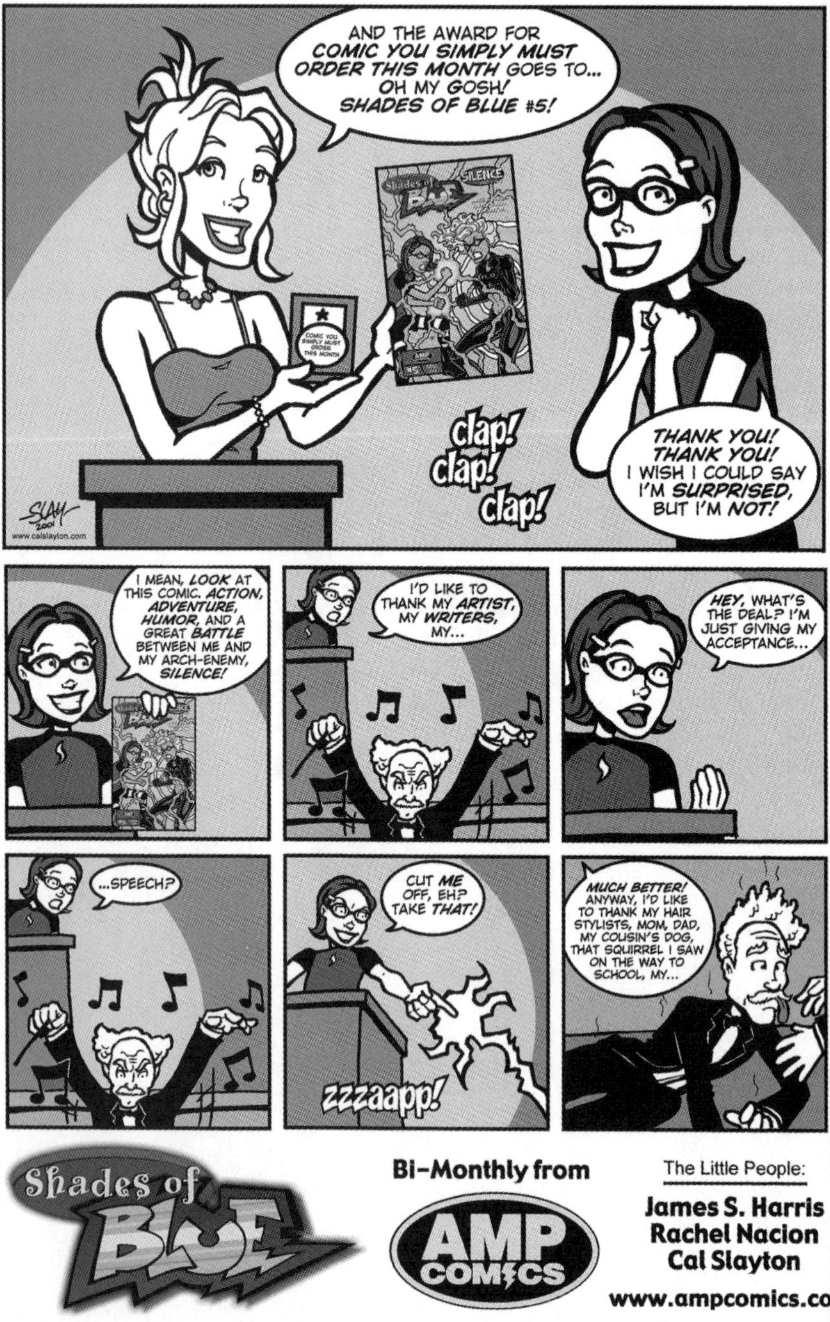

AND THE AWARD FOR COMIC YOU SIMPLY MUST ORDER THIS MONTH GOES TO... OH MY GOSH! SHADES OF BLUE #5!
COMIC YOU SIMPLY MUST ORDER THIS MONTH
SILENCE
Shades of BLUE
clap! clap! clap!
THANK YOU! THANK YOU! I WISH I COULD SAY I'M SURPRISED, BUT I'M NOT!
SLAY 2001
www.calslayton.com
I MEAN, LOOK AT THIS COMIC. ACTION, ADVENTURE, HUMOR, AND A GREAT BATTLE BETWEEN ME AND MY ARCH-ENEMY, SILENCE!
I'D LIKE TO THANK MY ARTIST, MY WRITERS, MY...
HEY, WHAT'S THE DEAL? I'M JUST GIVING MY ACCEPTANCE...
...SPEECH?
CUT ME OFF, EH? TAKE THAT!
zzzaapp!
MUCH BETTER! ANYWAY, I'D LIKE TO THANK MY HAIR STYLISTS, MOM, DAD, MY COUSIN'S DOG, THAT SQUIRREL I SAW ON THE WAY TO SCHOOL, MY...

Shades of BLUE

Bi-Monthly from

AMP COMICS

The Little People:

James S. Harris
Rachel Nacion
Cal Slayton

www.ampcomics.cor

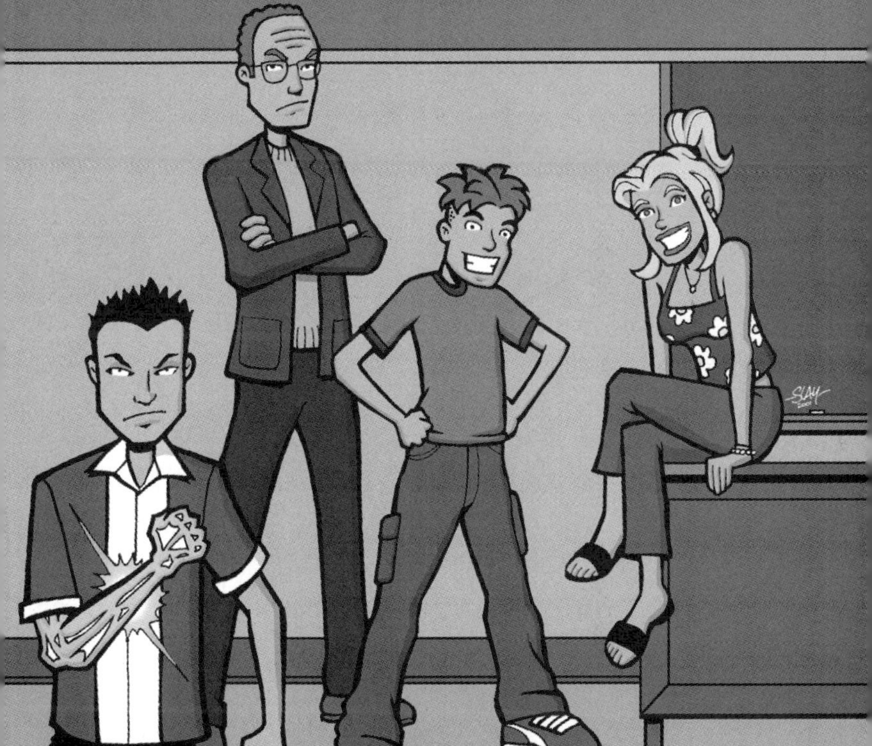

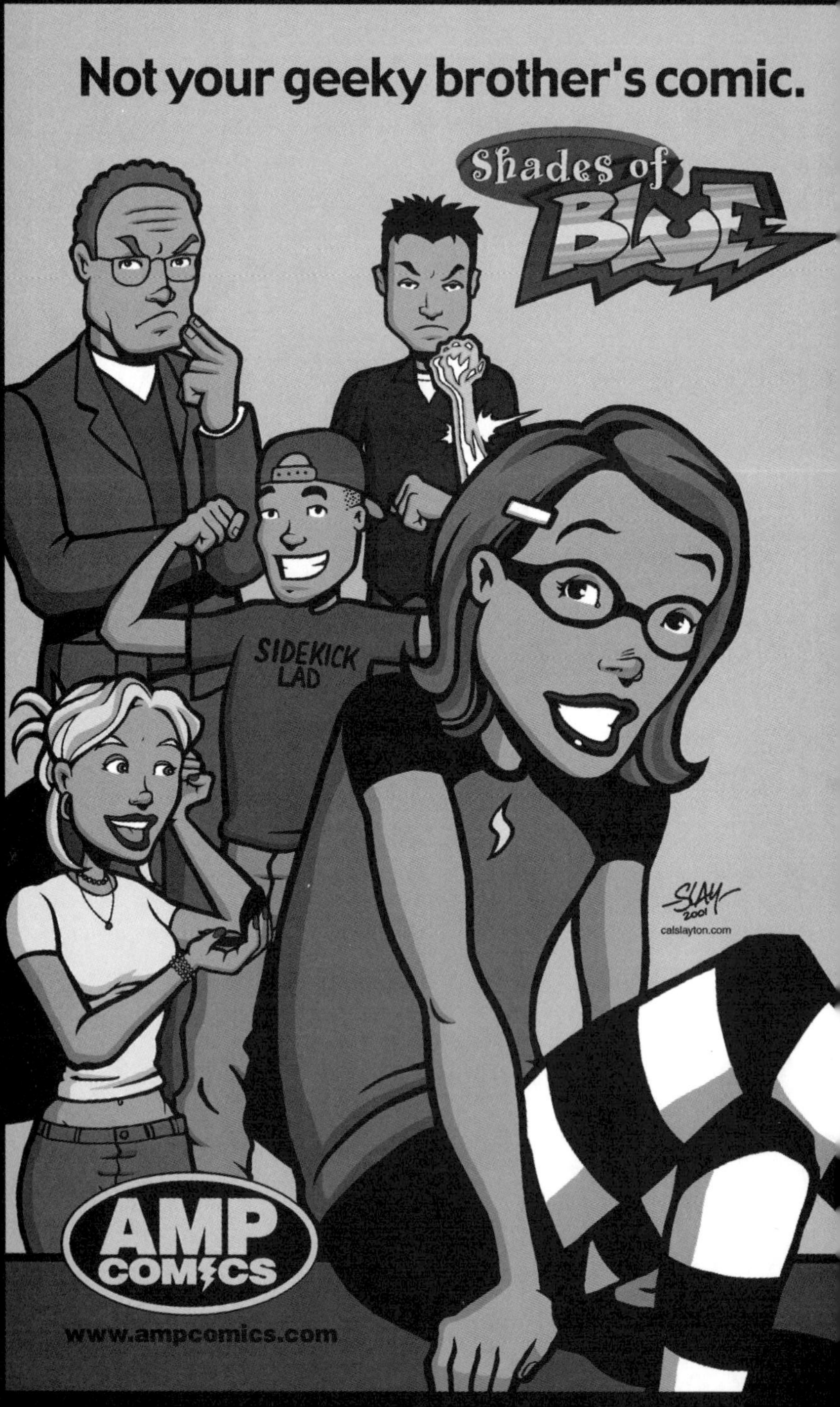
Not your geeky brother's comic.
Shades of
BLUE
SIDEKICK
LAD
SLAY
2001
calslayton.com
AMP
COMICS
www.ampcomics.com

Shades of BLUE™
SKETCHBOOK

TAKE A PEEK INTO THE SKETCHBOOK OF SHADES ARTIST *CAL SLAYTON*

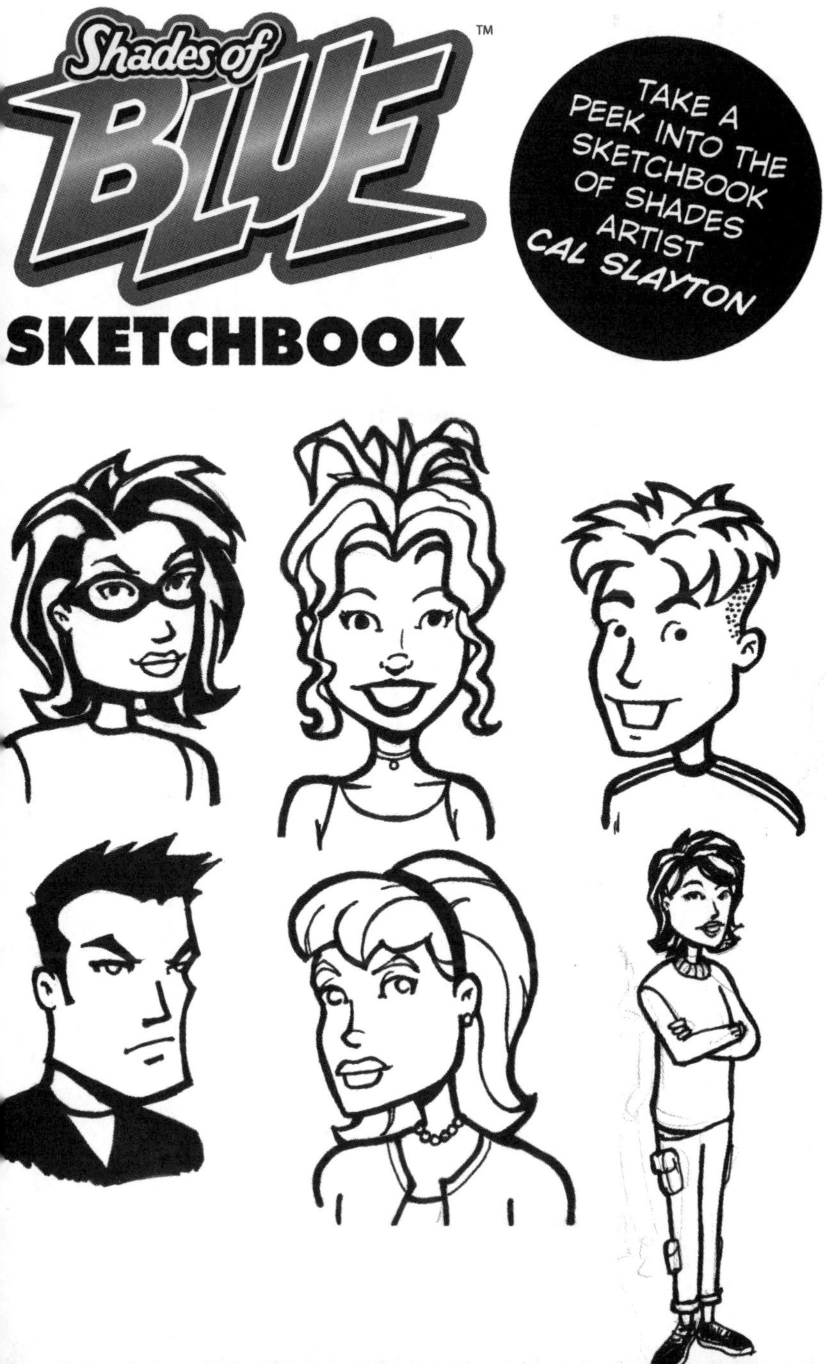

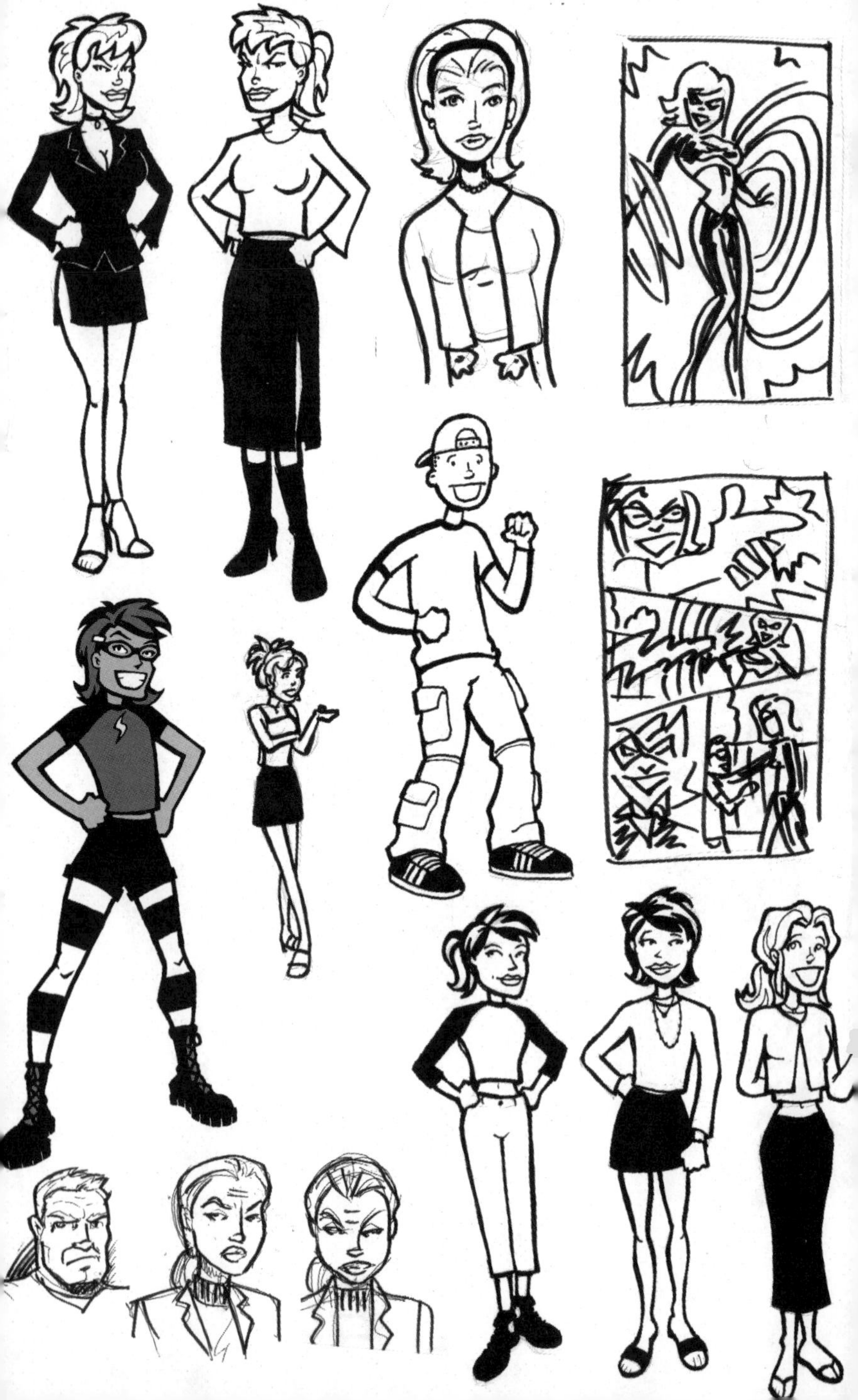

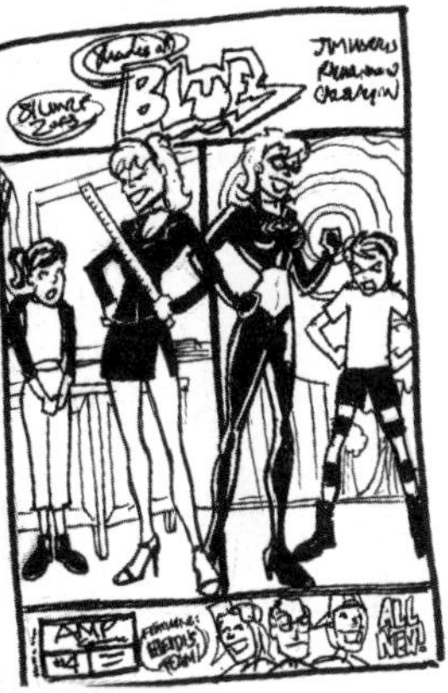
Shades of
BLUE
AMP
ALL NEW!

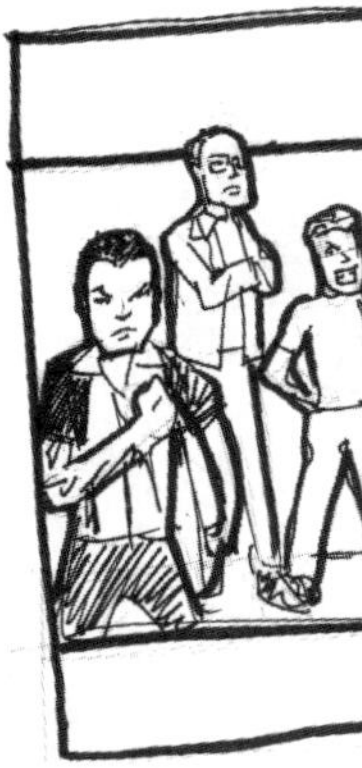

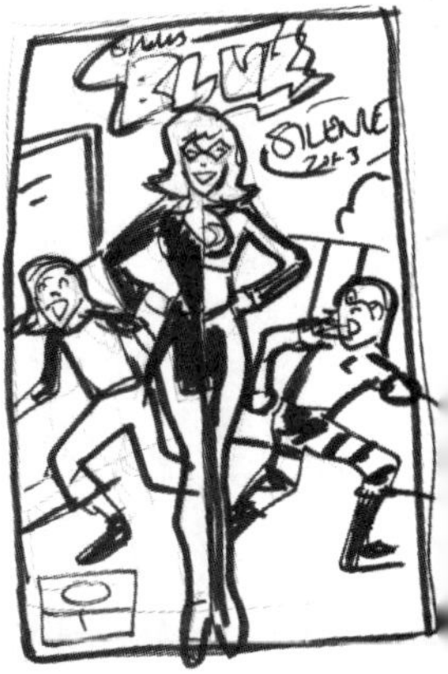

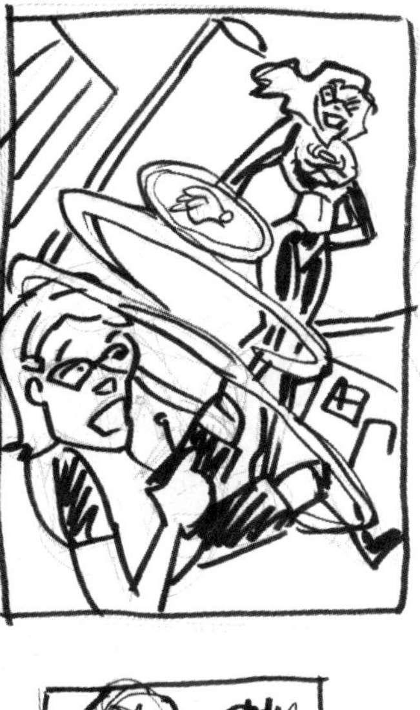

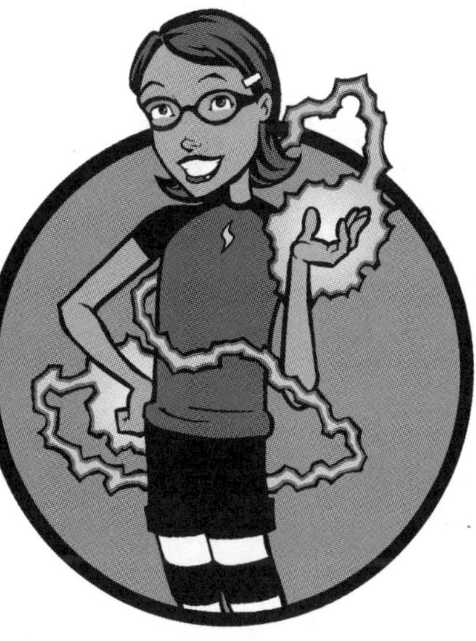

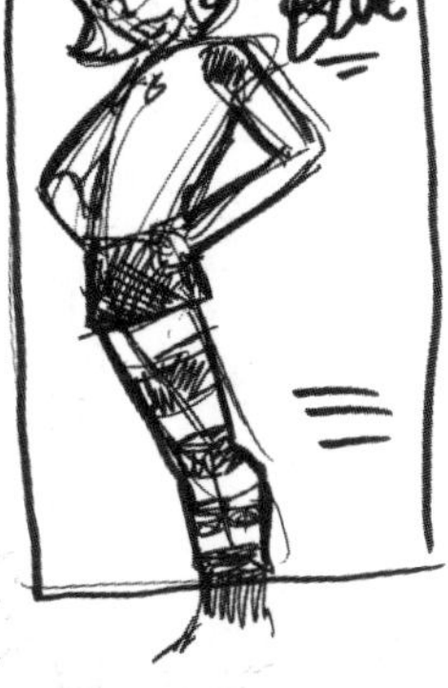

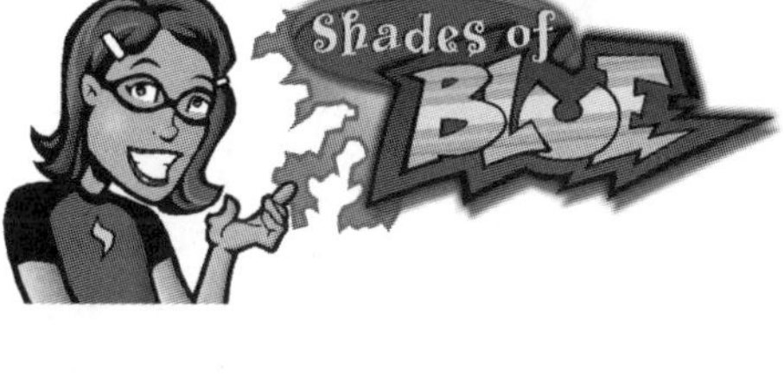
Shades of
BLUE

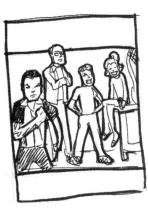

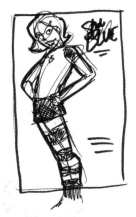

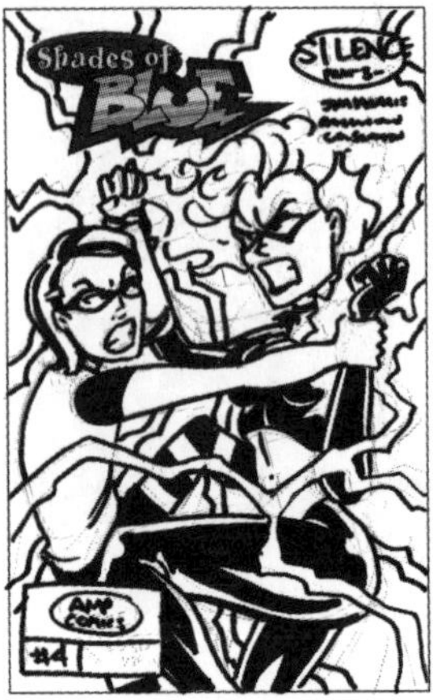
Shades of
BLUE
SILENCE
AMP
COMICS
#4

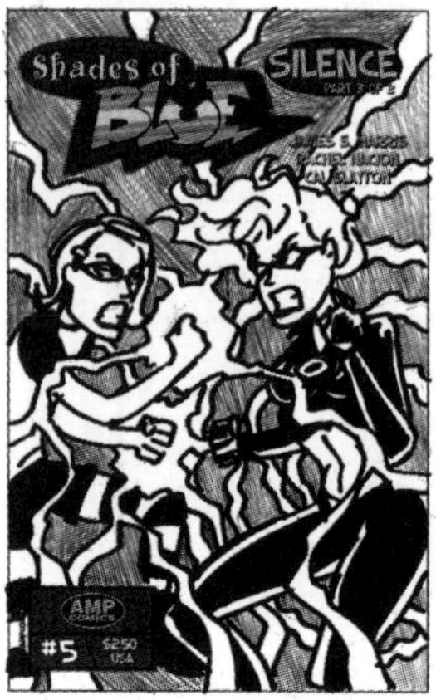
Shades of
BLUE
SILENCE
PART 3 OF 3
AMP
COMICS
#5
$2.50
USA

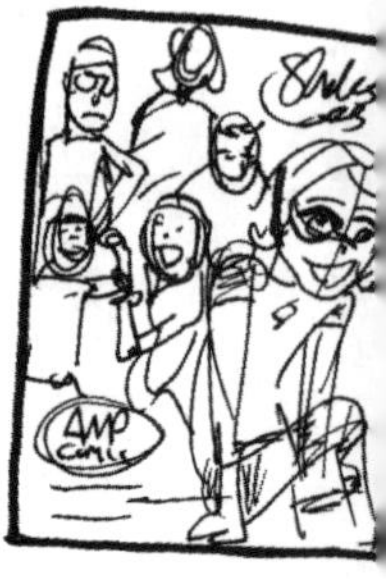
AMP
COMICS

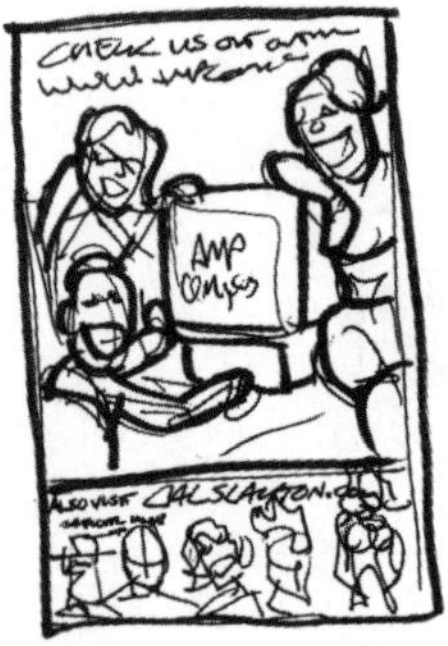
AMP
COMICS
ALSO VISIT CALSLAYTON.COM

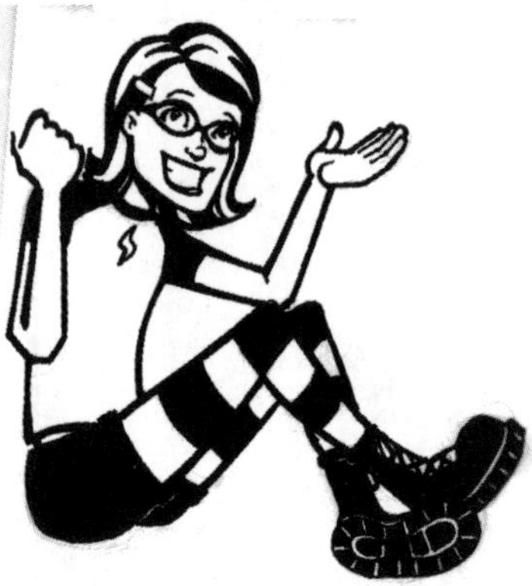

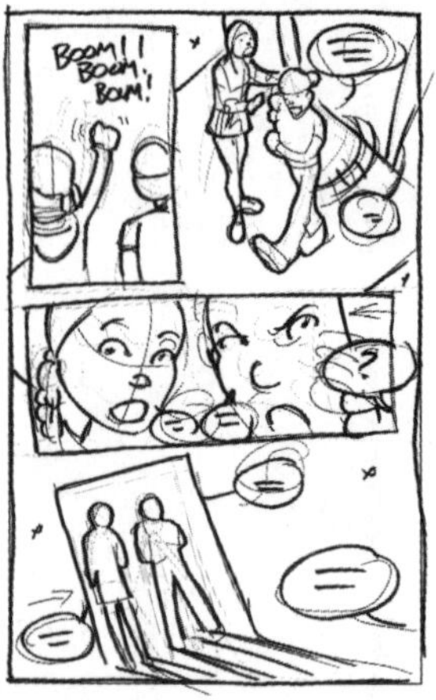
BOOM!!
BOOM!
BOOM!

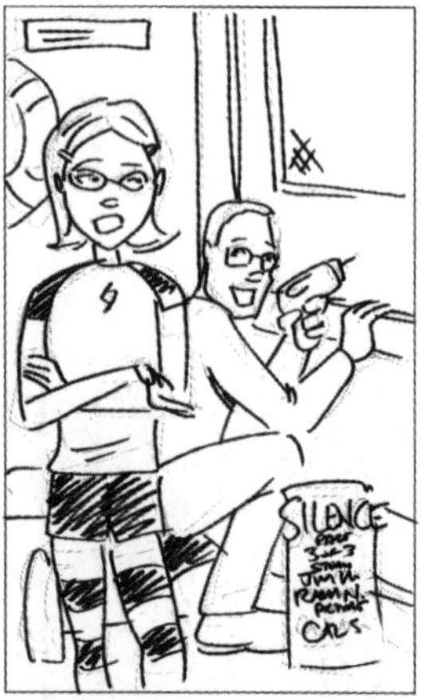
SILENCE

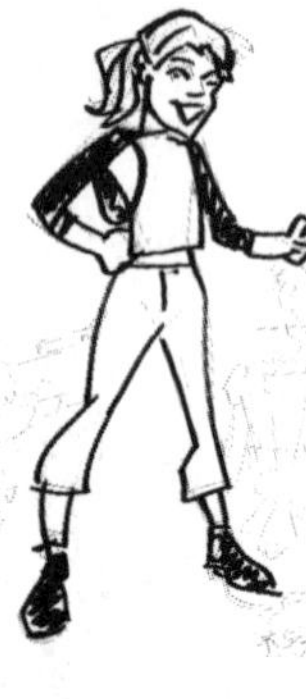